Innocent Ecstasy

Innocent Ecstasy

*How Christianity Gave America
an Ethic of Sexual Pleasure*

—◦◉◦—

Updated Edition

—◦◉◦—

PETER GARDELLA

OXFORD
UNIVERSITY PRESS

OXFORD
UNIVERSITY PRESS

Oxford University Press is a department of the University of Oxford. It furthers the University's objective of excellence in research, scholarship, and education by publishing worldwide. Oxford is a registered trade mark of Oxford University Press in the UK and certain other countries.

Published in the United States of America by Oxford University Press
198 Madison Avenue, New York, NY 10016, United States of America.

Library of Congress Cataloging-in-Publication Data
Names: Gardella, Peter, 1951– author.
Title: Innocent ecstasy : how Christianity gave America an ethic
of sexual pleasure / Peter Gardella.
Description: Updated Edition. | New York : Oxford University Press, 2016. |
Includes bibliographical references and index.
Identifiers: LCCN 2015042164 (print) | LCCN 2016012878 (ebook) |
ISBN 9780190609405 (pbk. : alk. paper) | ISBN 9780190609412 (updf) |
ISBN 9780190609429 (epub)
Subjects: LCSH: Sex—Religious aspects—Christianity. | Sin, Original. |
Sexual ethics—United States. | United States—Religious life and customs.
Classification: LCC BT708 .G37 2016 (print) | LCC BT708 (ebook) |
DDC 261.8/3570973—dc23
LC record available at http://lccn.loc.gov/2015042164

1 3 5 7 9 8 6 4 2

Printed by WebCom, Inc., Canada

To
Professor Sydney E. Ahlstrom,
without whom I could not have begun,

and to
Lorrie Greenhouse Gardella,
without whom I would not have finished.

Contents

Preface to the Updated Edition   ix

Introduction   1

1. Catholic Sensuality   7

2. Protestant Reactions   23

3. Medical Christianity   37

4. Medical Prophets   65

5. Evangelical Ecstasy   76

6. The Song of Bernadette   91

7. Redemption through Sex   126

Conclusion: History and Theology (1985)   146

Since 1985: Redeeming the Body   159

Afterword: Projecting the Future   183

Notes   195

Bibliography   227

Acknowledgments   239

Index   241

Preface to the Updated Edition

WHEN AMERICANS HAVE sex, they expect ecstasy and freedom from guilt. The first edition of this book, published in 1985, traced the expectation of *innocent ecstasy* to a long Christian struggle to overcome the association of sex with original sin. It told the story of Catholic, Protestant, and evangelical Christians, some of whom were also novelists, doctors, psychologists, and advocates of birth control. This 2016 edition adds a new chapter, "Redeeming the Body," which explores how three movements outside the churches—popular music, gay liberation, and recovery from sexual abuse—have expanded innocent ecstasy during the past thirty years, while continuing the Christian theme of redemption and the Christian sense of mission. It also adds an Afterword dealing with contemporary developments and offering thoughts about the future.

In the June 2015 Supreme Court decision legalizing gay marriage, the opinion by Justice Kennedy made a dramatic statement in favor of a right to love. The final paragraph of that opinion asserted that in marriage, "two people become something greater than once they were," and that "marriage embodies a love that may endure even past death." This can fairly be called religious language. Justice Kennedy's words evoked the realm of "nonrational commitments that hold life together," as I have defined "religion" in earlier books.

The word "religion" derives from the Latin *ligare*, to bind, and refers to obligations. When people say that they are "spiritual but not religious," they mean that they revere some form of energy (*spiritus*, wind) but admit to no obligations, or at least to no system of obligations, relative to that energy or its source. In affirming gay marriage, the Supreme Court was allowing a spiritual force, love between persons of the same sex, access to the status of marital love, which is inherently religious. The Court participated in the movement of religious discourse beyond the churches, synagogues, and other institutions of formal religion. By doing this, the

Court continued a trend that marked the whole last century of development in the American ethic of sexual pleasure. During the last century, the mainstream of American religious discourse, and especially of religious discourse about sex, has moved into popular culture.

In January of 1986, less than eight months after *Innocent Ecstasy* was published, the Rock and Roll Hall of Fame inducted its first ten performers, beginning with Elvis Presley. Of those ten, nine had evangelical Protestant backgrounds. Two of the most prominent rock stars, Elvis and Jerry Lee Lewis, were raised Pentecostal and never stopped singing about their faith. Over the years since 1985, Aretha Franklin, Michael Jackson, Prince, and hip-hop artists such as Tupac Shakur and Kanye West have continued to combine religious redemption and sex in their songs. Madonna, who had her first number one hit, *Like a Virgin*, in 1984, has performed three decades of religiously saturated and sexually provocative songs and videos and live shows. Stefani Germanotta, who performs as Lady Gaga, has taken up Madonna's mantle in the twenty-first century.

Beginning in the 1980s, the AIDS crisis lent increasing urgency to the movement for gay rights, extending the reach of innocent ecstasy both in popular culture and in religion. In May of 1985, the Centers for Disease Control and Prevention announced that 10,000 cases of AIDS had been identified in the United States, and that 4,942 of those diagnosed with AIDS had already died. The play *Angels in America* made gay rights a religious cause. The goal of gay marriage transformed the status of LGBTQ people in the United States. Religious groups responded quickly, though they had not begun the revolution. Some Christian churches and leaders married gay couples long before states recognized such marriages as legal.

The ideal of innocent ecstasy encouraged honesty about sex that contributed to a new awareness of the prevalence of rape, childhood sexual abuse, and clerical abuse, and of the possibilities for recovery. In 1986, recovery gained its greatest platform when Oprah Winfrey's Chicago talk show went to national syndication. Winfrey grew up in evangelical churches, but moved beyond them as a young woman. Through Winfrey's work, and that of other popular therapeutic experts, a potent combination of innocence, religion, and sex developed among those discussing recovery, and especially recovery from sexual abuse. A theme of recovery underlies the phenomenon of *Twilight*, a series of novels and movies by a Mormon woman, in which a virgin redeems a family of vampires. *Twilight* fan fiction produced *Fifty Shades of Grey*, in which another virgin redeems a sadomasochist and victim of childhood abuse.

Despite the movement of religious discourse into popular culture, the Christian crusade to overcome original sin remains visible in the American ethic of sexual pleasure. The struggle of Luke Skywalker, Han Solo, and Princess Leia against the Dark Side of the Force in *Star Wars*, an epic which began to appear on movie screens in 1977 and continues through 2016, is a metaphor for redemption from original sin. When *Avatar* became the highest-grossing movie of all time in 2009, it drew its power from a Tree of Life on a planet named Pandora that was Eden without even a thin disguise. To understand Lady Gaga, gay marriage, and American attitudes toward Internet pornography and virtual sex, to which this book will turn in its new chapter and in the Afterword, it is necessary to understand the history of the doctrine of original sin. That is where the first edition of *Innocent Ecstasy* begins.

Innocent Ecstasy

Introduction

THIS BOOK DESCRIBES how Christian influences, working through popular culture, led Americans to seek ecstatic pleasure and to expect freedom from guilt in their sexual relations. The story begins with the obligations to orgasm in marital sex that emerged in Roman Catholic moral teaching during the eighteenth and nineteenth centuries. It continues with chapters on the sexual sensationalism of anti-Catholic literature, the mixture of Protestant theology and medical theory in Victorian sexual advice, the impact of evangelical rapture on expectations of sexual pleasure, the model of womanhood that evolved in connection with devotion to the Virgin Mary, and the role of sexual mysticism in the birth control movement and in American versions of psychoanalysis.

Underlying the whole story is a single theme: the struggle to overcome original sin. From Catholic moralists to Victorian doctors, and from American Methodist women to St. Bernadette of Lourdes, the protagonists of this narrative all believed that human beings came into the world already tainted by sin, and that this disordered condition involved the corruption of human sexuality. In different ways, they all worked to alleviate this corruption. Their success so far exceeded their intentions that by the 1920s, when birth control advocates and psychologists joined the crusade to redeem sex from sin, a revolution had begun that would make any hint of a connection between sex and original sin unacceptable to American public opinion. Today, sixty years later, all that remains of traditional doctrine on sex and sin is the persistent demand that sex be *proved* to be innocent. The force of obligation that once repressed sex now attaches to the ethic of sexual pleasure that I call "innocent ecstasy." An example will help to define that ethic.

While I was writing this book, I attended a sermon on "Maximum Sex," preached by Josh McDowell, a traveling evangelist of the Campus

Crusade for Christ. He attracted about two thousand students to the largest auditorium on the campus of Miami University in Oxford, Ohio.

McDowell began by talking about his courtship of his wife. "I don't know whether I was thinking with my hormones or the Holy Spirit," he said. "I think they go together."[1] He promised the same harmony, with maximum sexual pleasure, to anyone who accepted Christ, married another Christian, and followed a few rules. With practiced ferocity, McDowell denounced "those who think that a woman is less sexually responsive than a man." If women did not enjoy sex, it was because their men were neglecting "physical and verbal caressment," and then "rolling over and going to sleep" after a brief sexual encounter. In a good Christian marriage, both husband and wife would know that "intercourse is basically a spiritual act." They would begin and end sex with prayer. The "extra-sensitivity" to each other that grew out of their spiritual union would tell them how much preparation they needed before intercourse. Those who heeded McDowell's call to "put Jesus Christ right in the center of your sex life" would find that success in the quest for sexual pleasure followed naturally.

On most points, McDowell defended conservative Christian teaching. He denounced premarital intercourse; he condemned abortion. He even mentioned original sin, to show the way beyond it. Accepting forgiveness though Jesus Christ would set sex free from sin, and therefore from all feelings of guilt.

By teaching that good Christians should feel no guilt while cultivating "maximum sex," McDowell endorsed the twin sexual goals that other Americans have long accepted: *innocence* and *ecstasy. Innocence* in this context means both the absence of guilt and a positive sense of healthiness. For some it may imply inexperience, youth, or even virginity; different individuals hold different beliefs as to whether innocent sex requires marriage, heterosexuality, or any other condition. The whole culture, however, approves of an attitude of innocence toward sex. Some people view guilt feelings as a symptom of psychological sickness; others see such feelings as a sign that something is wrong with the relationship or the action that provokes guilt. No sexual counselor, from Josh McDowell to Dear Abby to Masters and Johnson, recommends living with guilt. Indeed, the demand for innocence is frequently made in militant terms. When speaking on the subject of sex, Americans tend to assume a prophetic stance, denouncing abuses in the name of an ideal. The ideal of innocence does not allow acceptance of sex as one aspect of fallen nature.

Ecstasy means an intensity of feeling that transcends physical capacity, obliterating the boundaries of self-consciousness. The word *ecstasy* derives from Latin words meaning "out of" and "to stand," thus pointing to a state of being literally beside oneself, or carried away. Ecstasy is always momentary but not always sexual. Evangelicals seek ecstasy in the religious experience of being born again, being healed of disease, or speaking in tongues. Runners testify to the ecstasy of running through "the Wall" and into unconsciousness of pain. In sex, Americans usually identify the moment of ecstasy with orgasm.

To understand how revolutionary the ethic of innocent ecstasy really is, it is only necessary to turn to traditional statements on sex and original sin. A good example is the ninth Article of Religion of the Church of England, also found in the Book of Common Prayer of the Episcopal Church in America.

> Original sin ... is the fault and corruption of the Nature of every man, that naturally is engendered of the offspring of Adam; whereby man ... is of his own nature inclined to evil, so that the flesh lusteth always contrary to the Spirit; ... And this infection of nature doth remain, yea in them that are regenerated; ... And although there is no condemnation for those that believe and are baptized; yet the Apostle doth confess, that concupiscence and lust hath of itself the nature of sin.[2]

For fifteen hundred years, from the time of St. Augustine (*d.* 430) to the twentieth century, Christians believed that original sin corrupted every aspect of life. Theologians did not simplemindedly identify sex with sin; the "concupiscence," or insatiable desire, of human beings expressed itself in many ways. But no one, whether reborn in Christ or not, was regarded as exempt from the "infection of nature." Christians hoped for forgiveness, not innocence. In this life the most saintly human would remain, in Martin Luther's phrase, *"simul peccator ac justus"*—*both* justified and a sinner.[3] Luther himself seems to have enjoyed sex, and he taught that men and women had a fundamental right to sexual enjoyment; but Luther also said that, ever since Eden, the act of intercourse was "horribly marred" by "the hideousness inherent in our flesh, namely, the bestial desire and lust," and that intercourse even in marriage was never free from sin.

Clearly, innocent ecstasy offers some advantages over this gloomy perspective. The process that led Americans to reject the association of sex with original sin almost surely also increased the pleasure that Americans have found in sex. Sixty years of positive advice cannot have entirely failed to improve the skills and the sensitivity of sexual partners. Much of this advice, from sources as disparate as Campus Crusade and the birth control movement, has emphasized the needs and desires of women, and it seems likely that women have come to enjoy sex more than they once did.

Outside the bedroom, the redemption of sex from sin has promoted cultural innocence. Young people who combine moral uprightness with explicit sexual appeal are now the most popular figures of American culture. Ordinary men and women have developed a durable sexual innocence— not hypocrisy, but a real capacity to undergo experience without becoming jaded, disenchanted, or even sophisticated. Women in particular now maintain their self-respect and their reputations despite attitudes, fashions, and behavior that would have marked them as "fallen women" in all previous Christian cultures, and that still mark such women in most of the world outside America. The new sexual freedom of women has transformed everything from the content of conversation to the atmosphere of the college classroom to the practice of the professions.

But innocent ecstasy has also inflicted some special miseries on American men and women, and these miseries can be traced directly to the struggle against original sin.

First, the effort to break the bond between sex and original sin demanded so many declarations of the sacredness of sex that many Americans began to approach sexual intercourse as a spiritual discipline. The "quality" of sex became a standard by which personalities and relationships were judged. When a publication of the Catholic Theological Society of America defined a moral sex act as "self-liberating, other-enhancing, honest, faithful, socially responsible, life-serving and joyous," it cataloged only a few aspects of the modern ideal.[4] Under the pressure of such demands, both divorce and marriage have increased in frequency, not so much because people revere marriage less as because they have come to expect more. Premarital intercourse has increased, partly because young people need to know how well they will perform in sex. Certainly modern culture has continued to distinguish between sex and love, but that distinction has neither relieved the pressure on love to express itself sexually nor mitigated the judgment on marriages that do not include sexual ecstasy.

Second, among those who contributed to the redemption of sex from sin, from Victorian doctors to evangelical Protestants to worshipers of the

Virgin Mary, most emphasized the redemptive power of women, of female symbols, and of passive desires. This emphasis on women carried over into advice on reaching sexual ecstasy that consistently recommended self-control to husbands and emotional abandonment to wives. The sexual desires of women have lost their associations with sin more completely than have the desires of men. This imbalance left women with the double task of embodying innocence and certifying sexual success, and men with the responsibility for satisfying women through sexual performance. Both men and women have come to resent their respective burdens.

Finally, experts on sex inherited their faith in liberation through orgasm from Christians who had found freedom from sin in moments of religious ecstasy. The quest for ecstasy in orgasm then led people to neglect sensuality. Western mystical tradition has always known that in ecstasy, the action of the senses is suspended.[5] In America, the pursuit of orgasm as the equivalent of religious ecstasy quickly became an ascetic practice, best performed by those who disciplined their bodies to be thin, clean, and odorless. Marabel Morgan, evangelical author of *The Total Woman*, urged wives to seduce their husbands every day for a week. But she also illustrated the gulf that innocent ecstasy set between sex and sensuality when she wrote that "sex is as clean and pure as eating cottage cheese."[6]

To what extent can we really give the credit and the blame for such a sexual ethic to Christianity? If by "Christianity" one means faith in the Christ of the Nicene Creed, the answer is "not at all." The same answer will hold for anyone who would limit the name of Christianity to some definition of true Christian faith. But if "Christianity" also means a set of organizations including the churches, voluntary groups like the YMCA, and schools founded and run under Christian auspices, then the responsibility of Christianity for our sexual ethic becomes more credible. And if "Christianity" has a yet more extensive meaning, doing justice to the cultural force of the Christian message, which has left half the world grappling with such concepts as the fall of humanity, the immaculate conception, the virgin birth, and the resurrection of the body, then it is impossible to imagine how an ethic of sexual pleasure *could* have arisen in the United States without the cooperation of Christianity.

Not every Christian, or every Christian group, contributed directly to the emergence of innocent ecstasy. Quakers and Unitarians, Old Calvinists and "High Church" Episcopalians, to name a few, have little place in this story. But our ethic of sexual pleasure would not be what it is without the influence of Roman Catholic moral theology, the Protestant piety of American physicians, the Methodist pursuit of perfect love, and the attractive power of the Virgin Mary. Of course, all of these Christian factors exerted their influence within the American social setting. Immigration weakened Old World customs, and industry made possible a popular culture that could teach new habits in one generation. That culture reformulated Christian themes and blurred the lines between denominations, creating an American version of Christianity that church historians have only begun to describe. The Christianity that shaped American sexual behavior was itself reshaped by the movement for women's rights, the growth of the reading public, the rise of the medical profession, the adoption of American values by Catholic immigrants, the adjustment of Protestants to the presence of Catholics, and the entrance of Methodists and evangelicals into the middle class.

The question of causality can become an infinite regress. Class conflict, scientific advances, cultural ideals, and devotional practices all affected American attitudes toward sex. But within the pattern of causes, one cause united all the others. Our sexual ethic has a religious quality that it could only have inherited from the Christian zeal to overcome sin and to experience salvation. As Tom Wolfe observed, Americans seek in orgasm "a spark of the Divine."[7] And as Professor Ahlstrom taught me in graduate school, the only rule of historiography that matters is to tell a plausible story.

I

Catholic Sensuality

Basic Doctrine

The first American writer to prescribe orgasm was the Right Reverend Francis Patrick Kenrick, Roman Catholic bishop of Philadelphia. In the third volume of his *Theologiae Moralis,* published in 1843, Kenrick wrote that a married woman had the right to bring herself to orgasm "by touches" after intercourse, if she had experienced no climax during love-making.[1] Kenrick also said that a husband who did not remain sexually active until his wife reached orgasm was guilty of a venial sin of omission and that it was a mortal sin for a wife to distract herself during sex to avoid having an orgasm.[2]

Although Kenrick wrote in Latin for an audience of priests, his work had practical influence as a textbook for confessors. Priests needed specific guidance for dealing with the questions married people might raise in the confessions of sin that the church required all Catholics to make at least once a year. Bishop Kenrick was no heretic or even a radical, but a model prelate appointed to repair a breakdown of authority in the Philadelphia diocese.[3] His importance within American Catholicism grew through the use of his moral text in American seminaries, and through his elevation to the post of Archbishop of Baltimore in 1851. For twelve years in Baltimore, Kenrick led his fellow bishops, occupying what was then the primatial see of the Roman Catholic Church in the United States. His pronouncements on sexual pleasure reflected normative Catholic teaching. To understand how Kenrick came to write so positively about sex, it is less important to explore the bishop's biography than to seek some comprehension of the tradition he served.

The most famous Catholic sexual doctrine, the duty of married couples not to impede conception, appeared long before any detailed Christian accounts of sexual behavior. Catholic tradition emerged out of centuries of competition with groups now considered heretical. Inspired by Gospel examples, and in some cases by radical pessimism regarding this world, various early Christians recommended approaches to sex that ranged from total abstinence to the allowance of promiscuity as long as conception did not result.[4] The eventual Catholic position, powerfully stated by Augustine in the fifth century, represented a middle way. Catholics affirmed the goodness of the world by accepting procreation, marriage, and intercourse. Yet they also maintained that sin had corrupted the human capacity for passion, and that passion should never so dominate marital sex that the partners would copulate for pleasure alone, closing off the possibility of conception.[5]

The affirmation of some spiritual meaning in bodily acts, even though the body was tainted with sin, became a lasting distinction of orthodoxy as opposed to heresy. Sin had obscured but not obliterated the traces of God's creative intention in the physical world, Catholics argued. Therefore, the church had a duty to discover God's intentions in the structure of the sexual organs and to teach the faithful how those organs should and should not be used. Out of these basic ideas grew the notion of a "natural law" governing sexual morality. Catholicism came to regard the natural law as another form of revelation, supplementary to the Scriptures.

By concentrating on the physical, experts on natural law reached conclusions that might surprise those accustomed to a moral standard that places more importance on the personality. For example, in the thirteenth century, when Thomas Aquinas drew up a hierarchy of sexual sins, he classified masturbation as a more serious sin than fornication between consenting partners, seduction of a virgin, and adultery.[6] Masturbation was more sinful because it omitted the object created by God for the sexual drive, the genital organ of the opposite sex. Masturbation was one of the "unnatural vices," all of which were more sinful than illicit copulation because they violated the law of nature, as well as the laws of society and of the church. More serious unnatural vices included (in ascending order of gravity) orgasm involving a nongenital organ of a heterosexual partner, homosexual acts, and bestiality.

In the eight hundred years between Augustine and Aquinas, the potential of natural law theology to say something positive about sexual pleasure remained undeveloped. Augustine's influence was paramount, and Augustine taught that sin had removed the capacity for pleasure very far from its natural state. People could still enjoy sex, but their pleasure depended on an unruly passion, often present when unwanted and sometimes absent even though mentally desired. Passion pressed its claims without reference to greater rational goods such as procreation and friendship, and it constantly tempted humanity to sin against these goods. This conflict between passion and reason was fitting both as a punishment and as a symbol for human disobedience to God. In the perfection of life before sin, humans would have enjoyed a more reliable and more rational pleasure in sex, without inner conflict or shame.[7] Thus far came Augustine, but his successors went further. Observation of the disrupted relationship between passion and reason led some to conclude that any consent of the soul to the pleasure of sex was sinful, although they expected that intercourse would make such consent nearly unavoidable. Thus, even married couples fell into sin while making love, at the moment when passion overcame their reason. Pope Gregory the Great said that married people should not receive communion after intercourse unless they had first done penance.[8] Later writers, including the standard theological authors of the twelfth century, argued that passion actually transmitted original sin by corrupting the seed with its heat.[9]

A forum for reassessing the morality of pleasure within specific sexual acts came into being during the sixth and seventh centuries, when handbooks to guide confessors began to appear.[10] The practice of private confession of sin gradually spread from monasteries to parishes, to become a universal obligation of Catholics at the Fourth Lateran Council in 1215. Private confession brought the doctrine of the church into more and more frequent contact with the realities of married life. But this contact could not change theory. Sexual pleasure with one's spouse remained a venial sin. Venial sin did not destroy the saving work of God's grace in the soul, as mortal sin would, but taking pleasure even in marital sex weakened and stained the soul and so required that the sinner do penance on earth or after death.

With the recovery of Aristotelian philosophy in the thirteenth century, of which the work of Aquinas is the great example, Catholic thought gained a principle that transformed its perspective on sex. Aristotle's *Ethics* argued that pleasure itself was neither good nor evil. Only intentional acts could be good or evil, and any pleasures associated with such acts derived their moral character from that of the acts in question.[11] Applying this principle to sex, Aquinas reasoned that because intercourse in marriage was a legitimate act, the pleasure produced by that act did not entail even venial sin.[12]

Thus began the tradition invoked by the American bishop Kenrick who noted in his general discussion of desire, "There are some more severe philosophers who reject all enjoyment, but, as St. Thomas [Aquinas] said, they counsel badly."[13] For Kenrick, passion could even add to the moral goodness of an act. Writing on "concupiscence," the technical term for the capacity for passion, he argued that consent to the passion resulting from a good act was itself another good act.[14] There were grounds here for concluding that passionate sex in marriage was morally superior to sex without passion.

Passion, Pleasure, and Sin

Yet Aquinas had not given Catholics unconditional freedom to take pleasure from sex. Both Aquinas and Kenrick still maintained that sin had injured human sexuality, at least in the sense of weakening the control of the rational soul over the body. If passion, or on a conscious level the desire for pleasure (i.e., the desire to enjoy passion), so dominated reason as to become the *only* motive for a sexual act within marriage, that intercourse was not a true marriage act, because it was not rightly motivated. Marital sex had three rational purposes: to produce children, to fulfill one's contract with one's partner, and to save oneself and one's partner from temptations to sexual sin.[15] For Aquinas and for Kenrick, spouses who engaged in intercourse solely for pleasure, without conscious or assumed reference to one of these rational ends, acted not as husbands and wives but as males and females.[16] Because their married status allowed sex, their sin was not mortal; but the deficiency of their intention meant that in the moment of passion, they incurred the guilt and stain of venial sin. Only true marital intercourse, informed by rational purpose, could be both free from sin and as passionate as the partners could manage.

The centuries from Aquinas to Kenrick saw scores of moral theologians, armed with post-Aristotelian reasoning and Augustinian distrust of passion, refining and developing Catholic teaching on sex. Not all were liberals: a school of rigorists emerged, some of whom contributed to the heresy called Jansenism by teaching that any act not motivated by a desire for the glory of God was sinful. Ranged against the rigorists were the laxists, particularly strong in the Jesuit order, some of whom fell under condemnation at the other extreme when they contended that no one could commit sin without the conscious intention of offending God.[17]

Advances continued despite the dispute. Because they consulted carefully with the married and with doctors,[18] moralists altered several readings of the natural law that had arisen from medieval conjecture. Pope Gregory the Great, for example, had forbidden sex during nursing lest the milk be spoiled or contaminated; authorities including Aquinas had condemned sex during menstruation out of fear that leprous children would result; many had sought to limit sex to a face-to-face position with the man on top, because they believed that any other posture had a contraceptive effect. These taboos and others were gradually broken down in the face of increasing knowledge.[19] Meanwhile, two conclusions essential to the Catholic discussion of sexual pleasure received precise and authoritative definitions. In 1546, the Council of Trent declared that concupiscence was the "tinder" of sin (*fomes peccati*), but was not formally sinful in itself.[20] This definition gave the Catholic polemicist Robert Bellarmine the opportunity to criticize Protestants for being too hard on human nature.[21] On the other hand, in 1679 the laxist proposition that marital sex "exercised for pleasure alone lacks entirely any fault and any defect" was condemned by Pope Innocent XI.[22]

Between the statements of the council and the pope, there was room to build a system; the accumulation of detailed knowledge had provided the material for a system, but through the first half of the eighteenth century, there was no single Catholic system of sexual morality. If a confessor read rigorist texts, he might judge an act, such as the assumption of a particular position in intercourse, a given type of stimulation with the hand or the mouth, or even a fantasy, to be *prima facie* evidence of motivation by pleasure alone. Other texts told confessors to allow married couples identical actions without demanding contrition and penance.

Resolution came with the monumental work of Alphonsus Liguori (1696–1787). Though assailed from both the laxist and rigorist sides during his life, Liguori came finally to be hailed as the Aquinas of moral theology and to exert an influence on nineteenth-century Catholic life unmatched by any other individual. He founded an order (the Redemptorists), wrote devotional works that continue to be printed and hymns that are still sung, attained renown as a preacher to the poor, and as a bishop helped to crush the last strongholds of Jansenism in Italy.[23] But Liguori obtained his most telling influence through his *Theologia Moralis*, first published in 1748, and then revised and expanded over several decades. In 1831, the Roman

Penitentiary, the central Catholic court for questions arising in the confessional, ruled that priests could apply Liguori's conclusions uncritically, "not weighing the elements and reasons on which his various opinions depend."[24] The commission examining the case for Liguori's beatification, the first step toward sainthood, had already pronounced his works free from error,[25] and he was canonized by Pope Gregory XVI in 1839.[26] In 1871, Pope Pius IX declared St. Alphonsus to be a doctor of the church. By that time, as one scholar has said, "In the manuals [of moral theology] St. Augustine was replaced without much struggle by St. Alphonsus."[27] Kenrick did make some interesting additions to the theological structure that Liguori had erected, but the American bishop professed that his intention in writing about sex was to follow "closely upon the footsteps of St. Alphonsus in this slippery place," even to the point of reproducing the saint's exact words on some questions, "lest any take offense at us."[28]

Liguori avoided the extremes of the rigorist and laxist schools by combining their intellectual principles. Rigorists decided moral questions by presuming that an act detracted from God's glory unless the more probable arguments militated for innocence; their position was called probabiliorism. Laxists, on the other hand, said that an act was innocent if *any* probable argument could be stated in its favor; their position was known as probabilism. Making use of scholastic method, Liguori first posed a question, then weighed arguments for guilt and innocence against each other, and finally ruled the act allowable if the arguments were equal. He called his principle equiprobabilism.[29] Because the method entailed consideration of every possible argument, the moral theology of St. Alphonsus became an encyclopedic work, valuable not only for the influence of Liguori's conclusions but also as an index to the history of Catholic opinion.

For example, because Liguori had so ruled, Kenrick said that a wife could innocently bring herself to orgasm after intercourse in which she had experienced no climax; but Kenrick gave no reason for this decision. In St. Alphonsus himself, one found the question: "If the man retracts himself after semination, but before the semination of the woman, may she immediately excite herself by touches to seminate?"[30] Liguori then cited five moralists who denied women this action under penalty of sin; they believed (following the biology accepted by Albert the Great, the teacher of Aquinas) that the woman's orgasm was not true "semination," because it released no seed and was not necessary for conception. Therefore, a complete sexual act had already occurred when the man seminated. The woman's self-stimulation would be beyond the bounds of natural law, and thus mortally sinful. On the opposite side, Liguori ranged twenty-two authorities who allowed wives this action on the grounds that it pertained to the completion of the marital act, which nature indicated should involve the orgasm of both partners. Among these twenty-two were some who added that the denial of this right would put wives in danger of sin in the form of later masturbation or adultery. "If women were required to restrain nature after such irritation," Liguori reported, summarizing this argument, "they would be continually exposed to great danger of sinning mortally, since usually the men, being hotter, seminate first."

This last appeal to realism won the approval of several later Catholic authors. Liguori himself did not accept it, pointing out that a man deprived of orgasm through incomplete coitus had no analogous right to relieve himself. Instead, Liguori's argument combined the contention that a woman's touches completed the marital act with a reply to the objections based on biology. Even if female orgasm (still called *seminatio)* was not necessary for conception, he found it probable that the wife's orgasm imparted some benefit or "perfection" to any child that might be conceived. As St. Alphonsus saw it, there must be some biological purpose for female orgasm, because "nature does nothing in vain." Both the definition of a marriage act and a probable argument from natural law therefore vindicated the woman in this case, and she was guilty of no sin. St. Alphonsus concluded his discussion with a reminder that would tend to promote mutual orgasm: "All concede that wives who are colder by nature may excite themselves before copulation, so that they might seminate while having marital congress."[31]

With advice of this sort, moral theology was moving into an entirely different world from that in which consent to pleasure had been venial sin and passion was held guilty of corrupting seed. Progressing beyond the allowance and recommendation of pleasure, Liguori and his successors developed a positive obligation of the married to pursue orgasm.

Kenrick's statements concerning this obligation were simple and clear: a husband sinned venially by neglecting to remain active until his wife's orgasm; a wife sinned mortally by distracting herself to avoid orgasm.[32] But behind these judgments stood the complex reasoning Liguori had applied to *amplexus reservatus*, an arcane form of intercourse in which a couple joined their sexual organs but restricted their motion to delay or to avoid climax. *Amplexus* has appeared among Albigensian heretics in twelfth-century France, among illicit lovers in French court circles of the same century, among married couples in Liguori's Italy, and among members of the Oneida Community in nineteenth-century New York.[33] For some it was merely a method of birth control; for others it expressed spiritual love through control of the flesh. For Liguori, *amplexus* provided an opportunity to examine more closely the relation of orgasm to a complete sexual act.[34]

Although St. Alphonsus conceded the practice of *amplexus* to the married, he expressed great concern for mutuality. Neither husband nor wife could practice unilateral restraint, under pain of mortal sin. Furthermore, in the event of a unilateral breakdown of restraint, as when the woman "might be in probable danger of seminating," the other partner was bound also to release.[35] A modern writer might well approve of these sanctions on psychological grounds; for one partner to maintain control while the other yielded to orgasm would not seem likely to foster a harmonious relationship. But Liguori grounded his judgments in the physical realm of natural law.

Pursuing the questions raised by a failure of discipline, Liguori asked whether a man who lost control of himself and ejaculated while attempting to practice *amplexus* thereby acquired any obligation to stimulate his wife to orgasm.[36] The consensus of moralists said no. Even those who felt that the woman's orgasm should be part of a complete sex act believed female orgasm to be unnecessary for conception, which was the ultimate end of nature in sex. They therefore ruled that the husband's omission was not sinful. But here Liguori demonstrated his independence of majorities. According to a corollary of equiprobabilism, no one could be allowed to omit an action on probable grounds if another probable argument indicated that damage to a third party might result. Release of the male seed introduced a third party by opening the possibility of conception. Therefore, Liguori decided that a husband in this situation must continue stimulating his wife, to provide any conceptus with the "perfection" probably imparted by female orgasm.[37] Omission of this duty would be venial sin.

Such reasoning had potential for applications beyond the limited context of *amplexus reservatus*. Explicitly stepping out of that context, Liguori reminded his readers that the consensus of authorities at least *allowed* a husband to continue to stimulate his wife after ejaculation in *any* act of intercourse.[38] Returning to the women, St. Alphonsus then dissented strongly from the permission, granted by a few, to a woman to avoid orgasm during ordinary sexual acts "by diverting her mind to other things."[39] Only in a mutual *amplexus* could wives so restrain themselves. In ordinary intercourse, this restraint often represented a contraceptive intention, because some women followed a folk belief that they could not conceive if they did not have orgasm. Even if there was no contraceptive intent, Liguori saw the avoidance of orgasm under such circumstances as a contravention of natural law and a probable occasion of damage to any child conceived, and therefore as a mortal sin.

One (undoubtedly unforeseen) consequence of the Roman ruling that confessors could employ Liguori's conclusions without weighing his arguments was that later moralists, among them Bishop Kenrick, emphasized obligations to orgasm but eliminated the connections to conception. In Kenrick's text, the husband's duty to continue stimulating his wife and the wife's duty not to distract herself were set forth in separate short paragraphs.[40] The context of *amplexus reservatus* and of "perfections" imparted to the fetus had vanished. In both cases, the encouragement of orgasm grew stronger and more unconditional by the omission of arguments.

An explicit shift of concern from conception to pleasure gradually strengthened the woman's right to procure orgasm for herself after her husband stopped his activity. Here again, Kenrick's text of 1843 simply stated the right, eliminating Liguori's discussion of whether female orgasm related to conception and his accounts of dissenting views.[41] The Dutch American Anthony Könings, whose 1874 text supplemented Kenrick's in American seminaries, endorsed the argument that women should not be required to restrain nature when men, "being hotter, seminate first," despite Liguori's rejection of this line of reasoning.[42] Meanwhile, the word *seminatio*, with its implication of a relationship between female orgasm and the release of seed for conception, gradually disappeared from moral texts. Both Kenrick and Könings still used the term, but in 1869, the French Jesuit Jean-Paul Gury, whose digest of Liguori became influential both in Europe and in America, introduced the phrase "in order to more powerfully complete her pleasure [*voluptatem*]" alongside *seminatio* in his discussion of this right.[43] By 1908, when an English Jesuit named Thomas Slater produced the first moral theology written in English (with the exception of sexual doctrine, which remained in Latin), *seminatio* no longer appeared at all, having been replaced by "in order to complete the venereal delight [*delectationem veneream*]."[44] New texts that affirmed the woman's right to bring herself to orgasm continued to be published in America through 1946; sometimes they retained *seminatio* in describing this right, but more often the descriptions made exclusive reference to pleasure.[45]

Despite its encouragement of orgasm, post-Liguorian Catholic theology still taught that the connection between pleasure and the sinfulness of human nature posed difficulties for the morality of sexual behavior. Pleasure in a good act was morally good, and probably conducive to physical good, but the definition of a good act still required couples not to have sex, in Liguori's words, "for a depraved end, for example on account of sensuality alone."[46] A woman could licitly complete her pleasure, but she could not licitly begin sexual activity without reference to one of the rational purposes of marital intercourse. To act for the sake of pleasure alone was to consent to the depravity of a fallen nature, in which passion subjugated reason.

Paradoxically, a majority of Liguori's allowances for pleasure *resulted* from his suspicions of fallen human nature. The reasoning underlying such allowances was that depraved nature often made demands that required extraordinary action if sins such as adultery or masturbation were to be avoided. For example, refusing sex to a marriage partner sometimes placed the one seeking sex "in danger of incontinence," and thus the refusal of sex "when seriously asked" was a mortal sin for the partner refusing.[47] Having intercourse "in an unusual place, such as a church or a public place," would ordinarily be sinful on account of the possible scandal to others or the sacrilege involved, but sex in such settings might be allowed in a case of "necessity."[48] Under most circumstances, a husband did not sin by omitting to seek sex from his wife; yet he would sin by this omission if the wife showed "any indication of her desire" by which she might seem tacitly to ask for sex, "because in women, on account of their innate modesty, such signs are taken for a true petition."[49] Husbands and wives had a duty to watch for the signs of desire so that sin might be avoided. Even if a spouse had taken a religious vow not to seek sex for a certain time, perception of a "danger of incontinence" in either partner meant that the spouse under the vow was not only allowed but also obligated to ask.[50]

Rules like these had a Biblical basis in Paul's admonition (I Corinthians 7:5) that husbands and wives not remain apart for long, lest they be tempted; but Catholic suspicion of sexual passion within fallen human nature fostered dramatically specific applications of Paul's advice. Within moral theology, passion figured as a source of unceasing pressure, constantly threatening to break forth into violations of the natural law.

On the other hand, natural law reasoning had the potential to leave the suspicion of depravity behind and to justify pleasure in terms of fulfilling the purposes of God in nature. Liguori approached this point when he added "the reason of health" to his list of the rational purposes of marital sex.[51] The purpose of procreation came from Genesis through Augustine, and the purposes of fulfilling a duty to one's spouse and of avoiding sin had their sources in Paul, but "the reason of health" could claim no authority other than the argument that sex was a good of nature. If health was sufficient as a purpose for marital sex, what happened to the doctrine that sin had removed human sexual pleasure from its natural context? Liguori sensed the difficulty and qualified his acceptance; "to use [sex] *solely* for the reason of health, however," was probably still venial sin.[52] Along another front, Kenrick advanced independently toward asserting the natural goodness of sex. In his list of reasons for a husband's obligation to seek intercourse, he replaced the negative purpose of helping the wife to avoid sin with a purpose of "satisfying the wife [*ad uxori satisfaciendum*]."[53]

According to John Noonan, a contemporary authority on canon law and moral theology, the Liguorian era was indeed a time of decision, during which the Roman Catholic Church nearly recast its teaching on the natural law of sexual behavior.[54] Noonan made this point in relation to the issue of contraception, but the same era also witnessed crucial battles over the moral status of sexual pleasure. Innocent XI had censured the proposition that "a marital act exercised for pleasure alone lacks entirely any fault and any defect," yet theologians persisted in the attempt to find a path around the papal teaching. Reinterpreting the doctrine that marital sex could be used to prevent sin, as Kenrick did in his positive version of the husband's duty, was the logical route. The main body of moralists took no notice of Kenrick, who published in a mission land and presented no argument in support of his new phrase. The Italian Jesuit Antonio Ballerini, however, touched off a general debate that had the same Pauline doctrine as its focus. Over the last third of the nineteenth century, in a revision of Gury's manual and in his own moral theology, Ballerini argued that the marriage act could not function as the "remedy for concupiscence," preventing sexual sins, unless that act could be done for the purpose of pleasure.[55] Recent moralists such as the Americans John C. Ford and Gerald Kelly, who wrote in 1964, have stated their belief that Ballerini won his point.[56] But a group of angry Redemptorists, calling themselves the *Vindicatores* of St. Alphonsus, assailed the Jesuit in 1874, and the positions found in twentieth-century moral texts (particularly those published in the United States) by no means demonstrated Ballerini's triumph.[57] Papal statements over the last fifty years have certainly commended the pursuit of pleasure as a secondary end of sex, but they have also given new prominence to the doctrine that married couples who have sex for pleasure alone commit sin.[58]

Natural law theology produced the first Christian defense of orgasm; it also weakened the Augustinian condemnation of passion, and thus contributed to the liberation of sex from original sin. Yet the whole development of Catholic thinking on sexual pleasure may appear misguided, or even perverse, from the standpoint of contemporary American ethics. From this standpoint, disputes over the moral limits of consent to fallen nature seem to miss the basic purpose of sex in marriage: to express love. For us, sexual pleasure in marriage can only be evil if it fails to express love. Even if our criterion of love results in the same conclusion that natural law theology would support in a specific case, the process by which we reach that conclusion represents a transformation of sexual morality. The purposes of marital sex accepted by Catholic theology, from procreating, to fulfilling a marriage contract, to avoiding temptation, or, for that matter, to strengthening health or experiencing pleasure, demanded no more than a rational intention and an appropriate physical act. But to judge the morality of sex by the criterion of love extended the discussion into the realm of emotional or spiritual dispositions.

Emphasizing psychological rather than physical considerations opened another route to the liberation of sex from original sin. Even though death, sickness, and the necessity for work implied that the *physical* world had fallen into disharmony, and even though that disharmony appeared in the unreliability and impetuous force of sexual passion, the claim to an innocent spirit could still prevail. This idea of perfection in spiritual love was central for those who would finally "redeem" sex in American culture. The history of Catholic doctrine on the psychology of sex thus became as relevant to modern sexual ethics as the defense of pleasure drawn from natural law.

Psychological Standards

Beginning with the laxist-rigorist debates of the seventeenth century, Catholic moral theology has demonstrated a growing concern with the mental states accompanying passion, and this concern had its influence on the texts of Liguori and Kenrick. The earliest manuals for confessors had dealt simply with physical acts, but Liguori both summarized an existent body of teaching on protection of the personal bond in marriage and added his own contribution to that teaching. He agreed, for example, with the consensus that imagining another partner while having sex with one's spouse was "mental adultery," and therefore mortal sin.[59] On the other hand, entertaining a fantasy about the copulation of another couple might be innocent if the spouse or spouses used the excitement of the fantasy to prepare for their own intercourse. Such fantasies could not involve known persons, however, because this might lead to an illicit desire for these persons. Acknowledging that he was the first moralist to consider the question of precoital fantasy, Liguori stated his conclusions tentatively, leaving further consideration "to the discretion of the wise."[60]

Often Liguori used mental criteria to weaken physical prohibitions. On the question of whether a man sinned if he inserted his finger into the anus of his wife during intercourse, the rigorist Tamburinius had said yes, indicting the act as a variant of the mortal sin of sodomy; but Liguori dissented, professing uncertainty "that this feeling [the *affectus* of sodomy] is contained in such an act."[61] A more remarkable example of tolerance based on consideration of mental states occurred in *The Practice of the Confessor*, a small volume of guidance sometimes bound with Liguori's moral theology. Here, St. Alphonsus noted that peasant males frequently did not realize "the special malice of adultery." If these men did not think of their extramarital relations (presumably with prostitutes) as mortal sins, Liguori advised the confessor not to disturb their ignorance:

> With those who are accustomed to this vice, it is not expedient to warn them of the evil of adultery, since the profit of the warning may be expected to be small, but will have such effect that the penitent will sin doubly, if he does not resist the desire of the flesh.[62]

Such concern for the consciousness of sin could cut both ways. Only two paragraphs after allowing adultery to the ignorant, Liguori taught that a wavering intention to commit sin added a separate sin of intention at each point of consent, even if there was only one consummated act. Fantasies during masturbation likewise involved a distinct mortal sin for each person imagined in the fantasy.[63]

But with all of Liguori's concern for sexual psychology, his doctrine on sex almost never mentioned love. This omission reflected a tradition that knew the difference between sex and love only too well. Women taught by Catholic moralists to give themselves sexually "as many times as the

men can bear"[64] probably saw more love in a husband's self-denial than in
his ardor, and celibate priests also recognized love more easily in sacrifice
than in enjoyment.

The single instance in which love did figure in Liguori's teaching on
sex in marriage was his discussion of the so-called imperfect acts: kissing, manual stimulation, and oral-genital contact. Because natural
law permitted orgasm only in coitus, no imperfect acts could licitly be
continued to the point of imminent orgasm. To Liguori, this meant
that some of these acts were forbidden altogether. Some moralists had
argued that "insistently moving a finger in the female vessel," or the
taking of the male organ into the wife's mouth, might be allowed if
done "in passing," or in preparation for intercourse; but St. Alphonsus
felt that both actions necessarily brought about an imminent danger of
orgasm, and therefore constituted mortal sin.[65] Yet here again Liguori
reasoned that the proper mental condition might result in innocence.
Any act, even with the "foreseen danger of pollution," could be done if
there was an urgent necessity "to foster love" (ad fovendum amorem).[66]
A sufficient need to foster love could arise from suspicion of adultery,
strong temptation to infidelity, or some other threat to the marriage.
Thus, even the isolated appearance of love in Liguori's sexual doctrine
was really negative, overshadowed by the expectation that extraordinary
means could be necessary to keep corrupt passion within the bounds
of marriage.

Love received more positive attention from Liguori's successors.
According to John Noonan, Jean-Paul Gury's 1869 digest of St. Alphonsus
was the first Catholic text that mentioned love as one of the rational purposes for undertaking marital coitus.[67] This is formally correct, but the
American Kenrick anticipated Gury by twenty-six years when he listed "to
foster love" among the reasons a husband might be obligated to attempt
intercourse.[68] And for Kenrick, the role of love went far beyond technical precepts. He introduced his section on marriage with a little sermon
on love, a feature unparalleled in earlier moralists and unequaled until
much later. "Love is enjoined upon the husband," wrote the bishop of
Philadelphia, "so that he might rule the wife by affection more strongly
than by authority."[69] Both spouses "ought to love each other especially,"
continued Kenrick; they should avoid any "singular affection" for another
even if that affection was not expressed in sexual acts. The positive bond
that Kenrick forged between love, sex, and general behavior in marriage
was something entirely new in Catholic moral theology.

The man sins gravely against the debt of love to his wife, ... in bearing himself so as to give his wife reason to suspect that she is loved less, in order to make her unhappy and miserable. Again, he sins in suspecting his wife for light reasons of having illicit commerce with another man, and in finding fault continually, and blaming her. He sins equally by treating her harshly, and neglecting her, because he wearies of her company. Hence the man who frequents taverns, theaters, and other places of this type, and does not return home until the night is already advanced; and who, not having known his wife, retires in another place; and who is absent many times for no necessary cause, gravely fails in that affection with which a wife ought to be pursued.[70]

Until the 1920s, no Catholic moralist equaled Kenrick in relating sex to a larger pattern of marital behavior centered on love. Because Catholic tradition offered no precedent for such an emphasis, a question arises regarding cultural influences: Did Kenrick's teaching on marriage derive its unique character from his American context?

Internal evidence suggests a positive answer to this question. Kenrick's moral theology abounded in explicit adjustments to conditions in America. A volume has been written analyzing his doctrine on slavery.[71] In matters relating to marriage, the most obvious adjustment appeared in his long paragraph on migration, a topic untouched by Liguori. An "undivided custom of life" ought to prevail among married couples, Kenrick taught; therefore, he required a wife to follow a husband who wanted to move, even if this meant "to leave her parents and her native land and to remain in a distant region."[72] However, he did not expect a wife to accompany a husband who wandered without definite aim, "unless she has married in good conscience to lead an uncertain life." The loneliness and fear of the immigrant and the pioneer echoed behind Kenrick's final admonition:

And if the husband wants to translate himself into distant lands, where they will lack the means of subsistence, the wife can influence him by entreaties, but scarcely can refuse to submit to him, for God will not be lacking to his pious efforts.[73]

The perception that Catholics in the United States needed instruction for new situations must have helped motivate Kenrick to write his moral theology. Love became part of the necessary adjustment. Marriage was a more personal matter in the New World than it had been in Europe; marriages depended more on the spouses alone as people moved away from traditional social networks and arrangements. Just as Kenrick eliminated some topics included by Liguori in his treatment of marriage, such as advice on marital obligations to a political exile and on fixing the terms of dowries, so the American bishop needed to say more than Liguori (or any other moralist) had said about personal love. The transition to the United States brought Catholic thought closer to the modern ethic of sexual pleasure, in which love emerged as the central moral question.

2

Protestant Reactions

Anti-Catholic Pornography

American Protestants made Catholic sexual doctrine more famous than the moral theologians ever intended it to be. More than a dozen collections of excerpts from Catholic moralists, translated as thoroughly as Victorian modesty allowed, issued from Protestant presses during the nineteenth century.[1] The ministers who edited these collections denounced "the incurable filthiness and brutalizing effects of Popery,"[2] but they also wrote more explicitly about sex than they ever had occasion to write otherwise. And they sold books.

Even more popular than direct attacks on Catholic teaching were the personal tales of supposed victims of Catholicism. Maria Monk's *Awful Disclosures of the Hotel Dieu Nunnery* sold three hundred thousand copies between 1836 and the Civil War, making it the most popular book written in America before *Uncle Tom's Cabin*.[3] Presenting itself as the autobiography of a woman who was born Protestant but who attended a Catholic school and became a nun, *Awful Disclosures* depicted life in the convent as a ceaseless round of forced sex and sadistic penances, presided over by priests who had access to the nuns by means of a tunnel from the rectory. If a nun became pregnant, the baby was baptized and suffocated immediately after birth, and the body was disposed of in a pit of lye. The whole ghastly system began in the confessional. As Monk wrote, "When quite a child, I heard from the mouths of priests at confession what I cannot repeat, with treatment corresponding. . . ."[4] During her novitiate, the priests progressed to questions "of the most improper and revolting nature, naming crimes both unthought of, and inhuman."[5] She grew accustomed to such interrogations and accustomed to believe that she needed her confessors to obtain forgiveness of sin, so Monk descended to the state of subjection in which she had sexual relations with three priests in a night, and then became pregnant by another. Having fled the convent to save the life of her unborn baby, Monk found ministers in New York eager to protect her. The Harper brothers went to court to win the right to publish her book.[6]

Though several ministers and newspaper reporters investigated the convent named by Maria Monk and discredited her story,[7] *Awful Disclosures* began a flourishing genre. Not only did hack writers enter the field for profit, but also such giants of American literature as Nathaniel Hawthorne and Harriet Beecher Stowe participated, in their own more decorous fashion. The subject of Catholic immorality entered the mainstream of American literature, where it remains today, as the popularity of *The Thorn Birds* and Andrew Greeley's novels indicates. During the nineteenth century and the first quarter of the twentieth, anti-Catholic pornography helped to provoke a defensive reaction among Catholic moral theologians in the United States, leading them to write apologies for dealing with sex and to take much more conservative positions on sex than their colleagues in Europe. On the other hand, accounts of Catholic corruption may have had a liberating effect on Protestants, who could use this literature to explore their own darker desires while reinforcing their sense of righteousness.

Sexual accusations against Catholicism contributed directly to the modern ethic of sexual pleasure by increasing the amount and the explicitness of discourse about sex. Among the more skillful practitioners of this combination of prurience and religious polemic was William Hogan, a priest who left the church after clashing with the bishop of Philadelphia (Bishop Kenrick's predecessor) over the claim that his parishioners, and not the bishop, owned the building where they worshiped.[8] Hogan asked his readers to imagine "a young lady, . . . on her knees, with her lips nearly close pressed to the cheeks of the priest. . . ."[9] The priest listens to the girl confess her hatred for a schoolmate; then, "scarcely able to conceal a smile in finding the girl perfectly innocent," he begins to ask questions. Has she ever had immodest thoughts? Does she ever think about men? After the girl admits her fondness for a cousin, the confessor becomes more specific. Has she ever slept with her cousin? How long did her thoughts of him continue? Did she have these thoughts by day or by night?

> In this strain does this reptile confessor proceed, till his now half-gained prey is filled with ideas and thoughts, to which she has been hitherto a stranger. He tells her that she must come to-morrow again. . . . Day after day, week after week, and month after month

does this hapless girl come to confession, until this wretch has worked up her passions to a tension almost snapping, and then becomes his easy prey.[10]

Many ex-priests used their status as experts to launch careers in anti-Catholic sensationalism. Samuel B. Smith claimed to have served as chaplain to a convent that specialized in hiding pregnant nuns from all over the country. In his weekly newspaper, *The Downfall of Babylon,* Smith combined his own adventures with selections from the racier parts of Liguori's moral theology, and the stories of Maria Monk and another "escaped nun," Rosamond Culbertson, who said she had been held captive in a convent in Cuba.[11] Alessandro Gavazzi, a priest who left Italy and the church after a failed revolt against the temporal rule of the pope, ran revival meetings at which he warned men not to let their wives and daughters come into contact with nuns and priests.[12] A Canadian priest named Charles Chiniquy wrote *The Priest, the Woman, and the Confessional,* which remains in print and available in some evangelical bookstores more than a century after its first publication.[13]

Former priests and escaped nuns never represented the elite of Catholicism, but Protestant writers in this field were often more distinguished. The Reverend George Bourne, a Presbyterian minister who was one of Maria Monk's editors, had the title of "Father Bourne" in the abolition movement, because he was the first American to advocate the immediate abolition of slavery.[14] In the novel *Lorette* (1833), Bourne described a frontal assault on virtue by Canadian Catholics. First a nun took the heroine, a girl named Louise, on a ride into the country, and delivered "a long eulogy upon the happiness of residing in a convent; where persons might enjoy every pleasure of life without restraint, unreproached, and exempt from the fear of discovery."[15] The nun brought Louise to an isolated house where two other sisters, "adepts in every species of vice,"[16] and a priest awaited her. "When they were alone with me and the priest, every attempt was made to induce me to join in their disgusting familiarities with him." Persuasion by example having failed, the victim was held captive for twelve days and subjected to the "blandishments" of the priest.

Continually did he torment me with his wicked proposals and forced caresses. He boasted of the authority of his church, the blessedness of his absolution, the comfort of enjoying a priest's favour, and the satisfaction of a nun's life, with its glorious reward.[17]

Fortunately for Louise, the priest never got around to violence. Burglars attracted by the priest's wealth broke into the house and set a fire, enabling her to escape.

Ned Buntline, the western writer who discovered Buffalo Bill Cody and Wild Bill Hickok, allowed no such luck to the victims of Catholics in his book, *The Beautiful Nun* (1866). There, a young woman named Ursula, imprisoned in a convent in New York, gave a letter for her father to a sympathetic nun named Cecilia, who managed to throw the letter from a window to some firemen. The firemen happened to be Protestants, and they tried to storm the convent, but they were prevented by twenty Irish police.[18] After Buntline described the fight between the firemen and the police, with the same spirit that brought the "western" to life, he turned to the punishment of Ursula and Sister Cecilia, who were taken out of the city to a mansion in Westchester.

In a room hung with black, seven men, masked in black crepe and wearing crosses on the left side of their chests, sat in judgment on Ursula. A thumbscrew did not succeed in making her renounce her faith and give up her Protestant Bible, even though her torturers applied the screw until it crushed a bone. The chief judge spoke:

> "Ah, even more obstinate than ever. Tear the dress from her shoulders, reveal her cherished beauties to our gaze, and then so mark her that all may know that she *has* been a Catholic."
>
> In a moment her shrieking, shuddering form was bared to the waist, and then taking a redhot iron from the furnace, the heartless executioner drew a cross upon her naked breast.[19]

Ursula had her hair torn out by the roots and was ultimately reduced to insanity by water torture. Sister Cecilia recanted at the sight of her. Buntline insisted that the story was true, just as he did in his stories of Buffalo Bill.[20]

Like most women in anti-Catholic fiction, Ursula and Cecilia had only a passive role. In the central plotline of *The Beautiful Nun*, however, Buntline broke this convention. Genita Morland, the nun of the title, infiltrated a family in which the wealthy father hated Catholics, though his wife and three daughters had secretly converted. Without revealing herself as a nun, Genita gained the position of tutor to the girls. Then she seduced their father, causing a divorce in which he was at fault, so that the wealth of the family devolved on the wife and daughters, and thus fell into the hands of the church.[21] To accomplish her mission, Genita employed considerable skill "in the art of reading and using human hearts," as well as physical attributes that Buntline lovingly described: "Her eyes were large, liquid, and brilliant as dew and black as jet. . . . Her red ripe lips slightly parted when she smiled. . . ."[22] Genita inherited a figure "rather slender in the waist, but with a magnificent bust" from her mother, who was stripped and whipped at the beginning of the book for trying to get Genita's father to leave the priesthood.[23]

Another active woman, a colleague of Genita in the Sisters of Charity, cultivated "an intelligent, cheerful, tidy look" and worked as a governess for the daughter of a political opponent of Catholicism, so that she could report on his activities. "American reader," warned Buntline, reaching for the moral of his tale, "beware lest a Jesuit spy has been shoved surreptitiously into your family. Be ever on the alert, our enemies never sleep."[24] Whether the servant looked prim or sensual, she might be a Catholic agent.

To move from Ned Buntline to Nathaniel Hawthorne might seem to violate cultural categories. Yet Hawthorne felt the same fear of and fascination with Catholicism, charged with the same sexual current that ran through *The Beautiful Nun*. In *The Marble Faun* (1860), Hawthorne had the heroine Hilda, as pale an example of Victorian maidenhood as ever appeared in fiction, kidnapped in Rome and held in a convent. Nothing comparable to the fates of Buntline's victims befell Hilda, but that did not keep her fiancé, an American sculptor named Kenyon, from entertaining lurid fears.

> For here was a priesthood, pampered, sensual, with red and bloated cheeks, and carnal eyes. With apparently a grosser development of animal life than most men, they were placed in an unnatural relation with women, and thereby lost the healthy, human conscience that pertains to other human beings, who own the sweet household ties connecting them with wife and daughter. . . . Here was a population, high and low, that had no genuine belief in virtue; and if they recognized any act as criminal, they might throw off all care, remorse, and memory of it, by kneeling a little while at the confessional, and rising unburdened, active, elastic, and incited by fresh appetite for the next ensuing sin.[25]

Hawthorne cast no doubt on the validity of Kenyon's fears. Instead, he dwelt for pages on the dungeons of Rome, "where Innocence might shriek in vain," and on the "grime and corruption which Paganism had left" in Rome, corruption that "a perverted Christianity had made more noisome." Kenyon reflected that "Hilda's sanctity" should draw divine Providence to protect her, but Hawthorne also made his hero recall that "many an innocent virgin has lifted her white arms, beseeching [Providential] aid in her extremity, and all in vain."[26] Although Hilda returned to marry her sculptor, and Hawthorne in fact accepted some aspects of Catholicism, as the chapter on Mary will demonstrate, *The Marble Faun* took the conventions of anti-Catholic fiction for granted. The plot hinged on the murder of a corrupt monk by a woman with whom the monk was enmeshed in a mysterious crime. Hilda would never have been kidnapped if she had not gone to the confessional to unburden herself of the secret that she had witnessed this murder.

Working closer to the center of American culture, somewhere between Ned Buntline's dime novels and the art of Hawthorne, Harriet Beecher Stowe also exploited the sensational potential of Catholicism. Her contribution to the genre, *Agnes of Sorrento* (1862), went through sixteen editions in twenty-one years.

While Stowe's heroine knelt and watched a procession in fifteenth-century Rome, two servants of a Borgia pope were watching her.

"There is the model which our master has been looking for," said a young and handsome man in a rich dress of black velvet, who . . . appeared to hold the rank of chamberlain in the Papal suite. . . .

"Pretty little rogue, how well she does the saint!"

"One can see that, with judicious arrangement, she might be a nymph as well as a saint. . . ."[27]

Agnes soon found herself in the "impure den" of Pope Alexander VI, from which she was rescued by her noble lover Agostino, at the head of a hundred men.

Confession had once again brought about sexual peril. Agnes went to Rome at the order of her confessor, Father Francesco, who sent her on pilgrimage to delay her marriage. Although Francesco had led a "dissipated and irregular life" until the preaching of Savonarola convinced him to renounce the world, his priestly ordination gave him the right to guide the innocent Agnes, the "right with probing-knife and lancet to dissect all the finest nerves and fibres of her womanly nature."[28] Naturally, this spiritual surgeon fell in love with his patient. His love began with no base desire: "insensibly to himself, the weekly interviews with Agnes at the confessional became the rallying-points around which the whole of his life was formed, and she the unsuspected spring of his inner being."[29] But when Francesco stood on his balcony at sunset and planned to send Agnes to Rome, to prevent her marriage and to convince her to enter the convent of St. Agnes where he was chaplain, Stowe revealed the more fleshly aspect of his love.

> Yes, she should ascend from glory to glory,—but *his* should be the hand that should lead her upward . . . *he* should be the guardian and director of her soul, the one being to whom she should render an obedience as unlimited as that which belongs to Christ alone.
>
> Such were the thoughts of this victorious hour,—which, alas! were destined to fade as those purple skies and golden fires gradually went out, leaving, in place of their light and glory, only the lurid glow of Vesuvius.[30]

Stowe described Catholicism as a dizzying maze of symbols and practices that could lead Agnes either to sainthood or to depravity. The convent Agnes often visited, where Father Francesco wanted her to stay, had been built on the site of an ancient temple of Venus, where "the unnatural vices of Tiberius" once held sway.[31] At the center of the cloister stood the nude statue of a nymph, a vestige of paganism that the nuns had placed in their fountain and baptized as "St. Agnes dispensing the waters of purity to her convent." St. Agnes had attained beatitude, as Stowe informed the reader, by choosing martyrdom rather than sex with a pagan. To concentrate the image further, Stowe described the statue in great detail, then showed her heroine "drawn towards it with a mysterious attraction." As Agnes sat by the fountain, preparing flowers for the altar of her patron saint, she became a second statue: "Unconsciously to herself . . . her head dropped into the attitude of the marble nymph, and her sweet features assumed the same expression."[32]

In the nineteenth century, Protestants knew that Roman Catholics were bringing an alien vision of woman and of sexual morality to the United States. Mormons, Masons, Indians, Communists, Fascists, and Muslims have all inspired comparable fears in Americans, and all have figured as villains in the literature of sexual threat. People have always projected the desires they cannot acknowledge onto their enemies. But the depth and range that anti-Catholic pornography attained has never been matched. The extent of the genre corresponded to the extent of social, cultural, and doctrinal competition between Protestants and Catholics in America.

Background and Results

No audience has ever been more predisposed to accept anti-Catholic pornography than the United States of the 1830s. Our experience of a pluralist culture makes it difficult for us to appreciate how Protestant that America was. Unlike Scotland, Holland, Geneva, or any other Protestant stronghold, the United States had no Catholic past. No cathedrals or customs reminded Americans of a time before the Reformation. Yet hatred of the Roman Catholic Church was the oldest theme of American culture. The eastern states were settled by the most extreme Protestants of Great Britain, crusaders against Catholicism who cherished the bitter memories of bloody Queen Mary, the Spanish Armada, the Gunpowder Plot, Oliver Cromwell, and the Catholic wives of Stuart kings. They burned the pope in effigy every November 5th until the Revolution, when George Washington stopped the practice to avoid offending the French.[33] For seventy years, the American colonists had fought France—and the Indians recruited by French Jesuits—for possession of the interior of the continent.

Most Americans had no personal knowledge of Catholicism to moderate their prejudices. Except for a handful of English Catholic aristocrats in Maryland, who lost control of their colony to Presbyterians in 1689, and another isolated group of English Catholics in Kentucky, there were no centers of Catholic culture in the United States. During the two centuries from 1630 to 1830, generations of Americans lived and died without knowing a Catholic.

Then, between 1830 and 1860, immigrants from Ireland and Austria transformed the American population. Immigration quadrupled from 150,000 in the 1820s to 600,000 in the 1830s, nearly tripled to 1.7 million in the 1840s, and reached 2.5 million in the 1850s.[34] The whole nation had numbered only 3 million at the Revolution. Because most of the immigrants were Catholic, by 1854 the Roman Catholic Church became the largest single denomination of Christians in the United States. By then Boston and St. Louis had more immigrants than natives; Chicago and Cincinnati were about half immigrant, and Milwaukee about one third. Ohio had no Catholic churches in 1816, but by 1834 there were twenty-two

Catholic churches in Ohio, along with a Catholic newspaper, a college, and a seminary.[35]

The immigrants appeared to threaten the political and moral character of the nation. The Reverend Lyman Beecher, the father of Harriet Beecher Stowe and a leader of public opinion in his time, observed that "since the irruption of the northern barbarians [into the Roman Empire], the world has never witnessed such a rush of dark-minded population from one country to another, as is now leaving Europe and dashing upon our shores."[36] Beecher feared that the pope and the Austrian emperor would use the immigrants to overwhelm both Protestantism and democracy in America. When Irish Catholic votes gave Democratic Party machines dominance in the cities, many native Protestants came to share Beecher's fear. Samuel F. B. Morse, who later invented the telegraph, gained his first fame by warning of a plot to move the Vatican to the Mississippi valley.[37]

Reactions went beyond words. In 1834, a mob set fire to the convent and school run by Ursuline nuns in Charlestown, Massachusetts, and the buildings burned to the ground while the local fire companies and several selectmen stood by. A score of Protestants and Catholics killed each other in armed clashes in the streets of Philadelphia in 1844. During the 1850s, the "Know-Nothings," a political party organized for the purpose of keeping Catholics out of public office, controlled the state legislatures of Massachusetts and Ohio and ran Millard Fillmore for president before merging into the Republican Party. A mob in Washington, DC, seized the block of marble that Pope Pius IX had donated for the construction of the Washington Monument and threw it into the Potomac.[38] Only the need for labor prevented passage of a law curtailing immigration. Had it not been for the capacity of America's open spaces and open economy to absorb vast multitudes, the United States might have been Ulster.

Besides economic and political competition, sexual fear fueled Protestant animosity toward Catholics. Suspicion of Catholic sexual morality began with the two practices that looked most exotic to Protestants, celibacy and the confession of sins. Few Protestants believed in the possibility of true celibacy. As Ned Buntline wrote, "Don't tell me that a cloister or convent cell, can shut out *Nature* from the heart of a woman. . . ."[39] Many saw the vow of chastity as a release from all sexual restraint. "The Romish priest leads a wandering, loose, licentious life," wrote W. C. Brownlee, pastor of the Collegiate Reformed Dutch Church in New York.[40] Brownlee argued that the impossibility of celibacy made the priest more subversive of American society, because each wicked priest undermined public morals.

> He has all the honest feelings and desires of humanity; he can never honour them in a lawful way. He steals a cup of guilty pleasure here, and another there; he is conscious of guilt: is a crushed down and debased being. . . . But some spirits can sustain any thing. They can live in habitual guiltiness; . . . and yet become sleek and jolly, and easy and contented. These are just the men to do the work of assault upon us, in this moral invasion. . . . By their doctrines they corrupt the public mind; by their morals they pollute a whole neighborhood.[41]

Without subscribing entirely to Brownlee's vision, most Protestants believed that celibacy made the Catholic system both more corrupt and more effective. They speculated that celibacy kept nuns and priests from developing loyalties to homes and families, and to the countries where they lived, thus ensuring total dedication to the church; yet Protestants also insisted, as Martin Luther had, that the vow of chastity presumed too much on grace to restrain nature.[42] In a six hundred–page *History of Sacerdotal Celibacy* published in 1867, the scholarly Henry Charles Lea first admired the contribution of celibacy to "the conquering career of the Church," and then compared the assignment of celibate priests to hear the confessions of women to putting "fire to straw" with the hope that "combustion will not follow."[43]

Confession exerted a peculiar fascination for nineteenth-century Protestants. A hundred years before psychoanalysis and magazine advice columns made explicit discussions of sex acceptable, the confessional was one of the few contexts other than seduction in which such conversation might occur. Even if no seduction took place, the thought of priests and women talking about sex provoked outrage and titillation.

Less obvious, but more fundamental, sexual fears concerned the sensuality of Catholic worship, and the Catholic view of how human nature was affected by sin and brought to redemption. In the first half of the nineteenth century, American Protestants had almost no experience of ritual in worship or of the adornment of churches. Even Episcopal churches tended to be very plain, because the Episcopalians who lived in America nurtured very Protestant sympathies. Horace Bushnell, one of the most prominent Congregationalist ministers in the country, never heard an organ until he went to Italy and visited the Catholic cathedral at Florence.[44] Few Americans had seen a painting or sculpture in any context, Christian or secular; most knew only the least cultivated forms of music, drama, and dance.

Against this background of sensory deprivation, the attempts at pomp and beauty presented by the immigrant Catholic Church seemed outlandish and immoral. Ministers pointed to the "purple, and scarlet colour" that priests and bishops wore in processions, and identified Catholicism with Babylon the Great, the Mother of Harlots predicted in the New Testament.[45] Novelists imagined the sensuality of Catholic worship hypnotizing those who would be victims of sexual assaults. In *The American Nun; or, The Effects of Romance* (1836), a Protestant woman explained why she had nearly converted:

> The human heart is prone to seek out sensible or tangible objects of adoration.... And the Catholics, too, know and feel their power; ... they use all the senses, enlist them one and all into their service; their pictures, their sculptures, their music, and their architecture, are all the most perfect they can obtain; and I have felt my heart throb with ecstasy, while I listened to the touching melody of their sublime chants;—and oh, how many prostrate themselves before the altar, melted and subdued by the harmony; and imagine *that* feeling is the true worship of God.[46]

Protestants felt certain that this kind of ecstasy had nothing to do with Christian faith. A hundred years earlier, during an explosion of revivalism that history called the Great Awakening, preachers such as Jonathan Edwards, George Whitefield, and John Wesley had shown Protestants the power of expressing emotions in worship; but those revivalists inspired emotions by the Word alone, by preaching on biblical texts, and they used emotions to lead people to confront their sinful natures and their need to be born again. Catholic worship inspired emotions by sensual means, among people who trusted that baptism had exempted them from punishment for original sin and eliminated the need for conversion. What could such worship accomplish, other than satisfying a depraved need for excitement? According to an official publication of the Presbyterians, Catholicism was "nothing more or less than the religion of human nature—the religion natural, congenial, and delightful to fallen man."[47] To American Protestants, the vestments and statues, the stained glass and paintings, the incense and chants of Catholics were not just exotic or distasteful customs—they were idolatry. Catholicism was not Christianity at all, but an insidious falsification, a corruption of the Gospel by collusion with the fallen nature from which true Christianity delivered people.

If people were saved by faith in God's Word alone, and if faith came as a gift of God in spite of the corruption of nature, as Protestants believed, then the whole Catholic system represented bondage to the flesh. Catholic theology pictured God bringing people to redemption through the physical world, teaching about invisible things by means of the visible, and imparting grace through material objects in the sacraments. With regard to sex, Catholic theologians developed highly specific doctrines because they thought it was their duty to interpret God's intentions in creating the physical structure of the genitals. To Protestants, this looked like more bondage. Protestants might enjoy sex, but neither sex nor any other bodily function or physical object could have positive religious significance for Protestants. The Bible was the only revelation of God they recognized. Sin had obscured the divine intentions in creation too completely for theology to find any "natural law" in the world other than the law of sin and death.

The reaction of American culture to Catholic moral theology, therefore, resulted not only from unfamiliarity and prurient curiosity, but also from a fundamental theological difference. To publish a moral theology in nineteenth-century America meant having to apologize for dealing with sex at all. At the end of his section on marital sex, Bishop Kenrick of Philadelphia defended himself against those who, "pretending to moral purity, abhor scrutiny of the facts of marriage."[48] Since no such critics existed in Catholic circles, the bishop must have meant Protestants. Kenrick then lamented the suffering that arose from the abuse of sex and argued that the uniqueness of Catholicism in having a comprehensive and detailed body of doctrine on sexual practice proved that Catholicism was "the only true religion in the world."[49] Obviously, Kenrick knew that his church was under attack for its sexual doctrine.

It was the turn of the twentieth century before Father Adolphe Tanquerey, professor at St. Mary's Seminary in Baltimore from 1887 to 1902, produced the second moral theology that drew on American materials and experience. The organization of Tanquerey's book represented prudery triumphant. To judge from the tables of contents of each of his two volumes, moral theology had nothing to say about sex. His treatments of marriage and the virtue of chastity occupied separate sections called "supplements," unlisted in the tables of contents, bound after the indexes to their respective volumes and separately indexed themselves. Within these supplements, Tanquerey reached conclusions that would have tried the patience of St. Alphonsus Liguori. All the allowances and recommendations of sexual pleasure built up over centuries of reasoning on the natural law still appeared, but were hedged about with warnings. Positions other than the missionary position in coitus were not sinful, but they were unhealthy. Wives could bring themselves to orgasm after intercourse, but the confessor should seek out masturbators. Intercourse during menstruation involved no sin, but priests should inform husbands that their wives "naturally abhor" sex at this time, and rightly, since it could result in infections of the penis and the vagina.[50] Oral sex ranked as "a more horrible kind of sodomy" than anal intercourse, and entailed more horrible possibilities of disease.[51] Although Tanquerey could not challenge the letter of Liguori's tolerant conclusions, which had received the approbation of the church, his work revealed a transformation of the whole spirit of Catholic teaching on sex.

Many causes contributed to this transformation. Within the Catholic Church itself, birth control and abortion became serious issues in the 1870s, and the renewed battle over the reproductive purpose of sex led moralists to emphasize control rather than pleasure. But this issue did not have such dramatic effects on European theologians as in the United States, where the anti-Catholic and antisensual culture reinforced the conservative trend. Tanquerey cited American health writers to support his warnings.[52] After Tanquerey, Catholic moralists in America continued to follow such writers until they reached positions far more reactionary than European Catholic theologians ever adopted. By the 1920s, the contrast became so pronounced that, while the leading Vatican counselor on sex, Arthur Vermeersch, was advocating simultaneous orgasm as the best outcome of marital intercourse,[53] an American moralist named John McHugh introduced his section on sexual doctrine with this sentiment:

> Now, sex pleasure has been ordained by God as an inducement to perform an act which is both disgusting in itself and burdensome in its consequences.[54]

Catholic theology fell from the liberality of Kenrick, with his Liguorian tolerance for nature and his personal concern for love, to the repugnance of McHugh in less than a hundred years. To explain this change requires an exploration of American culture, and especially of the perspective on sex that American Protestants developed from the close of the colonial period to the beginning of the twentieth century. Physicians, not ministers, invented this new theology, and Catholic moralists proved more receptive to the theories of Protestant doctors than to the assaults of the Protestant clergy. In the United States, Christianity again encountered the ancient thesis that passion transmitted original sin by corrupting the seed, but this time the outcome was different.

3

Medical Christianity

Sex and Sin in the Colonies

Colonial Americans received little expert advice on sex. Perhaps they would have refused advice, since the colonies were farming communities in which sex was familiar and large families were useful. Population grew, mostly through natural increase, from three hundred and sixty thousand in 1713 to nearly three million by 1776.[1] Maternal deaths in bearing a dozen or more children posed a more obvious problem than sexual morality or the pursuit of pleasure.

The prevalence of Protestantism made Catholic expertise irrelevant. To Protestants, theology meant the Bible in its Protestant interpretation, not natural law. This greatly simplified clerical advice on marriage. Preachers emphasized marriage as a divine command, from which no celibates were exempt, and admonished husbands and wives to yield their bodies to one another. But the Bible appeared to say nothing about female orgasm, positions in intercourse, or any other details of sexual practice. Some English authorities who were revered in the colonies, such as the Puritans William Ames and William Perkins, and the Anglican Jeremy Taylor, warned against "too sensual applications"[2] in the marriage bed, but the brevity and vagueness of their warnings demonstrated the limits of Protestant theory. Besides, abolition of the confessional eliminated the forum for private instruction and discipline that fostered more explicit teaching. Protestant doctrine was public doctrine. Protestant sexual doctrine could not address the details of sexual behavior until those details fell within the scope of public discussion.

As the Enlightenment brought rationalism to the colonies, Protestant silence on sex deepened. In part this was a matter of style: genteel abstraction displaced the earthy metaphor that had characterized

Reformation and Puritan preaching. More significantly, the new confidence in reason reflected an optimism about human nature that undermined the doctrine of original sin, so that the relation between sex and sin also became less vivid. In 1758, when Jonathan Edwards published *The Great Christian Doctrine of Original Sin Defended,* sex found no place in his discussion. For Edwards, selfishness was the sin into which humans were born, and "love to Being in general" was the virtue to which Christ redeemed them. Sexual desire (if Edwards had chosen to consider it at all) might have pertained to either state, depending on whether a given relationship participated in the divine gift of love.[3] The crucial point of debate on original sin had shifted to the question of legal responsibility for the actions of our first parents, with only subsidiary connections to the present condition of human nature. Neither Edwards and his followers, who defended God's right to judge all of humanity in the persons of Adam and Eve, nor the liberal opponents of Edwards, who denounced the injustice of guilt by inheritance, used sex as an important field of argument.[4]

Medicine began slowly to move into this vacuum of sexual expertise and theory, but social conditions limited medical influence. Throughout the colonial period, American physicians attained no professional organization, much less a systematic approach to sex or anything else. Healing depended largely on midwives and ministers. Meanwhile, the limitations of the hand-powered press, together with the weakness of systems for distributing books, confined the potential audience of medical authors.

One medical book on sex penetrated this colonial backwardness to achieve enduring popularity. *Aristotle's Master-Piece,* the work of an anonymous compiler who purported to disclose ancient secrets, first appeared in England in 1684.[5] Some later editions found their way across the Atlantic, and between 1760 and 1831, thirty-two American printings testified to the public's interest. *Master-Piece* engaged its readers with folklore about "monstrous births," the influence of a mother over the appearance of her unborn child, "directions and cautions for midwives," and remedies for venereal disease.[6] Mixed with all this was a basic appreciation of pleasure, justified by a pinch of Christian doctrine.

According to *Master-Piece,* both men and women possessed powerful sex drives that had apparently not been tainted by human depravity. Nature gave to girls ages fourteen or fifteen a surplus of blood, which "does by its abounding, stir up their minds to venery," so that "their desire of venereal embraces becomes very great, and, at some critical junctures, almost unsupportable."[7] With surprising accuracy, the English "Aristotle" gave even more importance to the clitoris than does modern medicine:

> Without this [the clitoris] the fair sex neither desire nuptial embraces nor have pleasure in them, nor conceive by them; and according to the greatness or smallness of this part, they are more or less fond of men's embraces; so it may properly be styled the seat of lust,
>> Blewing the coals of those amorous fires,
>> Which youth and beauty to be quench'd requires.[8]

"Aristotle's" theology concentrated on marriage, which he saw as the proper setting for quenching these "amorous fires." At the beginning of its first chapter, *Master-Piece* asserted not only that marriage had been "ordained in Paradise" but also that Eden "could scarcely have been paradise without it; for paradise is known to be a place of pleasure."[9] God's ordination of marriage in Eden was proof that sexual pleasure "doth with innocence consist."[10] Nor had the Fall destroyed the innocence of pleasure. Disobedience had entered the world with sin, and unfaithful spouses disobeyed the divine law of marriage, but no "infection of nature" tainted sex itself, despite what the Church of England said in its ninth Article of Religion. To enjoy sex in purity, a couple needed only to avoid adultery, remembering that the same God who intended that they be moved to copulate "by a powerful secret instinct" also intended "that every man should have his own wife."[11] Thus, no doubt without consciousness of his deed, the anonymous author of *Aristotle's Master-Piece* began the medical modification of traditional teaching on sex and original sin in the United States.

In the midst of "Aristotle's" American popularity, a more sophisticated medical theology appeared. Dr. Benjamin Rush (1745–1813), a Philadelphia physician and signer of the Declaration of Independence who became one of the founders of formal medical education in America, combined physiology with reasoning on sin that drew on both Edwards and liberal theologians.

Although he was a practicing Episcopalian, Rush had his children baptized as Presbyterians, because he felt that the American Episcopal Prayer Book of 1789 went too far in the direction of asserting infant regeneration through baptism. This was a distinctly Reformed objection, reflecting a strong belief in the power of original sin. Rush's diaries expounded on this belief. "Original or native sin," he wrote in 1809, "is favored by the ideas of pregnancy and parturition being diseases. Sin and suffering began together."[12] Here, defining the process that resulted from the sexual act as a disease helped Rush to confirm the existence of original sin. Later, justifying God's permission of such suffering as punishment for sin, the doctor used sex as part of an analogy to illustrate the responsibility of the whole human race for the evils of each individual. As disease affected parts of the body that were not responsible for contracting the disease, Rush observed, so members of the body of Christ suffered for sins they did not themselves commit. "Thus the feet suffer in the gout for the intemperance of the tongue, and the whole body for the sin of one part of it in contracting the venereal disease," wrote Rush. He then repeated Jonathan Edwards's ultimate defense of divine justice in permitting all to suffer for the sin of Adam and Eve: "To the Deity the whole human race probably appears as much a unit as a single human body appears to be a unit to the eye of man."[13]

The medical model for theology—or what some might call the reduction of Christianity to a religion of health—emerged clearly in Rush's *Three Lectures upon Animal Life,* delivered to his classes in physiology at the University of Pennsylvania and published in 1799. Urging his students to relate their work in medicine "to morals, metaphysics, and theology," the lecturer set an example of how to overcome the "erroneous belief" that these subjects belong exclusively to another profession."[14] General principles were essential to physiology, according to Rush, and general principles included theology. His own principles began with another idea borrowed from Edwardsean theology: the idea that life depended totally, at every moment of its existence, on external force. "Life is the EFFECT of certain stimuli," not a power inhering in matter, Rush insisted. From this postulate, he deduced that the human will had "no self-determining power"; that each individual remained alive only through God's "universal, and particular providence"; and that those who argued otherwise, seeking to find the power of life in the body, would "open a door for the restoration of the old Epicurean or atheistical philosophy."[15]

If Rush had gone only this far, he would have left a legacy of medical theory entirely at the service of Reformed religion. But the doctor carried physiology further, to the point of using physiology to explain how Christianity carried on its redemptive work. Redemption resulted from an economy of stimuli:

Atheism is the worst of sedatives to the understanding, and passions.... Religions are friendly to animal life, in proportion as they
elevate the understanding, and act upon the passions of hope and
love.... It will readily occur to you, that Christianity ... is more
calculated to produce those effects, than any other religion in the
world. Such is the salutary operation of its doctrines, and precepts
upon health and life, that if its divine authority rested upon no other
argument, this alone would be sufficient to recommend it to our
belief. How long mankind may continue to prefer substituted pur-
suits and pleasures, to this invigorating stimulus, is uncertain; but
the time we are assured will come, when the understanding shall
be elevated from its present inferior objects, and the luxated passions be reduced to their original order. This change in the mind of
man, I believe, will be effected only by the Christian religion....[16]

Nobler and more intense stimulation, not stricter restraint, would be required to bring the "luxated passions" to order. Nor were the higher and
the lower passions necessarily opposed to each other. As Rush argued in
this same course of lectures, there had indeed been a Fall, by which "passions and emotions of a malignant nature" began to compete with the
"love, hope, and joy" that had been the exclusive passions of humanity
in Eden.[17] Yet, even under sin, all passions, however unpleasant in themselves or "morally evil in their objects, remained "subservient to the purpose of promoting animal life." The doctor gave examples of "persons
who have derived strength, and long life from the influence of the evil
passions."[18] Hatred, peevishness, avarice, and ambition could keep people
healthy. The moral quality of passions did affect health indirectly, however; from a medical standpoint, Rush argued, love was superior to hate
because love exerted a stronger stimulus.

Aside from the importance Rush gave to passion in general, sexual
desire had no special place in his system. Observing that "lunatics"
often exhibited "an inordinate force of the venereal appetite," Rush did
not conclude that lust had caused their mental disturbance, but rather
that lust was one of the last props of whatever health they had. In works
in which warnings against sexual misconduct might have been expected, such as his *Sermons to Gentlemen on Temperance and Exercise*
(1772) and *Thoughts upon Female Education* (1787), Rush did not mention sex at all.[19] He never broke the Protestant silence on the details
of marital behavior; sex remained as peripheral for his intellectual

synthesis as it had for Jonathan Edwards. But the way Rush translated the Edwardsean concepts of original sin, redemption, and the dependence of all things on God into physical terms prefigured later forms of medical Christianity, in which sex would stand forth as *the* crucial passion in the drama of sin and redemption.

The Reduction of Sin to Sex

The prevalence of corn flakes on American breakfast tables is a rough index to the influence that the medical reduction of sin to sex eventually attained in the United States. For Dr. John Harvey Kellogg (1852–1943), inventor of the corn flake, and for the Seventh-Day Adventists under whose auspices Kellogg worked, breakfast cereals figured as part of a health regimen designed to cure original sin by reducing the force of sexual passion.

Behind Kellogg's cereal prescription lay a mixture of Bible history and scientific materialism. Because the sin of Adam and Eve was a sin of appetite, the first couple not only broke God's law but also disordered their own passions. Disordered passion became hereditary through its effect on sex. Disorder bred disorder, and the abuse of sex led to further sexual abuses, gluttony, greed, intemperance, and crime, so that continuous physical and moral decline marked the generations, as witnessed by the diminishing lifespans of the patriarchs recorded in Genesis. According to Ellen Gould White, the visionary foundress of Seventh-Day Adventism, this degeneration might well continue until the race "would become incapable of appreciating the great truths of redemption."[20] Reduction of the strength of passion thus was more than a health measure; it was also a religious duty. Writing "to wives and mothers" in a book that sold three hundred thousand copies between 1877 and 1910, Dr. Kellogg applied the Adventist perspective to marital intercourse:

> *The Origin of Evil.* 1. If a child is begotten in lust, its lower passions will as certainly be abnormally developed as peas will produce peas, or potatoes potatoes. If the child does not become a rake or a prostitute, it will be because of uncommonly fortunate surroundings, or a miracle of divine grace. But even then, what terrible struggles with sin and vice, what foul thoughts and lewd imaginations,—the product of a naturally abnormal mind,—must such an individual suffer![21]

No conclusion could have been more directly opposed to Benjamin Rush and *Aristotle's Master-Piece,* to Catholic advice to pursue orgasm for the sake of the child, or to modern assumptions about the healthfulness of sexual pleasure. Yet Kellogg was not a crank, but one of the most learned and skillful surgeons of his time. He and his church represented a revolution in medical thought, a revolution that shattered the silence of Protestant leaders on sex and thereby made a powerful, though unintended, contribution to the development of the modern ethic of pleasure.

Benjamin Rush saw disease as a constitutional state, reflecting imbalance and deficiency in the passions in general. Therefore, he prescribed not only the "invigorating stimulus" of Christianity but also "heroic" treatments affecting the whole person, such as bleeding away half the blood supply, or massive dosing with arsenic or mercury. But within decades after Rush's death, empiricism had triumphed over his systemic outlook. Kellogg lived in a medical world that sought the causes of disease in specific material agents, not general imbalance. Small doses of medicine, alterations of diet, and surgical interventions gradually replaced the heroic measures. This change in medical theory brought about a corresponding change in the medical diagnosis of original sin. Rush had reduced depravity to the derangement of passion; now empiricist physicians reduced it further, to the derangement of sexual passion. Sexual depravity by itself seemed sufficient to explain how people could be born with tendencies toward evil and suffering, and sufficient as well to dissolve objections against the justice of God's punishment of children for the sins of their ancestors. As scores of doctors (and theologians) came to argue, the crux of original sin was not abstract justice but physical law. Whoever sinned in sex automatically entailed his or her sin on all generations, without any mysterious judgment on God's part, and whoever sinned in any other respect affected his or her sexual nature.

The identification of a limited, material basis for human depravity produced tremendous therapeutic optimism. No longer would the pious physician have to wait for "the invigorating stimulus of Christianity" to perform its slow work in the world. Prescriptions for diet, sexual practice, sleeping habits, clothing, exercise, and surgery all became panaceas for the fundamental disorder of the race. Such optimism has remained a consistent feature of sexual medicine in the United States from the 1830s through our own time.

The sexual diagnosis of sin became predominant during the second quarter of the nineteenth century, the era when the social and material conditions for American mass culture were just coming into being. As population flowed west, Irish and Germans filled the ports, and industry drew people from the countryside to the cities and created new classes of managers and laborers, a corps of evangelists and entrepreneurs strove with remarkable vigor to give direction to their young nation. The Protestant churches responded by supporting national agencies such as the American Bible Society, the American Tract Society, the American Sunday School Union, the American Home Missionary Society, various antislavery groups, and dozens of other networks for promoting morality and education. Publishers set up national operations, printing and distributing books simultaneously in New York, Cincinnati, and Chicago.[22] Magazines began to bring women in every city the same images of fashion. As individuals sought their own fortunes, they also contributed to the creation of a common culture. Before Samuel F. B. Morse knit the nation into a whole with his telegraph, and before he made a name for himself in anti-Catholic literature, he tried to earn a living as a painter by touring up and down the eastern seaboard, charging admission to see his reproductions of masterpieces from the Louvre.[23] The same beneficent and entrepreneurial spirit that moved in Morse, the Bible Society agents, and the Harper brothers also moved the health experts who arose to address the public on the question of sex.

First among his peers was Sylvester Graham (1794–1851), whose name still lives in America through the cracker he prescribed. The descendant of two generations of Connecticut clergymen, Graham began his career as a Presbyterian minister in New Jersey but soon left the pulpit to work for a temperance society.[24] He gained public prominence with his *Lectures to Young Men on Chastity*, published in 1834, which he delivered before paying audiences on a circuit of eastern cities. In his lectures, Graham fueled the masturbation phobia that would plague adolescents into our own century; he proposed vegetarianism and "Graham" (unbolted) flour as curatives for sexual disease; and he based the whole system on an etiology of evil that revealed how far he had come from Presbyterian orthodoxy. The creed of his former church taught that people were born totally depraved, in spirit and in body, but Graham concentrated on physical causes and cures. He opposed the view that sin made disease and pain inevitable. In place of resignation, he offered a diagnosis of "voluntary depravity":

> of all the animals … proud, rational man is the only one who has depraved his nature, and, by this voluntary depravity, rendered this life a pilgrimage of pain, and the world one vast lazar-house for his species.[25]

Sex transmitted the effects of voluntary depravity. According to Graham, "the pure state of nature" for humans would have included a periodic rise of sexual desire, no more frequent "than that of other species of animals, of the same class, whose period of pregnancy is the same."[26] Since this was manifestly not the human condition, some principle of evil must have taken root in humanity. Graham identified this evil as the insatiability that sexual desire attained through abuse: "the moment man begins to violate the laws of constitution and relation, . . . that moment he begins to deprave his instinctive propensies, and to develope [*sic*] a power of appetite which, the more it is yielded to, the more it is increased. . . ."[27] Indulgence of passion was therefore not obedience to nature, but acquiescence in chronic disease. This acquiescence would lead to "the worst of consequences," which Graham detailed: increased suffering for the individual from a variety of maladies ranging from tuberculosis to insanity to cancer of the womb, and an inheritance of yet more intense depravity for the race.[28]

By making original sin voluntary, Graham obtained the best possible platform from which to preach to antebellum America. As he repeated such phrases as "excessively depraved as mankind are," he borrowed authority from Reformed religion; yet Graham could also assert the goodness of nature and the possibility of freedom from evil. Two of the most successful contemporary ministers, Charles Grandison Finney and Nathaniel William Taylor, worked along similar lines, but their thinking on voluntary sin lacked the principle of inheritance that came from concentrating on sex. After Graham, American health writers began to address original sin with more insistence and more assurance than theologians.

"We think, sometimes, of Eve,"[29] mused Dr. William A. Alcott (1798–1859), who was the first respectable physician in the United States to become known primarily as a writer on sex. Alcott continued his reflections on Eve, and "her great work of declension," throughout *The Young Wife* (1837), *The Young Husband* (1839), *The Physiology of Marriage* (1855), and *The Moral Philosophy of Courtship and Marriage* (1856). For him, sex functioned as the "fulcrum" on which the world had been sunk into sin, and by which it would have to be raised again. "Here, emphatically, the soul that sins must die," he wrote, mixing the rhetoric of Genesis into a discussion of the temptations of courtship. "Moreover, . . . the sins of the parents are visited upon those who come after them."[30]

When Alcott used the word "sin" to describe violations of his rules for healthy living (which included a ban on spicy food, coffee, tea, "amorous looks" between the married, and anything else that might stimulate desire), he knew that he was departing from Christian tradition. Sometimes he apologized, professing inability "to express the idea intended in a better way."[31] But more often, the doctor bluntly acknowledged his intention to revise theology. In *The Young Husband*, Dr. Alcott gave free rein to his sense that his audience needed a medical interpretation of religion. "When will the world understand the whole intention of Christianity?" Alcott asked. "When will it be fully and clearly seen, that the salvation and sanctification of man includes his whole being—body, soul, and spirit . . . ?" The answer was that, until physicians succeeded in enlightening the public about the hereditary connection between passion and sin, "the whole object of the divine mission to our earth" could not be accomplished.[32]

Other medical advisors went beyond Alcott by denouncing all non-medical views of original sin. "Theologians talk of original sin, . . . when seeking to account for a person's vices," noted Dr. Dio Lewis, a Boston physician whose work received praise from Harriet Beecher Stowe. The theologians were mistaken, Lewis argued, because the true way of explaining vices was "to trace them to their ante-natal source"—the sexual excesses of parents. The doctor himself traced this connection in *Chastity; or, Our Secret Sins* (1874).[33] For Dr. James Caleb Jackson, who treated Ellen Gould White and her Adventists at his sanitarium in Dansville, New York, the charge that medical treatment of sin implied materialism might be understandable, but was also unscientific. Confronted with "the simple, unvarnished truth . . . that human beings *are born depraved*," Jackson wrote in 1861, the practitioner of medicine or religion must look to bad health habits, and especially to "the misuse or abuse of the sexual organism." This offered the only way "to understand the origin of the perversities and depravities which human beings show."[34]

Mary S. Gove, who combined the administration of water-cure spa and a girls' boarding school with the publication of a health magazine at her headquarters in Lynn, Massachusetts, spoke to theology with even more authority. "Well-meaning Christian ministers" battled against sin without effect, Gove charged in her *Lectures to Women on Anatomy and Physiology* (1846). The ministers failed because they "have been wholly ignorant of the physical means of preventing this evil."[35] From Gove's perspective, there was really no such thing as "original sin"; there were only sexual abuses that affected the passions, producing "that physiological, phrenological, and consequently, moral disorder, characterized by many by the term *total depravity*."[36]

Although Augustus K. Gardner (1821–1876), Harvard-trained professor of "diseases of females," was a Unitarian whose theology should not have recognized original sin, Gardner resurrected the concept when dealing with sex. His *Conjugal Sins against the Laws of Life and Health* (1870) warned the married that their desires were not natural, and therefore could not be "physically right." If people lived in a state of nature, desire might be a safe guide to practice, but under our actual conditions, the "lustful cravings of our pampered selves" only revealed how depraved humanity had become.[37] Elizabeth Blackwell (1821–1900), the first female graduate of an American medical school, added her voice to this diagnosis. From *The Laws of Life* (1852) through *The Religion of Health* (1871) to *Medical Responsibility* (1897), Blackwell reiterated her judgment that the clergy could never bring souls from sin to redemption without attention to the programs of education, exercise, and public health reform that she prescribed.[38] Because the depravity of sex generated all human depravity, theology could not do without medicine.

The Religion of Health in Protestant Theology

For three centuries before doctors began to address a mass audience, Protestant theologians had walked a narrow line between traditional assertions that sex shared in the universal corruption caused by sin and the more extreme view that sex transmitted sin. Swayed by the new prestige of empirical medicine, many theologians lost their balance.

"The doctrine of physiology therefore is the doctrine of original sin," pronounced the Reverend Horace Bushnell in 1858, "and we are held to inevitable orthodoxy by it, even if the scriptures are cast away."[39] Bushnell (1802–1876) was one of the great men of American Christianity, a Connecticut Congregationalist whose books and sermons made Romantic philosophy available to a generation of churchgoers, and whose practical advice shaped religious education into our own time. Yet Bushnell's collaboration with the science of his day contributed to the reduction of original sin to its physical effects, and thus furthered the American transformation of Christianity into a religion of health. In *Nature and the Supernatural* (1858), the pinnacle of Bushnell's efforts to unite science and religion, spiritual life was consistently subordinated to physical models.

Here Bushnell began by adducing the disorder of human "passions, tempers, and appetites"[40] as evidence of original sin—an exercise typical of all theology since Apostle Paul. But he went on to affirm the medical conclusions that this disorder was physically inherited and might therefore be physically cured. He justified God's permission of hereditary depravity with the argument that a corrupt race provided better material for redemption than a race of innocent individuals, who would fall individually and who would have to be saved individually. Inherited depravity raised the hope that redemption could also be inherited: "as corruption or depravation is propagated, under well-known laws of physiology, what are we to think but that a regenerate life may be also propagated; and that so the scripture truth of a sanctification from the womb may sometime cease to be a thing remarkable, and become a commonly accepted fact?"[41]

This vision of physical redemption permeated Bushnell's *Christian Nurture* (1847; expanded edition 1861), which revolutionized Christian education and became his most influential work. Arguing that children should be raised as though they were already saved, not taught to regard themselves as damned and to await the moment when God would save them, Bushnell speculated that Christianity would redeem the world not by means of revivals and missionaries, but by "The Out-Populating Power of the Christian Stock."[42] Grace could do more than rescue individuals; it could produce a Christian People, who would not convert but physically displace "the feebler and more abject races."[43] Here, the medical reduction of Christianity reached its *reductio ad absurdum*, in a gross contradiction of Christ's injunction to preach the Gospel to all nations.

For Bushnell as for the doctors he followed, sexual repression was the price of such triumphalism. Alongside the dream of a healthful Christian People stood the nightmare of retrogression caused by the abuse of sex. Nurture must begin with the restriction of the parental sex life as soon as a child was conceived, Bushnell urged, lest the fetus "have the sad entail of any sensuality, or excess, or distempered passion upon him."[44] After a child was born, its diet should include only foods that would not feed the fires of passion:

> The wrong feeding of children, ... puts them under the body, teaches them to value bodily sensations, makes them sensual every way, and sets them lusting in every kind of excess. The vice of impurity is taught, how commonly, thus, at the mother's table.[45]

If parents followed the advice of *Christian Nurture,* on the other hand, they could have confidence that their children would be "penetrated bodily, all through, by the work of the Spirit."[46] Their "appetites" would be "more nearly in heaven's order, their passions more tempered by reason."[47] Horace Bushnell thus participated in the dietetic Christianity of Graham and Kellogg.

Not all Christians in the United States accepted Bushnell's theories. In fact, opponents drove *Christian Nurture* off the book list of the Sunday School Union, although its popularity eventually made it a classic. Two men who found Bushnell too modern were Leonard Woods (1774–1854), the defender of Congregational orthodoxy at Andover Seminary, and Charles Hodge (1797–1878), who performed an analogous function for Presbyterians at Princeton. Both Woods and Hodge protested against reductions of original sin to physical phenomena. They pointed out that the passions of sinful humanity *were* sinful, but only in the same sense that the whole man—mind, spirit, and body—was corrupted by sin.[48] Neither Woods nor Hodge entertained the hope that hygiene, diet, or continence could in any degree alleviate this corruption.

But the future of American religion did not belong to the Reformed orthodoxy of Andover and Princeton. Bushnell and his liberal followers, with their hope of overcoming original sin through racial progress, captured the imagination of middle-class Protestants. A far more important opponent to the liberals than Woods or Hodge was Charles Grandison Finney (1792–1875), the Presbyterian revivalist who became the honored ancestor of modern evangelicals. It was Finney's new style of evangelism, featuring the call to come forward and declare for Jesus, against which Bushnell was reacting with the educational program of *Christian Nurture.* Religion for Finney *was* the declaration for Jesus, the dedication of human will to the will of God. The traditional view of original sin struck Finney as the primary impediment to decisions for Christ, because concentrating on sin as a state of being discouraged potential believers by making them think that God had to give them a new feeling before they could be Christians.[49] In his *Lectures on Revivals of Religion* (1835), the great evangelist took issue with all who believed that sin meant anything more than actual disobedience:

Religion has been too much looked upon as something separate from obedience to God. And hence people set themselves down in inaction, and wait for God to do a work in them, instead of setting themselves at work to obey God. This notion of physical depravity, and physical regeneration, and physical sanctification is the great curse of the church.[50]

It would seem that no one could have stood further from medical Christianity than Charles Grandison Finney. For him, even Jonathan Edwards and his Calvinist heirs were tainted with adherence to "physical depravity." Both Edwards and Leonard Woods came under fire in Finney's *Systematic Theology* (1846) for making sin seem too physical.[51]

Closer attention to Finney's statements on sin and Christian life, however, reveals that medical Christianity had penetrated even to the heart of nineteenth-century evangelicalism. In considering the hereditary effects of that disobedience he named "sin," Finney foreshadowed Dr. Kellogg and the Adventists:

> The physical organization of the whole race has become impaired, and beyond all doubt has been becoming more and more so since intemperance of any kind was first introduced into our world.... Especially is this true of the human sensibility. The appetites, passions, and propensities are in a state of most unhealthy development.[52]

Finney insisted that this corrupt "sensibility" was not itself sinful, but he gave physical corruption a crucial role in each individual's fall into actual sin. He pictured the "sensibility" developing in children before the capacity to reason. After a season of innocent sensory gratification, reason developed. Then an occasion arose when the child wanted something that contradicted its newfound sense of the rational good, which Finney regarded as the voice of God in the soul. At some such point, inevitably but freely, every human being chose an object of selfish desire over the greater good perceived by reason, and thus committed sin. A habit of choosing sin became established—again inevitably but freely—until the person in question reached a point at which deliverance could come only through a conscious decision to obey God, in reliance on the ever-present power of the Holy Spirit.[53]

After the decision for obedience was made and the power of the Spirit accepted, one might think that the corrupt sensibility would lose its influence over the reborn Christian. Finney was a perfectionist. He did not agree with the Anglican Articles of Religion that sin remained, "yea, in them that are regenerated"; he did not subscribe to the Lutheran formula of *simul justus et peccator* ("at the same time justified and a sinner"). Rather, Finney and the entire school of revivalism he founded, down to the present, have preached the possibility of real and complete freedom from sin in this life. The spiritual struggle of a Christian was not a struggle against "present sin," as Leonard Woods insisted in a debate with Finney, but resistance to temptation.[54] The will was the crucial actor in the drama of redemption, and the will could be perfectly at one with God.

Yet the body intruded powerfully into Finney's account of Christian perfection. Seventeen lectures on perfection appeared in Finney's *Systematic Theology*, and the last of them warned against physical impediments to attaining perfection.

> There is an importance to be attached to the sanctification of the body, of which very few persons appear to be aware. Indeed unless the bodily appetites and powers be consecrated to the service of God ... permanent sanctification as a practical thing is out of the question. ...
>
> Few people seem to keep the fact steadily in view, that unless their bodies be rightly managed, they will be so fierce and overpowering a source of temptation to the mind, as inevitably to lead it into sin. If they indulge themselves in a stimulating diet, and in the use of those condiments that irritate and rasp the nervous system, their bodies will be of course and of necessity the source of powerful and incessant temptation to evil tempers and vile affections.[55]

At Oberlin College, where Finney served as professor and president, and from which he sent forth succeeding ranks of evangelists into the world, the Graham diet protected students against "vile affections."[56] Medicine led evangelical theology, even though the tenets of that theology appeared to deny the existence of physical depravity. Only the insistence of Princeton and Andover theologians that original sin could never be eradicated really contradicted the promise of medicine to conquer original sin through control of passion.

Thus, Horace Bushnell and Charles Grandison Finney, respectively the most representative figures of the liberal and evangelical camps of nineteenth-century Protestantism, both contributed to the reduction of original sin to sex. But the religion of health did not stop there. In addition to capturing both sides of the mainstream, the message of redemption through control of passion also played an important role in the new churches that America produced in abundance.

To cite the clearest example, Christian Science, from its birth with the publication of Mary Baker Eddy's *Science and Health* (1875), expressed this nineteenth-century consensus in its purest form. Belief in the creative power of matter was the original sin, according to Mrs. Eddy. If people understood that Spirit, not matter, created all life, they would reach a condition in which marriage would be purely spiritual.[57] Mrs. Eddy restrained those of her followers who attempted to enter this state too quickly. Reproduction without sex remained impossible because lack of faith in the power of Mind polluted the spiritual atmosphere.[58] But the founder of Christian Science never placed this accomplishment beyond the theoretical power of faith, and, more significantly, she embraced the goal of completely overcoming physical sex. No other religious movement so clearly reduced religion to health as Christian Science did, and no church adhered more faithfully to the teachings of Victorian medicine on the subjugation of the body, the avoidance of stimulating substances, and the moral harmfulness of passion.

Another example from outside the mainstream was the Campbellite movement, stemming from Alexander Campbell (1788–1866), whose life and work gave rise to two major denominations, the Disciples of Christ and the Churches of Christ. Campbell presented original sin exclusively as "the triumph of passion."[59] Whether the story of the Fall was understood "as literal or symbolic," he wrote, "one thing is obvious":

> and that is all and alone important to know, and that is the nature of the trial. . . . In one sentence, whether [Adam's] spirit shall retain the sovereignty with which God had invested it, or his passions usurp the government.[60]

Having failed this test by accepting the tempting fruit, Adam became a slave to passion. His condition resembled that of a healthy man gone insane, retaining his faculties but in "a state of derangement." Lucid moments occurred, but these were "followed up by strong and long continued exhibitions of the triumphs of passion and prostration of reason and goodness."[61] When Adam and Eve had children, their offspring differed from the original state of the first man "in this one fact, viz.: His reason first controlled his actions—passion first controls theirs."[62] Thus, every child since the expulsion from Eden has struggled with a defect "which no education, intellectual or moral, can perfectly subdue." God mercifully permitted "the conflicts of reason and passion" to wear out the "animal life" in humanity, so that people would die and so be delivered from passion.[63] The prohibition on eating blood, given by God to Noah (a prohibition that Campbell believed should remain in force among Christians), served somewhat to mitigate the tyrannical power of passion.[64]

Like Benjamin Rush, Alexander Campbell saw Christianity doing its redemptive work by offering worthy objects to desire. As the first Christians arose from baptism, they found that "the sacrifice of Jesus" had, "like the touch of a magnet, turned their affections toward the skies."[65] The adults whom Campbell baptized also found that "their affections were placed on things above, and not on the things of earth." But unlike Rush, the nineteenth-century evangelist placed no trust in human passions in general as supports of life and health. Campbell's followers flowed into the same movement toward repression that absorbed most of the vital energies of American Protestants in Campbell's time.

Even further than Christian Scientists and Campbellites from the center of Protestant culture in the United States were the numerous, now overstudied communal groups of the nineteenth century: the Mormons, the Shakers, the Oneida Community, the Transcendentalists of Brook Farm and Fruitlands, the German pietists of New Harmony, and others. The colorful sexual practices of these groups, who tried everything from celibacy to polygamy to group marriage, have diverted attention from the more mundane behavior of Presbyterians and Methodists. But the secret of the proliferation of cults lay within the same process that transformed the mainstream. The whole age was wrestling with the problem of redefining original sin; everyone's answer to the question had something to do with sex; and those who found the secret of overcoming sin therefore gave evidence of their triumph by revolutionizing their sexual lives, the health habits that influenced their passions, or both. Far more significant than the vegetarian experiment at Fruitlands was the almost universal adoption of abstinence from alcohol as a test of Christian faith.

The theory of evolution evoked still more capitulations of theology to medicine. Many theologians welcomed Darwin, because he seemed to ratify the vision of life straining upward, out of animal existence and toward the Spirit, which they had been developing for decades before the *Origin of Species* (1859). Evolution completed the reduction of original sin to physical passion. As the Reverend Theodore Thornton Munger (1830–1910), a student of Bushnell, put it, "We must be born again, not merely because we are wicked, not because of a lapse, but because we are flesh."[66] Sin was no "strange, mystic fact" of the spirit, resulting from a primeval transgression, but simply the animal in all of us. "We carry the animal with us," wrote Lyman Abbott in his *Theology of an Evolutionist* (1897), "and some have a very small man's head on a very large beast's body."[67] Rare was the theologian, such as the Reverend Newman Smyth of New Haven or Professor George Harris of Andover, who could accept evolution without redefining original sin as a retrograde physical tendency manifest in sex.[68]

Christian tradition from Augustine through Edwards had known original sin as an ineradicable flaw in the spirit, which affected the body indirectly, however profoundly. With their failure to defend this conception, American Protestant leaders forfeited any distinctive witness in the struggle over human nature that raged around them during the nineteenth century. Leadership passed to physicians and scientists, while ministers occupied themselves explaining the "real," "scientific" meaning of traditional symbols.

The Fear of Passion and Sexual Practice

The same fear of passion that drove Americans to reduce original sin to sex also produced remarkable perspectives on sexual practice. Medical justifications of this fear revealed the crude empiricism of the age. Doctors would observe that "there are symptoms closely allied to epilepsy in the crisis of the venereal act"[69] and infer that orgasm caused epilepsy; or they would notice masturbation among inmates of prisons and asylums and conclude (reversing the conclusions of Benjamin Rush) that "self-abuse" caused insanity and crime.[70] As ministers joined the denunciations of passion, they recited the pathology at second hand. "Here is the fruitful parent of epilepsies, tabes [tuberculosis], and as it is now asserted, of leprosy itself,"[71] reported the Reverend William T. Duryea, speaking on "Social Vice and National Decay" before the 1895 meeting of the National Purity Conference.

Orgasm gained new prominence, and prescriptions for sexual practice gained new specificity, because medical warnings began to focus on the nervous system. Earlier medical writing on sex had speculated about a weakness caused by losing semen;[72] in fact, an eighteenth-century French doctor named Simon André Tissot began the masturbation phobia with his estimate that losing one ounce of semen equaled a loss of forty ounces of blood.[73] But nineteenth-century American science rejected Tissot, instead tracing all evil to the nervous shock of orgasm.

As usual, Sylvester Graham said it most vividly. The phrases Graham used to name orgasm—"venereal paroxysm" and "convulsive paroxysm"—conveyed his sense of danger. Sweeping along the nerves "with the tremendous violence of a tornado," an orgasm stimulated the "convulsed heart" to drive blood "in fearful congestion, to the principal viscera," damaging all other organs. Frequent orgasm would induce a general "prostration":

> The nervous system, even to its most minute filamentary extremities, is tortured into a shocking state of debility, ... the muscles, generally, become relaxed and flaccid; and consequently, all the organs and vessels of the body, even to the smallest capillaries, become exceedingly debilitated; and their functional powers exceedingly feeble.[74]

Because Graham believed that this condition resulted from excitement rather than from loss of semen, his warning extended beyond men to women and reached even those who felt nothing more than heightened desire. Desire by itself "disturbs and disorders all the functions of the system," according to Graham's argument. Entertainment of what he called *"adultery of the mind"* (giving medical significance to Christ's condemnation of lustful thought) could cause "general debility, effeminacy, disordered functions, and permanent disease, and even premature death, without the actual exercise of the genital organs!"[75]

There was one consolation for the married: although sexual excitement held as many dangers for them as for anyone else, the inevitable cooling of their ardor would make excitement less frequent and less intense. "Promiscuous" intercourse, Graham observed, entailed an excited imagination, injurious in itself, and "convulsive paroxysms proportionably violent and hazardous to life."[76] The intense pleasure of these paroxysms also motivated illicit lovers to "that frequency of commerce that produces the most ruinous consequences." On the other hand, Graham continued,

> between husband and wife, where there is a proper degree of chastity, all these causes either entirely lose, or are exceedingly

diminished in their effect. They become accustomed to each other's body, and their parts no longer excite an impure imagination, and their sexual intercourse is the result of the more natural and instinctive excitements of the organs themselves;—and when the dietetic, and other habits are such as they should be, this intercourse is very seldom.[77]

As to exactly how "seldom" the wise married couple could safely engage in their calm intercourse, Graham admitted variations according to physical condition. Young men who worked in strenuous occupations might safely indulge more freely; those suffering from epilepsy or tuberculosis should not have sex at all. But even for the "healthy and robust," Graham advised that "it were better for you, not to exceed . . . the number of months in the year."[78] No one, however healthy, could have intercourse more than once a week without endangering his own life and his partner's, and bequeathing "an impaired constitution, with strong and unhappy predispositions," on his children.[79]

Dozens of pages could be filled with medical warnings that equaled Graham's. Radicals warned as vehemently as conservatives. Dr. Charles Knowlton (1800–1850), who served three months at hard labor for describing contraceptive douches in his *Fruits of Philosophy* (1832), did hope to facilitate sexual enjoyment through his advice. But the same book that defended contraception admonished newlyweds that "many young married people . . . have debilitated the whole system, the genital and nervous systems in particular; have impaired their mental energies; have induced consumptive, and other diseases; by an undue gratification of the reproductive instinct."[80] Even Monsieur Larmont, who in 1859 claimed he could cure syphilis, and who would send diaphragms through the mail for five dollars, warned in his *Medical Adviser* that "Sexual commerce must not be prolonged or a fatal weakness may result."[81]

Advice on the frequency of intercourse varied, but without departing from the fundamental aim of controlling passion. Graham's ideal of once a month was moderate. Dr. John Cowan, who published his *Science of a New Life* in 1869, characterized those who followed such advice as victims of "perverted amativeness, coupled with ignorance of the laws of life."[82] Cowan prescribed total abstinence, with the exception of a yearly act of coitus, scheduled for August or September, for the purpose of conceiving a child to be born in the spring.[83]

As the century progressed, Cowan's position gained support, especially from those who believed that animal sexual behavior revealed the true standard of nature. To Elizabeth Edson Evans, author of *The Abuse of Maternity* (1875), a plea of "moderate" indulgence for any purpose other than procreation was merely the excuse of the "sensualist."[84] Endorsements of Cowan's book came from such leaders as suffragist Elizabeth Cady Stanton, abolitionist William Lloyd Garrison, and the Reverend Octavius B. Frothingham.[85] According to Dr. Annie J. Deering, Cowan's chapter on "the law of continence," in which he set forth the procreative standard, was "more than worth the price of the book to every earnest man and woman." Although Dr. Deering knew that strict limitation of intercourse would be unacceptable to many, she assured Cowan that "angels will bless you if man does not."[86] The hope that sex would someday be confined to procreative relations also figured in the works of Dr. James Caleb Jackson (1861), Dr. John Harvey Kellogg (1877), Dr. Mary Wood-Allen (1898), and Dr. Emma F. A. Drake (1901).[87] By the turn of the century, it had become commonplace for writers on sex to look forward to a day, in Elizabeth Evans's words,

> when . . . the pleasure attendant upon the animal function of reproduction shall never be sought as an end, and the sexual act shall be indulged at rare intervals, for the purpose of calling into existence a sufficient number of successors to the joyous inheritance of health, beauty, wisdom, and plenty, which shall have made the earth a Paradise.[88]

Writers on the pathology of passion evolved a consensus on the rules that should govern sexual practice. Doctors universally condemned coitus during menstruation or any part of pregnancy.[89] Nearly everyone warned against both *coitus interruptus* and the condom as contraceptive measures, because of the widespread belief that sperm had some cooling and healing effect upon the "agitated" womb.[90] Kellogg and others indicted sex during nursing, fearing "the transmission of libidinous tendencies to the child."[91] Some experts prescribed a period of abstinence extending from pregnancy through nursing, added a year after the infant was weaned so that the mother could recover, and thus ended by recommending one act of coitus every three years as the ideal sex life in marriage.[92] On the side of positive duties, doctors agreed on the bland diet and general health regimen, including exercise and separate beds, that had descended from Sylvester Graham.

From the evidence available, one cannot conclude that this prescriptive literature actually stopped Americans from having sex. Birth rates

among white women in the United States did fall throughout the nineteenth century, from an average of 7.04 children for every woman surviving to menopause in 1800, to 5.42 children by 1850 and 3.42 by 1900,[93]
but the decrease may have represented increasing use of contraceptive devices, which were far more prevalent than has generally been recognized,
rather than the effect of pressure to abstain from sex. Two small, personal
surveys, one taken by Dr. Celia Duel Mosher (1863–1940), a physician at
Stanford University, and the other by Dr. Robert Latou Dickinson (1861–
1950), a Brooklyn gynecologist, both indicated that married couples during
the last quarter of the nineteenth century copulated about as often as they
do today: that is, an average of about 2.5 times per week.[94] Of course, these
surveys were unscientifically small and selective. Mosher drew on her
own circle of educated women, and Dickinson surveyed his patients, who
were all urban and enlightened enough to be willing to consult a gynecologist. Perhaps the most convincing argument that people disregarded
prescriptions of continence is the observation of Carl Degler, the scholar
who discovered the Mosher survey, that the admonitory tone of the physicians suggested that the excesses they condemned were continuing.[95]

Whether Americans had intercourse less often or not, medical
warnings did produce some indisputable results. Some women came to
perceive passion as dangerous enough to demand a new operation: the
clitoridectomy, which attained popularity from the 1870s through 1900.[96]
The last clitoridectomy performed in the United States occurred as recently as 1948, as a "cure" for the habit of masturbation in a five-year-old
girl.[97] Although never accepted in Europe and rejected by many American
doctors, clitoridectomies appealed to some as the ultimate weapon against
pathological passion.

The vogue for clitoridectomies contradicts the belief that patterns
of sexual behavior belong to a changeless dimension of human nature.
Like the African custom of sewing shut the vagina, the Hebrew tradition of circumcising the penis, and the ritual intercourse of Tantric
Buddhists, these operations show how malleable and how political the
human approach to sex actually is. Males controlled what that approach
should be in nineteenth-century America, and males received more
advice on this point from doctors than from any other group. The doctors advised that intercourse should not be prolonged, even if it was
infrequent.[98] Because doctors did not expect women to enjoy sex, the
counsel to keep sex brief seemed to serve wives, even as it conserved
the strength of their husbands. There is reason to believe that men

followed this advice (or perhaps did not need it). When Kinsey surveyed American sexual habits in the 1940s, he discovered that the average reported time from intromission of the penis to ejaculation was two minutes.[99] Today, males have developed enough concern for female response to create a market for desensitizing creams and therapies for "premature" ejaculation; but the dominant concern, and likely practice, of Victorian men ran in precisely the opposite direction.

Trends in bedroom furniture, diet, and politics also indicated a rise in real sexual repression. Twin beds for married couples, recommended by doctors for reasons of health, became fashionable after the Civil War.[100] The success of corn flakes demonstrated that antisexual ideology could make a difference in eating habits, which must be at least as "natural" as sex. And other successful crusades, such as the temperance movement, the elimination of legal prostitution in several American cities, and the drive to raise the age of consent for sexual intercourse, grew alongside and strengthened the cultural sense of the dangers of sex.[101]

Finally, whatever physical events typified Victorian bedrooms, that cultural sense of danger must have affected the meaning of those events for married couples. Even if "nature" triumphed over all the forces of repression, and a couple managed to have what we, from our own conditioned standpoint, would consider a satisfactory sex life, they certainly encountered no support for their success. The skillful husband would have to ignore cultural standards that made his wife seem a prostitute and himself a rake. The orgasmic wife did not find *Redbook* or *Cosmopolitan* magazine ready to confirm her status as healthy and normal. In fact, feminist historians have noted a syndrome of physical prostration among the most intelligent and accomplished young women of the turn of the twentieth century, and they have attributed this to the contradictory messages that American culture sent such women.[102] One of the contradictions was the simultaneous affirmation of motherhood and denigration of sex. Such conflict must have affected sexual practice.

Constituencies of the Victorian Consensus

By promoting the fear of passion, doctors acquired new authority over a whole sphere of life. The representation of sex as pathological supported the claim that sex demanded special attention from experts, and the medical profession became the original and most loyal constituency for fearful and repressive perspectives on sex. This is not to say that doctors deliberately wrote falsehoods to generate business. Rather, they responded to a set of scientific and economic developments that made their warnings both plausible and socially useful, and in that response they also served their own interests.

Science transformed sexual medicine after 1845, the year that an Alabama country doctor named J. Marion Sims invented the speculum.[103] Employing his window on female anatomy, Sims perfected operations to repair the disastrous bladder and bowel damage that sometimes occurred during childbirth. Soon he left Alabama and, by 1855, his driving ambition and promotional skill had created the Women's Hospital of New York.[104] Sims thereafter pursued his career at the courts of Europe and among the first families of Newport. His achievements not only established gynecology as a medical specialty but also established the United States as the world leader in this field. Scores of doctors followed Sims into gynecology. By 1880, although American medical students still went abroad for training in most other specializations, the United States boasted an American Gynecological Society and eleven regional organizations: more than in all of Europe and Russia combined.[105] And from knowledge flowed the desire to intervene. More could be done about maladies affecting the sexual organs of women than about most medical problems at that time, and therefore, more was done. The vogue for clitoridectomy and ovariotomy grew in direct proportion to the rise of gynecology. Sex seemed more pathological as its pathology yielded to investigation.

All the advances of science might have met resistance, rather than the eager acceptance they actually encountered, had it not been for an economic revolution that also began during the antebellum decades. Middle-class women were becoming consumers rather than producers.[106] As the Industrial Revolution took hold, the virtues of the farm wife became less and less relevant for many women. Bearing huge families produced workers for the farmer, but only dependents for the businessman or professional. Manufacturing butter and cheese, clothing, and produce for sale had made women partners in production on the farm, but city wives became supervisors of servants and experts on purchasing the accoutrements of middle-class life. From the standpoint of the middle-class male, wife, children, and sex itself rose upward from the realm of practical realities, and into a romantic sphere of personal life. For women, sex and children were subordinated, sometimes as unavoidable liabilities, to the larger vocation of homemaking. The speed with which this reorganized family came to seem natural stands as a striking example of human flexibility.

Of course, the Industrial Revolution also turned many farm women into millhands. But the women who became consumers counted for more, because that same economic transition had produced the apparatus required for a mass culture. And in the magazines and books that poured from steam presses, to create a national consciousness in cities that grew beside railroad lines, women who worked in factories did not exist. Only women who consumed commanded attention. They were the readers, writers, and sometimes editors,[107] and their problems revolved around sex. Sex posed real dangers to these women. Childbirth under nineteenth-century conditions remained dangerous, and venereal disease remained incurable. The number of children that might result with frequent intercourse increasing the odds of pregnancy had become an economic disaster. So, fashion, expounded by and for women through the new media, came to demand the suppression of sex, and a class of physicians came into being whose function was to protect the middle-class couple from their own drives.

Some women became health experts themselves, adding their personal testimony to the dogmas male doctors had established. "If women had their way in the matter," wrote Elizabeth Edson Evans in *The Abuse of Maternity*, "this physical intercourse would take place at comparatively rare intervals, and only under the most favorable circumstances."[108] Much has been made of Dr. Elizabeth Blackwell's radicalism in asserting that sexual feeling was as strong in women as in men, but Blackwell distinguished between physical and mental feelings.[109] As one scholar has suggested, to insist that women felt less physical passion than men served women's interests in an age of adjustment to the loss of family participation in the making of marriages.[110] Being perceived as passionless enabled women to use sex more effectively in bargaining with men during courtship and marriage.

If, in addition to female health writers, one considers women like Harriet Beecher Stowe, Mary Baker Eddy, and Frances Willard (of the Women's Christian Temperance Union), who addressed sexual problems indirectly while leading other movements, it becomes evident that organized womanhood formed another constituency for the fear of passion. Most campaigners for women's voting rights from 1860 to 1919 opposed birth control and rejected the few feminists who called for free love.[111] Sexual restraint represented an ideal most women wanted, for eminently sensible reasons.

Organized Christianity formed a third constituency for the fear of passion. Doctors who wrote for the public on sex often worked for Christian groups. Thus, Dr. Kellogg ran the sanitarium at Seventh-Day Adventist headquarters in Battle Creek; Dr. Mary Wood-Allen superintended the Purity Department of the Women's Christian Temperance Union; and Dr. Emma F. A. Drake worked at revivalist Dwight L. Moody's prep school, Mount Hermon.[112] An occasional minister, such as the Presbyterian John Todd or the Methodist Sylvanus Stall, made a career out of warning people against the perils of sex. Sylvanus Stall recruited the most alarmist doctors to write for his "Self and Sex Series" and personally authored volumes on *What a Young Man Ought to Know* and *What a Young Husband Ought to Know*. From Stall's perspective, the most important thing for the young husband to know was how to examine himself, on the morning after intercourse, for symptoms of sexual excess.

> Do not wait until you have the pronounced effects of backache, giddiness, dimness of sight, noises in the ears, numbness of fingers and paralysis. Note your own condition the next day very carefully. If you observe a lack of physical power, a loss of intellectual quickness or mental grip, if you are sensitive and irritable, if you are less kind and considerate of your wife, if you are morose and less companionable, it would be well for you to think seriously and proceed cautiously.[113]

This purely physical advice marked a new stage in Christian sexual doctrine. Medical fear of passion had become so dominant that the minister no longer needed to buttress his warning with references to human depravity. Going beyond the reduction of original sin to sex, Sylvanus Stall wrote of sex without mentioning sin at all except to deny its relevance. "A strong sexual nature is not a curse," the Methodist insisted; "God made no mistake in making man what he is."[114] Apparently human nature, at least with regard to sex, remained as it had come from the hand of its Maker. Yet sex presented special danger, because God had "never intended that the lower nature should rule over the higher and better nature of man."[115] In fact, the original design of God connected sex with death. Surveying sexual life from algae through insects and animals to humanity, Stall concluded that "the inclination to beget descendants is a premonition of the physical dissolution which awaits the individual."[116] Thus, it was fitting that "the act itself is always more or less exhaustive," and that "increased activity of the reproductive system is secured at the cost of diminished force throughout the remainder of the entire body." Fear of passion survived the disappearance of original sin from Stall's theology. And Stall took care to foster acceptance of his ideas. His books carried endorsements from Episcopal Bishop John H. Vincent; Professor Herrick Johnson, representing the Presbyterians at McCormick Seminary; Congregationalist Charles M. Sheldon; and six medical school professors.

Reasoning like Stall's helped bring Catholics into the consensus of American Christianity on sex, because Catholics could now join in denouncing passion without having to identify concupiscence with sin. In the early years of our century, American Catholic authorities began to write that sexual pleasure was natural but dangerous and that shame also formed part of the natural endowment of human beings. The Jesuit Henry J. Spalding, oblivious to the Scriptural description of Adam and Eve as "naked but not ashamed," compared "the instinct of shame" in children to the oriole's knowledge of nest building, the bee's capacity to produce honey, and the ant's urge to store food for the winter.[117] Charles Coppens, a Jesuit who taught at Creighton Medical College in Nebraska from 1896 to 1905, and who played a key role in introducing modern medical fear to Catholic moral theology, wrote that "the effects of venereal excesses" included "tuberculosis, diabetes, cardial and nervous affections, epilepsy, hysteria, general debility, weaknesses of sight, langour and general worthlessness, hypochondria, weakness and total loss of reason";[118] yet Coppens also described sexual passion as "altogether natural in itself."[119] Balancing passion and reason, not wrestling with a fallen nature, was the problem that confronted the church in dealing with sex. From 1897 through 1921, Coppens's text on *Moral Principles and Medical Practice* remained close to the center of American Catholic moralism.[120] The same perspective informed Austin O'Malley and James J. Walsh's *Pastoral Medicine* (1906), another influential Catholic work. Assertions that both sex and shame were natural, combined with silence on original sin, medical warnings against desire, and encouragement of reason in its war with lust, continued to inform Catholic teaching on sex through the recent work of Fulton J. Sheen.[121]

Thus, the fear of passion brought an end to the contrast between Protestant and Catholic on sexual matters. From the 1880s through the 1920s, when Protestants began a new rift by accepting birth control, the two great divisions of Christendom worked together to support sexual repression in the United States. Both agreed on the authority of the physician in sexual matters; both promoted the passionless woman as the ideal of sexual life. Neither mentioned the earlier conflict of their creeds on the question of sex and original sin, because neither now possessed an independent perspective on what the relation of sin to sex might be.

More than a static peace emerged from this consensus. In the aftermath of the displacement of original sin by medical fear, therapeutic optimism soared. Protestants from Horace Bushnell and Charles Grandison Finney through Mary Baker Eddy, Alexander Campbell, and the devotees of various cults had all become perfectionists during the nineteenth century, under the influence of the religion of health. Their successors could dispense even with that vestige of sin that had clogged the "animal" nature. The simultaneous rejection of passion and of belief in original sin became characteristic of liberal Protestants of the twentieth century. Catholics expanded their vision of perfect freedom from sin, previously limited to a handful of ascetics, to embrace all humanity on the condition of enlightenment with true doctrine.[122] Conventions to promote "social purity" gave Protestants and Catholics the opportunity to share their conviction that purity and civilization worked together, in a natural alliance, for the perfection of the race.[123]

Fear of passion ended in hope for perfection. At first, this hope was encumbered with sexual repression and with the ethos of the upper middle class. But those who associated perfection with ecstatic experience, and those who translated ecstasy into orgasm, would build on the Victorian foundation. While official teachers settled into a coalition, popular movements in medicine, evangelical Protestantism, and Catholic devotion pressed on.

4

Medical Prophets

Presbyterian Yoga

The girl was only seventeen, but she had not left her bedroom for four months. Years of exercise, prescribed to strengthen what her culture called a "delicate" constitution, had culminated in debilitating pain in her head and back. Brought home from boarding school, she developed a chronic cough; her lungs seemed never to be clear. Many doctors attended her, but their bleeding and dosing induced no improvement. Gradually, she lost the strength even to sit up in bed or to use her arms. At this crisis, the family called in an irregular practitioner, Dr. Andrew J. Ingersoll, who ran a clinic at Corning, New York. The year was 1871.

"I saw that her prostration was caused by the suppression of sexual life by the will,"[1] Ingersoll observed, anticipating Freud by twenty-five years. But unlike Freud, Ingersoll thought of religion as both part of the problem and as part of the solution. He undertook the girl's case "because there seemed hope that she could be led to look to Christ for the restoration of that [sexual] life."[2]

Combining the urgency of an evangelist, the insight of a psychoanalyst, the precision of a moral theologian, and the detachment of a social critic, Ingersoll exhorted his patient.

> I told Miss N that she had considered her intellect God-given, but had despised her sexual nature; that God had made all parts of the body equally pure, and that she sinned every time she thought of sex with shame; and that the cause of her illness was the false feeling in which she had been educated.[3]

Miss N was convinced. She began, as the healer recommended, "looking to Christ for the redemption of sexual life,"[4] and quickly recovered her health. By the time Ingersoll published her case history, she had been well for six years.

Of the dozens of cases described in Ingersoll's only book, *In Health*, Miss N's was among the most dramatic, but it was also typical. Nearly three fourths of the subjects of his novel form of faith healing were young women whose symptoms suggested what Freud would have called hysteria. But even when the subject was a widowed clergyman, or a masturbating boy, or an ailing older wife, Ingersoll's approach remained the same. He would urge the patient to greet each impulse of sexual feeling with "thankfulness" and "good will" and to offer these feelings, with the rest of themselves, to Christ for redemption. The advice grew out of the doctor's own experience. Yet so many connections bound Ingersoll's system to his era that he cannot be understood apart from a more general movement, a perfectionist movement that carried both medicine and Christianity toward the ethic of innocent ecstasy.

To begin with Ingersoll is to begin with the presuppositions of medical orthodoxy. Natural law looked as absolute to Ingersoll as to any other doctor, and its prohibitions seemed just as clear. "Every thought or deed in opposition to having children is a sin against the soul, and is productive of disease,"[5] he wrote. Connections between disease and sin permeated the body and the mind. Being ashamed of sex was the sin that had nearly killed Miss N; practicing withdrawal to prevent conception was another sin, to which the doctor "unmistakably" traced "cases of rheumatism, paralysis, and insanity."[6] He quoted Dr. Horatio Storer of Boston, one of the champions of the fear of passion, in support of his warnings against any abuse of sex.

But Ingersoll never warned against sexual pleasure itself. In fact, he made the acceptance of pleasure the essential criterion for physical health and spiritual well-being. This peculiarity, which the Corning healer came to share with increasing numbers of adventurous health experts as the nineteenth century rounded into the twentieth, arose not from Ingersoll's medical reading but from his religious experience.

Born in 1818 on a farm near Hammondsport, New York, Andrew Ingersoll nurtured aspirations to the Presbyterian ministry.[7] His father, "a Jacksonian democrat and a strong Presbyterian," considered Andrew a weak child, and so urged him toward the pulpit for reasons both positive and negative. Guided by the local minister, the young man began to study, but he soon became "bewildered by the entangled controversies of theologians,"[8] and especially by those controversies surrounding original sin, the predestination of the saved, and the experience of the second birth. Ingersoll drifted into the heresy of universalism and, simultaneously, into sickness. His studies left him physically unfit even for clerical life.

It was his mother, who was noted for her skill in healing, who rescued Andrew from this wretched state. Mrs. Ingersoll taught her son a method of relaxation that enabled him to recover his strength. Andrew soon discovered in himself an ability to cure "headache and other complaints"[9] by touch. In finding his own health, he found a career as well.

The crisis that would give Ingersoll's medical theology its distinctive emphasis began when a neighbor asked Andrew to see his wife. Up to this point, Ingersoll had treated only males, leaving the women to his mother, but she was not available. Andrew "feared lest in the treatment he should have any wrong thoughts,"[10] and so refused. The anxious husband, however, continued to pressure the young practitioner, and one evening while relaxing at home, Andrew heard "something from deep within him that seemed to say, 'If you surrender your soul in deep desire for help, I will keep you pure in thought.'"[11] He accepted the case, and cured not only the woman but also himself. From that time forward, Ingersoll never needed to fear "entertaining lustful thoughts" toward a female patient. The deepest sources of his sexual feelings had been cleansed.

Still the young doctor had no settled religious belief, and no explanation for the voice that had freed him to treat women. Then two adolescent males came to Ingersoll, complaining of addiction to masturbation. They were subject to all the terrors that Victorian medicine held out before the victim of "self-abuse." Ingersoll found himself, without reflection, telling these boys that they could not be cured until they gave themselves wholly to Christ. As he spoke, he saw that his patients were already feeling the punishments of the damned "that will be eternal unless they seek His power."[12] Thus, the former candidate for the ministry dropped universalism forever. That evening Ingersoll took his own advice, "fully surrendered to Christ," and realized that it was the power of Christ that had kept him pure in his medical work. Out of this conversion experience grew the theology that informed all of Ingersoll's later life and practice.

A biographer has described the most immediate result, Ingersoll's new view of salvation:

> Since then [the conversion] he believed that all his spiritual growth came through first intrusting his sexual nature to God's keeping; and his teaching has been that this sexual life is the sustaining force of body and mind, and that through this life, if it is reverenced as a heavenly gift, the spirit of the Creator will work the regeneration of body and soul, which is the second birth.[13]

Those who followed the doctor's example and attained what Ingersoll called "sexual redemption" would come to know that sex was the "very essence" of humanity, "being the life in us that begat us."[14] This pansexualism was not far from that of the fearful physicians who had reduced original sin to sex; indeed, Ingersoll agreed that sex was the medium "through which we inherited the original sin."[15] But while others looked for redemption from this corrupt power, Ingersoll found his redemption through the acceptance of sex. *In Health* gave specific directions for welcoming sexual feelings:

> All sensation of sexual feeling should be committed or yielded to Christ. To do this there should be thankfulness for it, and mercy and good-will toward it, at the moment there is consciousness of it; and not only in thought should there be a desire that Christ keep it, but this desire must be accompanied by resignation of the will to Him, and a consequent relaxation of the nervous and muscular systems.[16]

Relaxation, the opening of the soul that allowed Christ to come in, often entailed a change of attitude toward the sexual partner. Many wives came to Ingersoll complaining "that their husbands' love is low and animal,"[17] but he gave them none of the support in rejecting sex that they would have received from physicians who suspected that passion caused disease. The Corning healer prescribed total "yielding" to every impulse toward sex within marriage. "Sexual desire should be implied in the love of a woman for her husband," he wrote; "she should not consent to marry a man for whom she has no desire."[18] In Ingersoll's view, American culture had gone entirely wrong on this question, and produced a generation in which "most women, and many men" believed that "purity consists in having no consciousness of sexual life."[19] After he told suffering wives that they would not become less pure by enjoying sex, Ingersoll found them willing to "admit that their husbands' ideas of sexual life have been nobler than their own."[20]

Nor did Ingersoll's therapy cease when he obtained such admissions. His treatment also fostered relaxation through a physical method, by which the will could become disposed to trust in Christ and in sexual feeling. The method was that which his mother had taught, and which had restored Ingersoll's own health in adolescence. Called "hanging the head," this practice began with the instruction "to drop the head toward the chest, to sit with every muscle relaxed, and to let go all will over the muscular system."[21] The doctor likened the desired position to that of "some persons ... when asleep in their chairs," but in "hanging the head" the individual remained awake, with the intention of entering a special mental and physical state. Breathing was the key. "Such a position," Ingersoll wrote, "induces a truly natural, involuntary breathing by which the inhalations, instead of being expelled entirely through the nostrils, half utilized, are diffused through the body."[22] The pure spirit of air would then "carry out ... the perspiration or morbific matter constantly renewing in the system, which if retained causes death." Although long practice might be required before a person could "drop the head with ease," the promised result would be well worth the time. Ingersoll described the condition thus attained with an allusion to Wordsworth:

> In such high hour
> Of visitation from the Living God
> Thought was not.[23]

Ecstasy—a trancelike, self-obliterating experience of "visitation from the Living God"—was the heart of Ingersoll's therapy. Hanging the head cured psychosexual disease by releasing, in the moment of ecstasy, that free movement of breath that hatred and suppression of sex had restricted. After their breathing became free, patients not only lost their hysterical symptoms but also became capable of finding physical ecstasy and spiritual meaning in sexual relations. *In Health* substantiated this vision of complete redemption with ten closely printed pages of testimony from a minister who said that Ingersoll's exhortations on sexual life, combined with the practice of hanging the head, had saved his marriage, brought him the assurance of salvation, and augmented his power in the pulpit.[24]

Next to women, clergymen were Ingersoll's most numerous patients. "Theological students condemn the sexual life more bitterly than any other class of men," he commented.[25] Lamenting the fate of a Presbyterian minister who had despaired of his salvation and died insane, the doctor observed that "his condemnation of sexual life had turned it into lust, and through the darkness of lust he could see no hope for himself."[26] When a widowed minister came to the clinic "deploring his own high state of passion," Ingersoll saw in his condition the combined effects of the clerical and female patterns of rejecting sex. "You had a wife who despised that nature in you"[27] was the diagnosis, and the minister was astounded at its accuracy. Remarried to a woman who enjoyed sex, and having come to accept it himself, this clergyman found peace.

His contact with such ministers brought Ingersoll back to the religious questions that had troubled his youth. He now realized that traditional theology had literally made him sick because it did not offer complete redemption from sin. Perfectionism—belief in complete freedom from sin in this life—and sexual redemption implied each other in Ingersoll's system. "Nearly all Christians," he reasoned, admitted sexual feeling "to be the most powerful faculty man possesses"; yet these Christians did not accept sex, because they ascribed it to "the animal nature, which cannot be born again."[28] What ordinary Christians were missing was the realization that "the second birth will create in them the spiritual condition of our first parents before the Fall," a condition in which "everything was pure; sexual life was holy."[29] From this perspective on sin and conversion, Ingersoll explicitly attacked the ninth article of the Episcopal Articles of Religion. The statement of that article, that original sin was an "infection of nature" that "doth remain, yea, in them that are regenerated," seemed to Ingersoll to be grounded in Manichean distrust of the body. Asserting that "all mankind are intuitively believers" in the Manichean heresy, which condemned the material world and the flesh as intrinsically evil, the doctor presented redemption through sex as the fulfillment of true Christianity. To any who argued that liability to suffering and death proved the continuing sinfulness of all humans, Ingersoll replied that suffering and death were not sins; sin was a matter of motives, and Christ, if allowed to redeem sexual life, could transform all motives into love.[30] Once this transformation had occurred, sexual desire would express itself directly only when appropriate. Otherwise, sex would remain in the background, as the source of other powers. No sin or guilt would remain in connection with sexual acts or with the unfolding of sexual energy in life.

Never did Ingersoll condone the slightest relaxation of the commonly held Judeo-Christian standards for acceptable sexual acts. Complete freedom from sin, and freedom to accept sex in oneself and to enjoy sexual acts in marriage, did not mean freedom from the law. Yet there was real radicalism in this doctor's prescription for sexual practice. He expected moral perfection, a complete absence of guilt and shame, and ecstasy. He foreshadowed modern sexual ethics.

Other Voices in the Wilderness

Although Andrew Ingersoll was undeniably outside the mainstream, both because his clinic was isolated in the back country of New York State and because his methods were bizarre, he was by no means unknown or unaffected by other writers. *In Health* first appeared, as a strange harbinger, in 1877, but the book went through three additional editions in more receptive times, during the 1890s. Important people read *In Health*: the fourth edition carried testimonials from John Ruskin and John Greenleaf Whittier, as well as reviews from many Pennsylvania and New York newspapers. And the doctor drew on common sources to support his credo of perfection and ecstasy. The text of *In Health* quoted Ruskin, Wordsworth, and Horace Bushnell's *Nature and the Supernatural,* among other classics of the time.

Throughout the nineteenth century, the hope for perfection charged America's intellectual atmosphere. Most of the medical expressions of this hope entailed severe sexual restraint; most perfectionist doctors looked for a "good time coming" in which marital sex would occur for purposes of conception only. But there were others besides Ingersoll who linked perfection with ecstasy.

One of the most influential was Dr. Edward Bliss Foote (1829–1906), whose household health manual, *Plain Home Talk,* enjoyed wide distribution from 1870 through the 1880s. Confronting the issue of sex and its relation to original sin, Foote insisted that shame and social restriction intensified hereditary depravity. Damming up the sexual impulse caused reactions into vice that scarred future generations, inspiring them to be ashamed of sex, and thus perpetuating a cycle of shame. The remedy was at hand: "if the fall of man led him to envelop himself in fig-leaves, it seems to me that we had better all get up as soon as we can."[31] Freedom of discussion and knowledge of biology could destroy shame and eradicate sin. "While regeneration may be necessary for those who are already born morally and physically accursed," argued this medical theologian, "let us so look to the laws governing *generation* that regeneration will be rendered unnecessary."[32] Here was Horace Bushnell's hope for "consecration in the womb" restated; but Foote founded that hope on the ecstasy of parents in their sexual congress rather than on the restrictions of Bushnell's "Christian nurture" of children.

Describing the method for achieving ecstasy, Foote waxed nearly as mystical about the laws of physiology as Ingersoll had about "hanging the head" and yielding the will to Christ. "There can be no question that *physiological law is God's law*,"[33] he asserted. And physiological law demanded complete reciprocity between the partners in pleasure: Foote called this the Golden Rule applied to sex.[34] Reciprocity was basic because all sexual attraction arose from an electric current generated by the alkaline organ of the female and the acidic organ of the male. True partners would gauge each other's electrical potential in courtship (a warm handshake was enough for this). In marriage, they would take any waning of mutual pleasure as a sign that too frequent intercourse was reducing the polar opposition of their organs, and so they would rest until attraction became spontaneous.[35] The husband might also heed the doctor's admonition that "the clitoris and erectile tissue," rather than the inner vagina, was the usual source of "pleasurable sensation" in women.[36] Of course, the husband could generate a facsimile of passion by sheer friction, but this, in Foote's view, brought intercourse "down on a par with that horrible practice—masturbation."[37] Real, healthy passion was always both spontaneous and mutual.

Foote seemed confident that people would find his path to perfection. People could overcome shame in themselves, enjoy their sexual connections, and pass on an untainted heredity to future generations. As the natural result of free speech about sex, Foote predicted, "what is now called Christian civilization will eventually become, in fact, what it is now only in name."[38] Despite the shame that the doctor saw all around him, and which he diagnosed as the essence of depravity, a glorious future beckoned.

> Indeed our civilization, instead of being Christian, is only the shadow falling before the incoming Christianity, and that shadow is yet so dark and obscure in many of its aspects, that it is but little more than the monstrous caricature of the beautiful spirit whose approach produces it.[39]

What Christian ever expressed hope for the millennium more vividly than this "secular" physician, who promoted contraception and denounced restrictive laws? Innocent ecstasy was finding its prophetic voice.

Meanwhile, several other health writers kept a surprising range of physical knowledge before the Victorian public, while absorbing the perfectionist tendency of their age. Most notable was Frederick Hollick, an itinerant lecturer who illustrated his talks with anatomical charts in color,[40] and who published *The Marriage Guide* in 1850. Hollick knew not only the clitoris but also the female capacity for multiple orgasm. "This is sometimes carried on to a great extent," he wrote, a hundred years before Masters and Johnson, "each one becoming more vivid than the others, till fainting ensues."[41] Hollick noted that "the wild fanaticism of a camp meeting, or protracted revival meeting" could induce orgasms in women, who might remain "totally insensible to the nature of what they experience."[42] As a doctor he disapproved of such behavior, believing that natural law made orgasm healthy in sexual intercourse and unhealthy in any other context. His perfectionism appeared in his representation of the proper management of sex as *the* critical influence "upon individual action, and upon the destinies of nations."[43] The negative influence of those who regarded sex as "immoral and unworthy of rational beings" merely intensified human depravity.[44] On the other hand, rational teachers like himself performed a function that would "hasten the time when the mere animal instinct will be controlled, at least sufficiently to prevent evil, by the intellect."[45] Sin was avoidable.

With Hollick, medical advocacy of sexual enjoyment lost many Christian references and much imagistic power but gained social consciousness. Hollick saw the sexual significance of evangelical religion, though he did not share that faith. He also saw that popular culture would advance into more liberated views of sex ahead of medical experts. Doctors conspired to make sex "*a professional mystery,*" thus preserving their monopoly, he charged;[46] but public pressure would eventually induce doctors to offer themselves as teachers. Assuming the heroic pose that would become the norm for sex researchers, Hollick asked to be remembered:

> Let this [his pioneer work] be borne in mind, so that when eminent medical professors write popular books on sexual Physiology, and eminent Publishers give them to the world, as they certainly will, though they now affect to be shocked at them,—it may be known how they have been *forced* to do so, and credit may then be given to those who did it *before them* and *drove them to it.*[47]

Other doctors who advanced the cause of sexual pleasure through the Victorian age included William Hammond, Denslow Lewis, and Robert Latou Dickinson. A former surgeon general of the US Army, Hammond distinguished himself by publishing a book in 1887, *Sexual Impotence in the Male and Female*, that not only recognized orgasm in women but also classified the lack of orgasm in a married woman as a form of impotence requiring treatment. If a discussion with the husband, the content of which Hammond did not specify, failed to produce results, the doctor provided a complete prescription for a pill containing marijuana, strychnine, and aloes that the woman was to take three times a day![48]

Denslow Lewis jeopardized his medical career by giving a speech at the annual meeting of the American Medical Association, in Columbus, Ohio, in 1899, in which he tried to tell his fellow physicians how they could teach the husbands and wives in their care to enjoy sex more. Apparently Lewis succeeded primarily in provoking angry replies, such as that of Dr. Howard A. Kelly, a professor of medicine at Johns Hopkins:

> I do not believe mutual pleasure in the sexual act has any particular bearing on the happiness of life; that is the lowest possible view of happiness in married life.... Its discussion is attended with more or less filth and we besmirch ourselves by discussing it in public.[49]

Robert Latou Dickinson (1861–1950), the gynecologist whose survey of sexual activity has already been mentioned, had a medical career that extended from this high Victorianism into the era of Kinsey. Not only did Dickinson survey the sexual habits of his patients, but he also approved of and encouraged passion. When Dickinson published his observations, he made his position clear: "Passion is the crucial stuff of which the fabric of marriage is made."[50] From the descriptions that Dickinson provided of his practice, it appeared that he often "urged a free sexual expression of love in marriage," that he gave instructions on how to stimulate the clitoris in and out of coitus, and that he sometimes was the first person to tell a woman of her capacity to have orgasm.[51]

Behind Dickinson's sense of mission was his fervent Christian faith. As a man of twenty-eight, he wrote to Sarah Truslow, his fiancée, describing a vision he had of Christ "as the most perfect of several young men living together in good fellowship in Clinton Street." This Jesus of New York was the embodiment of physical and moral harmony. "He worked easily and didn't get tired and slept and ate well," wrote

Dickinson. "In talking over personal purity he said he knew what a fellow's temptations are and could help other men."[52] Sarah wanted them to become missionaries, but Dickinson argued that his best field of witness lay in caring for the "sick poor" and training other doctors to do likewise. An obvious moralism appeared in his justification of sexual research: "One man or woman saved from reckless wickedness is worth all the science."[53] In a speech on behalf of birth control in 1929, he described himself as "an Episcopalian and a lover of nature," and as a "father confessor to human beings who love."[54]

Robert Latou Dickinson obtained some influence. He was the first doctor to help organize the fight for freedom in dispensing contraceptive instruction and devices; he provided anatomical drawings for the leading gynecology textbook of the 1890s.[55] But Dickinson did not lead the movement toward modern sexual ethics. He could not publish his research until 1931, after the Comstock laws had lapsed and the crucial transformation of attitudes had already occurred. As he spoke on birth control, Dickinson deferred to a "dignified, auburn-haired nurse,"[56] Margaret Sanger, who had gone to prison to win the right of doctors to give advice on contraception. And Sanger also had her forerunners, who prepared society to accept her message.

When recalling the doctors who preached the liberation of sex throughout the nineteenth century, one must remember the limitations inherent in such work by health experts. The medical outlook was inevitably conservative, for both ideological and social reasons. Because writers on health concerned themselves with bodily functions, they naturally concentrated on physical methods. Even Ingersoll, for all his faith in sexual redemption, could do nothing unless his patients would "hang the head." Technical description of physiological facts and theories was the stock in trade of Foote, Hollick, and the other fringe physicians who wrote in favor of sexual pleasure.[57] Furthermore, those who sought physical advice belonged to a limited audience, defined by suffering or pathology with regard to sex. The tiny minority of radical doctors shared this audience with more conservative physicians, who would guide their patients toward repression. Before doctors could effectively teach the enjoyment of sex, some other, more extensive influence would have to move America beyond the fear of passion.

5

Evangelical Ecstasy

The Rapture of Rebirth

"Things will be different," he interrupted, his gloved hand moving to brush snow from her cheek, his fingers pausing near her knitted cap before he spoke again. "Because I'm different, Sara.... Now I know how Vivian made it through all those pain-filled days. She held fast to her faith in Christ, and now I understand why.... She knew the answer I was too blind to see."

"Answer?" Sara asked, holding her breath in anticipation, her voice a whisper.

"A personal relationship with Jesus. Only he can give us the ability to accept what cannot be changed ... knowing that a greater being is looking out for us ... believing in the individual's right to take a stand." He tweaked her nose as he spoke, his eyes glittering as he referred to her determination to stick by her beliefs. Sara felt her cheeks burn with color, her lashes lowering, her hands moving to his arms.[1]

SCENES LIKE THIS have been shaping American sexual expectations for a hundred and fifty years. When publishers began to market Christian romances a few years ago, the idea seemed novel, but in fact, the heroine who won a man for Christ and for herself was a staple of nineteenth-century romantic fiction.

Behind such heroines stood the pervasive influence of evangelical Christianity, the historic mainstream of American religion. Protestant evangelists reached a larger audience than doctors, priests, novelists, magazine writers, or any other group in the United States before the advent of the motion picture in the 1920s. The term *evangelical*, which now denotes only a minority of Christians, then described all Methodists and Baptists, most Presbyterians and Congregationalists, and a large percentage of Episcopalians. What united evangelicals across denominational lines was their zeal to promote emotional experiences of commitment, or conversion to Christianity: the sudden acceptance of a new spiritual power, transforming the personality from the inside out, that today has become the special mark of those who claim to be "born again."

The model of rebirth was so well known and so important that it can hardly have failed to exert an influence on American attitudes toward sex. As an illustration of the potential of this type of religious experience to affect sexual practice, an extreme example offers the advantage of clarity. Consider Aimée Semple McPherson (1890–1944), an evangelist who preached to the nation on radio. McPherson belonged to the Pentecostal movement, which meant that her rebirth included the gift of speaking in tongues; but her story of how she received this gift revealed feelings common to evangelicals. In 1908, after struggling through a long night of prayer, McPherson arrived at this consummation in the morning:

A quietness seemed to steal over me, the holy presence of the Lord to envelop me. The Voice of the Lord spoke tenderly:

"Now, child, cease your strivings and your begging; just begin to praise Me, and in simple, child-like faith, receive ye the Holy Ghost."

... Without effort on my part I began to say: "Glory to Jesus! Glory to Jesus! GLORY TO JESUS! ! !" Each time that I said "Glory to Jesus!" it seemed to come from a deeper place in my being than the last, and in a deeper voice, until great waves of "Glory to Jesus" were rolling from my toes up; such adoration and praise I had never known possible.

All at once my hands and arms began to shake, gently at first, then violently, until my whole body was shaking. . . .

How happy I was, Oh how happy! Happy just to feel His wonderful power taking control of my being. . . .

Almost without notice my body slipped gently to the floor, and I was lying stretched out under the power of God, but felt as though caught up and floating upon the billowy clouds of glory. . . .

My lungs began to fill and heave under the Power as the Comforter came in. The cords of my throat began to twitch—my chin began to quiver, and then to shake violently, but Oh, so sweetly! My tongue began to move up and down and sideways in my mouth. . . . Then, suddenly, out of my innermost being flowed rivers of praise in other tongues as the Spirit gave utterance (Acts 2:4). . . .

I shouted and sang and laughed and talked in tongues until it seemed that I was too full to hold another bit of blessing lest I should burst with the glory.[2]

To reduce this reception of the Spirit to mere sexuality would do violence to the truth of what McPherson experienced. But McPherson herself referred to seven parts of the body in her account; she went on to compare the Holy Spirit to an electric current. Any interpretation should at least note this physical dimension and admit the parallels between this conversion and the descriptions of orgasm provided by modern medicine.

As a condition for her religious ecstasy, McPherson first had to abandon self-consciousness and self-restraint ("cease your strivings . . ."). Such abandonment did not come easily to McPherson, both because her pride resisted it and because she knew that her family disapproved of speaking in tongues. Neither did the analogous abandonment of self in intercourse come easily to women who sought sexual fulfillment despite cultural opposition. Doctors from Ingersoll's clinic to the laboratory of Masters and Johnson have attempted to duplicate the effect produced by the divine voice that told McPherson to relax and receive. In both types of self-abandonment, a conviction that some higher good demanded the overcoming of restraint has proved crucial. Neither the gift of tongues nor female orgasm comes to the inhibited except through faith.[3]

Once McPherson relinquished control, simple repetitive action ("Glory to Jesus!") brought her to a state of excitement that affected her whole body ("rolling from my toes up"). This was the spiritual analog of the condition physiologists have named the plateau: a preorgasmic stage most reliably reached through simple, repetitive stimulation, which builds up a critical amount of tension without bringing about release.[4] From this point, in physiological terms, a woman may either go on to orgasm if stimulation continues or spend an hour or so in a gradual return to normality.

McPherson also stood at a point of decision. Had she become distracted or begun to resist, she might have come this far without receiving the Spirit.

Fresh action brought McPherson a positive resolution. When "the Comforter came in," He worked on the spiritual plane with the same timing that sex therapists since the 1920s have recommended to husbands; He entered at the plateau.[5] McPherson's feelings mounted and, filled to repletion, she released bodily tension in spasmodic, uncontrollable muscular contractions. Her lungs, vocal cords, and tongue all participated in the release. For McPherson, the contractions expelled words, "rivers of praise in other tongues"; in sexual consummations, the contractions have expelled blood from tissue and tension from nerves.[6] Both classes of events have disclosed to their subjects the infinite quality of ecstasy, a quality that makes it seem impossible that one could live for long at this level: "I was too full to hold another bit of blessing lest I should burst with the glory." And both the gift of tongues and orgasm have commonly convinced people that they have been reborn.[7]

Though McPherson's rebirth was not sexual, it paralleled the emotional and physical pattern that women followed when they became orgasmic. Thousands read and heard of Aimée Semple McPherson's reception of the Spirit; thousands saw it represented in the "tableaux" she acted out during evangelical campaigns. And these thousands, without thinking consciously of sex, absorbed a pattern of feeling that may have led them to connect sex with the consummation of life. McPherson taught that fulfillment came through ecstatic experience and showed how such experience looked and felt. When the psychologists and birth control advocates came in McPherson's wake, they found an audience prepared for their gospel of sexual ecstasy.

And they were prepared in more than one sense: besides unconscious patterning, that morning of rapture also produced an ideology capable of supporting the quest for ecstasy in sex. McPherson became a herald of victory over the consequences of sin, and the victory she proclaimed came through immediate experience, eliminating the need to await results either from medical therapy or from the evolution of Christian civilization.

Certainly McPherson preached restraint, just as the doctors did, with regard to minor vices. She spoke of dancing, motion pictures, and parties as so much "velvet" covering the "claws" of sin.[8] Sadly reviewing her own youth, she depicted herself as nearly ruined by "the oyster suppers, the strawberry festivals, the Christmas trees, and always the concerts to follow" sponsored by such groups as the Salvation Army and the

Temperance Union.[9] These condemnations of ordinary social life became standard among Pentecostals; some scholars have interpreted them as attempts by country people to resist the encroachments of city culture.[10] But for McPherson and others of her school, both Pentecostal and simple evangelical, self-denial also fostered concentration on more intense pleasure. When "in the Spirit," as she always was at revivals, McPherson herself could dance, and act on the stage, and sit down at a piano and sing, producing "strange, and sometimes weird heavenly chords that never man could produce in the natural."[11] Evangelicals used restraint as a platform from which to reach for ecstasy.

Ecstasy made McPherson a healer. After receiving the Spirit, she could pray the prayer of faith over the sick and expect instantaneous results.[12] Through such faith healing, evangelicals would spread the religion of health among a constituency far broader than that addressed by medical experts. Today's evangelical movement continues to emphasize healing, maintaining the alliance of therapy and ecstasy that began early in the twentieth century.

Finally, ecstasy gave Aimée Semple McPherson the strength to change the limits of her gender role into resources. She first received the Spirit through the ministry of a man, the Pentecostal evangelist Robert Semple, whom she married and then accompanied on a mission to China. When Semple died abroad, leaving his young wife with an infant, Aimée fell into the worst depression of her life. Still in this state, in which she had begun "to lose out spiritually and wander away from the Lord," she remarried.[13] But her new domestic life only deepened her depression. "Time after time I tried to shake myself from my lethargy ... and busy myself with household duties," she wrote. All such efforts were in vain. McPherson described herself roaming through the house her husband had purchased in Rhode Island, trying to glean contentment from the "shining, polished floors," the "soft Axminster and Wilton rugs," the "mahogany parlor furniture," "big brass beds," "steam heat," and "softly shaded electric lights,"[14] but in the end this litany of domestic objects evoked the same feelings as the dances and dinner parties of McPherson's youth. They impeded the Spirit, without offering any fulfillment that equaled the rapture McPherson had known. Borrowing money from her mother, she left home to lead a revival meeting in Kitchener, Ontario. Letters from her husband demanded that she return to "wash the dishes," "take care of the house," and "act like other women," but McPherson resisted.[15] Soon he came to bring her back, got the Spirit instead, and began to accompany her on the trail of country roads that were home for the traveling evangelist.

By 1927, those roads led to McPherson's own International Church of the Foursquare Gospel, with ninety thousand contributing members and a $1.5 million temple in Los Angeles. From the "Angelus Temple," McPherson broadcast her message to the nation: a message that purported to be nothing more than the pure Christianity of the early church as recorded in the Acts of the Apostles, but that conveyed undeniable undertones. Those who heard the Gospel from McPherson also heard that life could be fulfilled in a moment of ecstasy, that religion should be therapeutic, and that a woman could exercise leadership. McPherson played up her femininity, curling her long blond hair and dressing in flowing white robes, except when she donned a costume for a "tableau." She spoke in a breathless whisper, exploiting the microphone, and she got her message across.

Because a sexual scandal eventually turned McPherson's fame into notoriety, and because her theology looked childishly simple in print, she has not received much serious attention from historians. But the church she founded survived her death, joining a stream of Pentecostal churches that continues to broaden in America today. The future of Christianity in the United States lies as much with McPherson's heirs as with her detractors.

Methodism and Sanctification

Even in 1908, before Aimée Semple McPherson attained any personal influence, she exemplified a widespread pattern of religious development. Working far below the social and intellectual notice of well-endowed churches and seminaries, the combination of ecstatic experience and female leadership permeated popular Christianity. The new Pentecostals who arose at the turn of our century did not invent this combination. Rather, they rode the momentum of a movement that began within Methodism, the most popular form of Protestantism in America from 1820 through 1920. McPherson's own religious roots reached back through her mother, a Salvation Army soldier, to a maternal grandmother who "talked much of the mighty power of God manifested in the early Methodist Church," and who joined the Salvation Army because there "it was nothing uncommon to see men and women slain [by the Spirit] as in the church of John Wesley's day."[16] John Wesley (1703–1791), the founder of Methodism, deserved as much credit as anyone for McPherson's spiritual power.

Methodism was distinguished from other Protestant traditions by Wesley's reworking of the doctrines of sin and grace. Wesley began as an Episcopal priest who wished to reach the poor that his church neglected, but he ended by preaching new doctrine. He taught that the grace that could set people totally free from sin was always available to them, if only they would accept it. He adapted the Anglican Articles of Religion for Methodist use by eliminating the statement that sin remained as an "infection of nature" even in the redeemed.[17] Defining what he called "Christian perfection," Wesley wrote that the perfect Christian would find that "no wrong temper, none contrary to love, remains in the soul."[18] He depicted perfect Christians confessing, "I feel no sin, but all love. I pray, rejoice, give thanks without ceasing."[19] Wesley clung to the doctrine of perfection throughout decades of controversy and a career in which he delivered forty thousand sermons, traveling the equivalent of nine times around the earth. Christian perfection proved to be the special contribution of Methodism to theology.

It was in America that both Methodism and Christian perfection flourished most dramatically. The frontier of the United States furnished an ideal setting for the Methodist preacher. Outdistancing the Congregationalists, Presbyterians, and Episcopalians, who required a town big enough to support a church and a minister, Methodist "circuit riders" visited every hamlet and farmhouse in a territory, organizing lay-people into "classes" for prayer and mutual discipline. From a membership of about fourteen thousand, or one in two hundred Americans, at the end of the Revolutionary War, the Methodist church grew by 1845 to embrace a million souls, or one in twenty Americans.[20] During most of this period, Christian perfection produced little more than intensified moralism. The Methodist was more likely than his neighbors to have a conscience about using tobacco and alcohol, or owning slaves, because Methodists were supposed to be "going on to perfection."

But the doctrine caught fire at the hands of Methodist women during the 1830s. Female preaching in the lay classes had been a Methodist innovation of Wesley's own day. That innovation gave new life to the doctrine of perfection through the lay ministry of one extraordinary woman, Phoebe Palmer (1807–1874).

As the daughter of Henry Worrall, an immigrant from England who owned a certificate of Methodist membership signed by John Wesley himself, Phoebe Palmer grew up without ever developing a sense of sin. By her own account, written at the age of twenty, Miss Worrall could not recall herself "ever to have been willfully disobedient" or to have provoked pun-ishment from her parents.[21] Innocence actually caused problems in her re-ligious life. "So early in life was the love of God shed abroad in her heart," wrote Palmer's first biographer, that she fell into "perplexity" over when and how she had experienced conversion.[22] To be unable to recall the moment of conversion, in the evangelical atmosphere of the American 1820s, was to have doubts about whether or not one's soul was acceptable to God.

Christian perfection offered a resolution. What Phoebe wanted was not the struggle with sin that even Methodists saw in conversion, but a more intense experience of fulfillment. At thirteen, she "wrestled with the Lord till about midnight" on one occasion, then "sought the repose of her pillow" with feelings she expressed in these lines:

> I'll weary thee with my complaint,
> Here, at thy feet, forever lie,
> With longing sick, with groaning faint—
> O! give me love, or else I die.[23]

Unfortunately for Palmer, American Methodism in 1820 did not effec-tively teach the positive side of Christian perfection. The doctrine had fallen into disuse, partly because of controversy, but partly because of an editorial decision: the Methodist Conference of 1812 had voted, "purely in the interest of size and convenience," to omit Wesley's doctrinal tracts, including "Of Christian Perfection," from the basic Methodist book, the *Discipline*.[24] The conference did not get around to publishing the tracts separately until 1832. Meanwhile, a Boston Methodist, the Reverend Timothy Merritt, published a manual on perfection in 1825. Inspired by Merritt's work, classes began to discuss perfection, and in 1835, Sarah Worrall Lankford, Phoebe's older sister, claimed to have attained this state.[25] Lankford started a women's prayer meeting in her home to help others gain perfection. In this class, women learned to focus their minds on a single promise of the Bible, to seize upon that promise as though "au-dibly uttered from the heavens"[26] to each of them personally, and then to let go all consciousness of sin, guilt, and self to make room for the Spirit. Phoebe, by now Phoebe Palmer because of her marriage, attended her sister's meetings and in 1837 reached perfection herself.

"Ye are not your own, ye are bought with a price, therefore glorify God in your body and spirit which are his (1 Corinthians 6:20)." This was the first Scripture on which Palmer set her heart, according to her account in *The*

Way of Holiness, an introduction to Christian perfection that went through thirty-four editions by 1854.[27] "Body and spirit" was the crucial phrase, the phrase that taught Palmer that redemption should include her whole being. "Here she saw God as her Redeemer," recalled Palmer, writing of herself in the third person, "claiming, by virtue of the great price paid for the redemption of body, soul, and spirit, the present and entire service of all those redeemed powers."[28] Beginning "to anticipate, with longings unutterable," the fulfillment of this promise in her own life, Palmer noted that her emotions became deeper but not more "distressing."[29] The quest for perfection demanded no heightened consciousness of sin. Resolved to continue in prayer until "the desire of her heart was fulfilled," Palmer turned again to the Bible.

"Be ye holy" leapt from the page of 1 Peter 1:16. "With unutterable delight, she found the comprehensive desires of her soul blended and satisfied" in this command.[30] She called on the hosts of heaven to witness her intention to surrender herself entirely. Yet she paused, wondering how she would know if her gift was accepted.

> Still her insatiable desires were unsatisfied; and yet she continued to wait with unutterable importunity of desire and longing expectation, looking upward for the coming of the Lord.[31]

Palmer now saw that she alone was to blame for her unfulfilled state. She had searched herself for feelings, expecting to find the assurance that accompanied perfection, before exercising the faith that perfection required. Rather than hoping that God *would* receive her or trying to discern evidence that he *had*, she simply needed to believe that he *did* receive her at that very moment. Again the Scriptures told Palmer what to do: "The kingdom of heaven suffereth violence, and the violent take it by storm (Matthew 11:12)."[32] So she offered herself, violently enough:

> O Lord, I call heaven and earth to witness that I now lay *body, soul*, and *spirit*, with *all these redeemed powers, upon thine altar, to be forever* THINE! ... From this time henceforth I *am thine—wholly thine!*[33]

Instantly, Palmer felt herself "plunged ... into an immeasurable ocean of love, light, and power."[34] She had, once and for all, reached Christian perfection.

The desire to share this experience was the force that led Phoebe Palmer to become one of the most influential religious leaders of the second and third quarters of the nineteenth century. Uniting the prayer meeting that her sister had begun with another, she created the Tuesday Meeting for the Promotion of Holiness, which would continue under her direction for thirty-seven years. Palmer's husband, Walter C. Palmer (who fortunately was both prosperous and devout), would twice buy larger homes to accommodate the crowds of up to three hundred that gathered for these meetings. By admitting men to the meetings, Palmer greatly increased her sphere of influence: among the men who gained perfection at her home were Stephen C. Olin, president of Wesleyan University; Thomas C. Upham, professor of psychology at Bowdoin; three Methodist bishops (Janes, Hamline, and Peck); and John Dempster, founder of two seminaries. In the Businessman's Revival that swept New York in 1858, Palmer's meeting became a dynamo generating spiritual renewal. And this meeting spawned others, till by 1886 there were two hundred regular gatherings in cities across the country, modeled on the Tuesday Meeting in New York.[35]

After 1862, Palmer expanded her influence even further by editing a monthly magazine, *The Guide to Holiness*, which reached a circulation of thirty thousand. She and her husband accompanied Charles Grandison Finney on a revival tour of England, and traveled a circuit of revivals themselves. Finally, Phoebe Palmer left a permanent legacy in her books, especially *The Way of Holiness*, which continues to circulate among evangelicals today, and *The Promise of the Father*, her defense of the vocation of women to preach. The publishing house that the Palmers founded also sent forth books by other advocates of Christian perfection.

Palmer's meetings, her magazine, her preaching, and her books transformed the heritage of John Wesley. As one scholar wrote, Wesley's methods produced "a generation of seekers after Christian perfection; Mrs. Palmer's, a century of holiness professors."[36] Identifying the attainment of perfection with a single ecstatic experience was what brought about this change. Methodists following Wesley had believed in the possibility of perfection but expected to find it only after a long growth in grace; and Wesley himself said that a record of blameless behavior "for some time before this supposed change"[37] must be the first test of whether the grace of perfection had really been given. Phoebe Palmer, on the other hand, taught that God's work in perfection took place in an instant. Previous behavior did not matter, because however gradual a soul's progress toward perfect love had been, there must still be a moment when imperfect love became perfect. In handbooks and in massive tomes, Palmer and her followers argued that perfection must come at a definite point, or else there would be no qualitative difference between the condition of one still struggling with sin and the life of complete freedom.[38] Many names for perfection were coined to express the sense of this qualitative difference: some called it "perfect love" or "holiness"; others, "sanctification," "entire consecration," "the second blessing," or "purity." The multiplicity of names corresponded to the new multitude of believers.

When Wesley dealt with the question of whether the marriage of two perfect Christians would produce offspring born in freedom from sin, he wrote that such a marriage represented "a possible, but not a probable case"; he expressed doubt "whether it ever was or ever will be."[39] Clearly, perfection seemed a very rare thing in Wesley's time. But Phoebe and Walter C. Palmer considered themselves a married pair of perfect Christians, as did many who attended the meetings in their home. Compressing the grace of sanctification into an ecstatic moment made perfection seem so much more attainable that every good Methodist expected to find it. Another innovation that helped spread the doctrine was Palmer's insistence on the duty of everyone in perfect love to profess their perfection in public.[40] Though Wesley had warned (in 1747) that one should never speak of perfection "to them that know not God," lest they blaspheme, nor even to other Christians "without some particular reason,"[41] American Methodists of the nineteenth century believed themselves bound to testify on pain of losing the blessing itself.

Neither John Wesley nor Phoebe Palmer held that parents could pass perfect love to their children. "Grafts on a crabstock produce excellent fruit," Wesley wrote, likening the perfect Christian to a crabapple tree onto which God had grafted a more succulent species. "But sow the kernels of the fruit and what will be the event? As mere crabs as ever were eaten."[42] Not until the belief in original sin was more entirely lost, among the heirs of Wesley's spirit who translated sanctification into sexual terms, would a doctrine of inherited grace come into its own.

Palmer took a long step toward this translation by reinterpreting Wesley on the relation of perfect love to the body. Wesley had said that the body was the reason that perfect Christians still made mistakes, even on religious and moral subjects. Though involuntary or mistaken transgressions of God's law could not be actual sins, they were still "materially" sinful,[43] and they showed that people no longer possessed the original constitution of humanity as it was in Eden. "These defects are the mere natural result of the present imperfect and corruptible state of the body," Wesley wrote.[44] Even perfect Christians would continue to make mistakes, because "we cannot now think at all but by the mediation of those organs which have suffered" in the punishment of original sin.[45] Attempting to improve on Wesley, Professor Thomas Upham argued that the human will, and the other desires and powers of an embodied soul, actually died at the moment God sanctified the person.[46] Phoebe Palmer disagreed fiercely with Upham in a series of letters. Carrying Upham's departure from Wesley a step further, Palmer contended that God neither destroyed human nature nor left the body as it had been; rather, the grace of perfect love accepted all bodily drives and turned them into holy channels. The formula of placing "body, soul, and spirit"[47] upon God's altar became Palmer's refrain.

Acceptance of the body allied Methodism with the religion of health, but without the drastic and repressive consequences that came from seeking perfection through orthodox medicine. Palmer took care to remind herself and others that the Christian should rely on Scriptural promises, not bodily feelings, for evidence of perfection. But few, if any, members of the movement begun by Palmer professed sanctification without ecstasy. Nor did any publicly dispute the notion that living in freedom from sin led them to keep certain therapeutic rules, such as abstinence from alcohol and tobacco, maintenance of a cheerful disposition, and regard for the body as a gift from God. Even Palmer herself, despite her insistence that feelings had no *necessary* part in perfection, wrote of the body when describing her reaction to the idea of losing the "second blessing": "My heart recoils at the thought:—yes, and my nature, too, for it also partook of the living intensity with which it was sought."[48] One day "an aged professor" exclaimed to Palmer that he wished he could be as happy as she; Palmer replied "that she did not *dare* to be otherwise than happy."[49] Seventy years later, Aimée Semple McPherson taught the same duty.[50] And today, the healthy smile and the blow-dried hair of the American evangelist maintain this association between moral, physical, and emotional perfection.

Evangelicals set the religion of health ablaze with missionary enthusiasm. In their hands, the promise of health became available immediately and to everyone, without repression and without expert assistance, through the spirit of perfect love. As the Reverend Mr. Stockton wrote for *The Guide to Holiness*:

> Love is the excellence of all things.... Genuine self-love is good and glorious. It is not partial; but includes the whole nature, physical, intellectual, moral—and the whole interest, eternal as well as temporal.... It labors to prepare the body for immortal glory and grace; to discipline the mind for the attainment of boundless wisdom and knowledge; and to cleanse and refresh the heart, even here, with the first gushings of the final fullness of perfect holiness and joy.[51]

A mixture of faith in complete redemption, strict rules of behavior, and ecstatic experience became characteristic of the American evangelical by the middle of the nineteenth century. So potent was the appeal of this mixture that ecstatic perfectionism transcended denominational lines and began to gain adherents outside Methodism almost as quickly as within. Writing to *The Guide to Holiness*, a Presbyterian woman reported that she had to become willing to testify to complete redemption in her own church before the grace was given to her. Once she accepted this duty, she received her reward. "I find in God all that my soul desires," she wrote; "I rest, and yet continually desire; I feast, yet pant for more."[52] A Congregationalist wrote from Maine to describe a year-long struggle for perfect love, culminating in three months during which "so intense was the contest, so burning my desires ... that nature began to falter." After her prayers had been answered, this woman produced an entire theory of Christian perfection as the fulfillment of the soul, which she said could attain infinite happiness only through participation in the infinite desires of God.[53] A Baptist testified that her father was so vehemently opposed to the doctrine of perfect love that he had forced her to wear "those ornaments which ... the spirit of God had taught me was [sic] wrong"; but such "frivolous vanities" counted for nothing when the second blessing came to her:

> I arose, but scarcely had got upon my feet when my soul was so filled that my body was not able to sustain it. I fell prostrate to the earth, lost in wonder, love and praise. I felt the indubitable seal, the signature of divine love.[54]

Meanwhile, Phoebe Palmer wrote to Frederick Dan Huntington, a prominent convert from Unitarianism to the Episcopal Church, in an effort to convince Huntington that he need not feel *continual* ecstasy to claim complete redemption.[55] John Wesley's special doctrine had gained recognition across the whole spectrum of American Protestants.

Behind the rapid spread of this doctrine lay the secret of the influence that Methodist ecstasy exerted on American society at large, and also the secret of the movement's disappearance as a distinct element in American culture. Ecstatic perfectionism proved susceptible to remarkably secular expressions. For example, Phoebe Palmer's inspiration led to the formation of a National Camp Meeting Association in 1867. The association ran interdenominational meetings at sites such as Martha's Vineyard and the New Jersey shore—thus beginning the history of these places as summer resorts. Traders flocked to these attractive temples. By 1878, one revival meeting on the Jersey shore reported that "thirty-eight eye-glass and pack vendors, twenty-one prize package vendors, three Punch and Judy shows, four bird shows, two gymnastic shows, one hundred ninety-nine back peddlers, seven flashy shows, and fifty-six tramps" had been among those "fined, put off or turned away" by the authorities.[56] Such a congress of entertainers implied the presence of an audience that wanted entertainment. And indeed, most of those who attended these revivals had already experienced sanctification. They came to testify, to sustain their ardor, to see their children get the blessing, and also to enjoy a vacation from the summer heat of the eastern cities. Ecstatic perfectionism helped make revivals for the already converted an enduring feature of American religion. But once revivals came to be occasions for cultivating ecstatic experience among those who already knew ecstasy, they ran the danger of degenerating to the level of mere entertainment themselves.

The 1970s would see a closer harmony between sanctification and entertainment than anyone imagined in the 1870s. Between those seasons of flourishing, however, came a period in which the Wesleyan movement dissolved into isolated churches and secular channels. As Methodists prospered and grew more sophisticated, they tended to drift toward more worldly satisfactions and away from the demands of Christian perfection. Meanwhile, the logic of sanctification carried others onward into the gifts of tongues and of healing. A splintering off of new denominations ensued, and by the first decade of our century, the Assemblies of God, the Church of God in Christ, the Church of the Nazarene, and innumerable other denominations outside the mainstream had become the primary vehicles of perfectionism.[57]

Evangelical Christianity itself went on the defensive during the early twentieth century, for the first time since the Revolutionary era. Continuing Catholic and Jewish immigration, the movement of population into the cities, the teaching of evolution in the public schools, and the rise of motion pictures, radio, and the automobile all combined to decrease the importance of evangelists and to undermine their message. For half a century, those who maintained the doctrine of rebirth in the Spirit rejected many of the most prominent aspects of American popular culture, especially the new ethic of sexual pleasure that emerged in the 1920s and after. Yet the hope of overcoming sin in a single ecstatic moment had left its mark on that sexual ethic. Phoebe Palmer and her heirs, down to Aimée Semple McPherson, did much to remove the suspicion that all passion was tainted by sin. They reached multitudes who could hear such a message only if it came in Christian terms, and who learned to release emotion in a Christian context. Though many of these people and their descendants drifted from the fold, they took with them an earnestness and fervor that John Wesley might have recognized.

Nineteenth-century perfectionism bore secular fruit, not only in summer visitors to New Jersey and Cape Cod, but also in movements and thinkers that began their search for perfection where Methodism left off. But before America became ready for their accomplishment, one more stage of preparation remained: the contribution that Roman Catholicism, the largest branch of Christendom in the United States, made by advancing the cult of the Virgin Mary.

6

The Song of Bernadette

American Messengers of the Beautiful Lady

Roman Catholics followed their own ecstatic women into the twentieth century. A series of Catholic girls, each claiming to have met the Virgin Mary in a vision, opened another route to the conquest of original sin, the way of the Immaculate Conception. The surge of devotion to Mary that followed the visions gave the Romantic ideal of woman a Christian form and projected an image of innocent, yet rapturous, womanhood that would touch Americans of all faiths.

American culture produced its most vivid picture of Mary consecrating ecstasy in the 1943 film *The Song of Bernadette.* Jennifer Jones won the Academy Award for Best Actress (despite competition from Ingrid Bergman in *For Whom the Bell Tolls*) for her portrayal of Bernadette Soubirous, the fourteen-year-old who saw the Virgin at Lourdes, France, in 1858. In the death scene that ended the film, Bernadette, her face aglow from the soft lights, passed into eternity, entranced by a final glimpse of the Virgin standing at the foot of her bed, while a priest read aloud from the *Song of Songs:* "Open to me, my sister, my love, my dove, my undefiled; for my hand is filled with dew, and my locks with the drops of the night."[1] Thus Hollywood made use of the most frankly sexual book of the Bible to emphasize the ecstatic element in Bernadette's life. The dark, intense beauty of actress Jennifer Jones, a beauty that did not surpass that of the original Bernadette, helped achieve the same effect.

The millions who saw *The Song of Bernadette* were secondary participants in an event that had already shown its power to move masses of people. Within weeks of Bernadette's first sighting of the Virgin, crowds of up to twenty thousand came to watch her kneel and pray.[2] Usually, all they saw was Bernadette entering a trance, losing consciousness of everything but the apparition that she called "the Beautiful Lady." The most dramatic outward manifestation came on February 25, 1858, when, directed by the Lady to bathe in a fountain, Bernadette uncovered a spring by digging in the earth with her hands. Since that day, pilgrims whose number has surpassed a million a year have used the water from this spring in the hope of being cured of disease. Devotion to Mary thus generated another form of the religion of health. Despite the isolation of Lourdes in the foothills of the Pyrenees, a major shrine, complete with church and hospital and bath houses, grew up around the spring. Bernadette's visions ceased after July 1858; she eventually entered religious life and died in a convent in 1879.[3] In 1933, the church declared her a saint.

Seven years after Bernadette's canonization, Franz Werfel, an Austrian Jew in flight from the Nazis, took refuge at Lourdes, where he observed the power of the shrine. After Werfel escaped, he wrote *The Song of Bernadette*, the book that gave Lourdes to the bestseller lists and to Technicolor. Because of Werfel's work, the influence of this appearance of Mary actually reached its peak at about the middle of the twentieth century.

The special character of that influence had to do with Bernadette's age and sex. Before modern times, adolescent girls had rarely touched off religious movements, even in connection with Mary. Although the Virgin had appeared on a number of occasions in the Middle Ages, she seemed then to favor veteran members of religious orders. Mary's appearance at Guadalupe in 1531 served to establish the spiritual center of Catholic Mexico, but the message of Guadalupe came through an adult male.[4] The emotional power of Bernadette's story, however, sprang precisely from the efforts of a girl to win belief from hostile elders, including her mother and the local officials of church and state. When Bernadette triumphed, and the doubters were convinced of her sincerity, she exemplified the Cinderella archetype. Just as the peasant girl might become a princess, so this child became a saint—by means of natural goodness and immediate experience, not through learning and gradual growth. Adolescent and preadolescent girls, including many non-Catholics, were still reading *The Song of Bernadette* as inspirational literature in the 1960s.

For those who were not adolescent girls, the identity of the visionary had another effect. It seems reasonable to surmise that the crowds who watched Bernadette kneeling in rapture, and the millions who read descriptions or saw re-enactments of the event, came away feeling that female ecstasy had some special relation to God. In his novel, Franz

Werfel left no room for doubt about the relation between the visions and Bernadette's physical being. Describing Bernadette's reaction to the first vision, Werfel imagined that the "utter sweetness" of the experience "penetrate[ed] her shivering body to the very points of her young breasts."[5] Bernadette functioned as a medium, a means of communication with the spiritual world; and, in Marshall McLuhan's phrase, the medium is the message. Although Saint Bernadette preached the need for repentance, although she kissed the ground on behalf of sinners during her trances and later embraced a life of penitence in the convent, still her message furthered the identification of female ecstasy with religious fulfillment.

According to Bernadette's descriptions, the Virgin she saw also exemplified girlhood and ecstasy. In the medieval legend of Mary's appearance to St. Bernard, the Virgin appeared as a mother, offering the saint milk from her breast. Other visionaries of that time told of Mary appearing as a queen, demanding loyalty and service.[6] But to Bernadette, the Virgin looked about sixteen or seventeen years old. She wore no crown, but distinguished herself principally by being "young and beautiful, exceedingly beautiful."[7] Mary appeared in a literal *ecstasis*, standing in the air above a rosebush near the entrance to a cave. In all the visions, her main activity was to join Bernadette in rapturous prayer.

When Bernadette asked her Beautiful Lady to identify herself, the Lady's answer connected all the messages of Lourdes to the conquest of original sin. "I am the Immaculate Conception," Mary said.[8] Bernadette had to ask her parish priest what the words meant. By this phrase, the Virgin affirmed what the Roman Catholic Church had formally granted her only four years before, in a proclamation by Pope Pius IX: that she, "in the first instant of conception was, by a singular grace and privilege of Almighty God in view of the merits of Jesus Christ, ... preserved exempt from all stain of original sin."[9] The sin of Adam and Eve had never touched Mary. Despite her descent from two human parents who had conceived her in the usual way, Mary had received the gift of absolute purity. The doctrine of the Immaculate Conception made the "infection of nature" passed on through sex seem less inescapable; Mary bore witness that a conception that was both sexual and pure had taken place at least once. For Roman Catholics, Mary became *the* woman who had overcome the bond between sex and sin.

Popular acceptance of the Immaculate Conception certainly was facilitated by the Virgin's claiming that title for herself in her most famous appearance. But even before Lourdes, other appearances had impelled the church toward this understanding of Mary's role. And, as with St. Bernadette, these appearances raised up young women, through ecstatic experience, to proclaim the Virgin's victory over sin.

These modern visions intervened in a very controversial course of doctrinal development. None of the Fathers of the church, with the possible exception of St. Ephraim of Syria (*d.* 373), wrote anything that can be taken to indicate belief in the Immaculate Conception of Mary.[10] Certainly Augustine had not held Mary exempt from the corruption transmitted to all through sex. But the contrast of Eve and Mary became commonplace, yielding much praise of Mary, with the implication that Eve and Mary made their opposite decisions (to disobey God in Eden and to accept God's will in the Incarnation) in a similar state of innocence.[11] Meanwhile, Mary attained a popularity as an object of prayer that nearly equaled that of her Son. Popular sentiment tolerated discussion of guilt in relation to her no more than in relation to Christ.[12] By the end of the sixth century, Christians of the East had settled on December 9 to celebrate the conception of the Virgin by her parents, Joachim and Anna. Later, advocates of the Immaculate Conception would argue that the very existence of such a feast testified to belief in something holier than the transmission of sin to another soul.[13] The celebration of Mary's conception spread to Europe during the fourteenth century; but in the West, devotional practice collided with a theology that, continuing the emphasis of Augustine, was centered on sin. Controversy flared, with Dominicans leading the forces who contended that Mary was conceived in sin and afterward saved by Christ, while Franciscans and others insisted that a sinful woman could not have been a fit medium for the Incarnation.[14] Assertions of Mary's innocence appeared to some to threaten the honor of Christ as Savior. On the other hand, Mary's reputation evoked as strong a protective response as would that of any mother. The seventeenth and eighteenth centuries witnessed the establishment throughout Spain, France, and Italy of a custom according to which men would swear to defend the sinlessness of Mary to the death.[15] In this "bloody vow," as it came to be known, theology and piety mixed with the remnants of chivalry. The vow was a sign that the cause of the Immaculate Conception had entered a phase of violent reaction, in which it might well have perished alongside other relics of the Middle Ages.

But in 1830, breaking three centuries of silence since the appearance at Guadalupe, the first modern appearance of Mary gained for the Immaculate Conception a foothold in the Romantic era. In the novice house of the Daughters of Charity at Paris,[16] Catherine Labouré was awakened by the specter of a little boy. It was 11:30, and the young woman feared to leave her bed lest she disturb the order of the house. Still, she arose and followed the ghostly child to the chapel and obeyed his instructions to wait until the Blessed Virgin appeared, Catherine and Mary spoke together, and the Virgin strengthened Catherine to fulfill an undisclosed mission. And on November 27, 1830, five months after the first vision, Mary revealed to Catherine the task she must undertake. This novice sister, then twenty-four years old and so uneducated that she had barely gained admission to her order, had to convince her superiors to distribute a medal bearing an image of the Virgin treading the serpent of sin underfoot, and the words "O Mary, conceived without sin, pray for us who have recourse to thee." By 1832, Catherine succeeded, and thus the Medal of the Immaculate Conception, commonly called the Miraculous Medal, appeared in the world twenty-two years before the Virgin's freedom from original sin became official Catholic doctrine.

Religious experience took another step beyond theology in the same Paris convent in 1840, when another novice, Justine Bisqueyburu, saw the Virgin several times. In the fall of 1840, Justine had a vision in which Mary asked for the distribution of a scapular—a piece of green cloth, hung around the neck by a string—bearing the picture of a heart pierced by a sword and the inscription "Immaculate Heart of Mary, pray for us now and at the hour of our death."[17] The Daughters of Charity began to produce this Green Scapular in 1846, again anticipating the declaration that Mary's heart was indeed "immaculate."

On September 19, 1846, Mary appeared on the mountain of La Salette in the French Alps, to Melanie Mathieu, aged fourteen, and Maximin Giraud, aged eleven, the latter one of the few boys caught up by the visions. These children came upon Mary sitting on the ground and crying. When the Virgin stood, Melanie saw her thus:

> She had white shoes, with roses round them of all colors; a gold-colored apron; a white robe with pearls all over it; a white cape over her shoulders, with roses round it; a white cap, bent a little forwards; a crown with roses round her cap. She wore a very small chain, on which was hung a cross, with a figure of our Lord; on the right were pincers, on the left a hammer. . . . Her face was white and elongated. I could not look at her long together, because she dazzled us.[18]

This Virgin personified the Romantic ideal of woman. Since Rousseau and Goethe, European writers had presented woman as a symbol for the spiritual mystery they found at the heart of nature. Her beauty, her emotions, and her innocence were like sacraments, connecting men with the basic power that informed the world. Christian insistence that sin had corrupted all of nature, including the nature of women, contradicted this Romantic ideal. But after 1830, in such romantic settings as the mountain of La Salette, the convent of the Daughters of Charity at Paris, and the grotto of Lourdes, the Virgin took the attributes of Romantic womanhood upon herself. Mary became young and beautiful, emotional and innocent. Mary revealed herself to the peasants that Romantics loved to eulogize. Mary brought Romanticism into the daily devotions of the Roman Catholic Church.

Too many visions occurred to include details on all of them except in a work devoted to the subject. Sister Apolline Andriveau heard Mary's instructions for a Red Scapular in 1846;[19] Father Pierre de Smet reported that Mary had appeared to a young convert at his mission among the Native Americans of Montana in 1841;[20] a laywoman named Adele Brisse founded a teaching order to fulfill the command she received from the Virgin near Green Bay, Wisconsin, in 1858.[21] French culture, the original matrix of Romanticism, took the lead in producing visionaries. Only later would Ireland (1879), Italy (1888), and Portugal (1917) bring forth their own examples of Mary's activity in the modern world.[22]

In France, the visions had immediate effects. According to a recent sociological study, the new popularity of devotion to Mary changed "the map of religious observance," renewing religious life in Paris and other "de-Christianized" locales.[23] Fashionable women took up scapulars, medals, and rosaries. The French Revolution of 1848 maintained an "equanimity" on the subject of religion that contrasted sharply with the anti-Christian violence of the 1830 revolution. And according to J. Michael Phayer, Marian piety provided a new tie to Catholicism that kept France loyal to the church, despite conflict with Catholic doctrine on divorce and birth control. In 1870, birth control became so widespread in France that the population no longer reproduced itself;[24] yet many who practiced contraception also went to La Salette and to Lourdes. Mary appeared to several more children at Pontmain in 1871 and to a lady's maid at Pellevoisin in 1876.[25]

Meanwhile, the Miraculous Medal, the scapulars, a new order of priests called the Missionary Fathers of La Salette, and even the French army carried the influence of Mary into the rest of the world. During the revolutionary upheavals of 1848, Roman mobs drove Pope Pius IX into exile, but French bayonets restored the pope as ruler of Rome in 1850.[26] When Pius IX declared the Immaculate Conception to be dogma in 1854, he was responding not only to French visionaries but also to the French archbishops, politicians, and soldiers who had seen the power of the visionaries.

In America, a council of Catholic bishops met in Baltimore in 1846 and voted to name Our Lady of the Immaculate Conception the Patronness of the United States.[27] Their action reflected the European development of devotion to Mary: many Catholic bishops and priests in America came from France and presumably communicated with French enthusiasts of the new devotion. But the new Patronness also suited a new direction in American culture.

The Romantic movement did not arrive in the United States until the 1830s, about half a century after the birth of Romanticism in Europe. It was accompanied by a confluence of events that exemplified what Hegel called "the cunning of history." Not only did American Romanticism and modern devotion to Mary emerge simultaneously, but also they emerged in the same decade that saw the first massive migration of Catholics to the United States, the first use of steam presses to produce a truly popular literature (including sexual advice), and the first stirrings of a movement to promote women's rights. The cultural life of the United States, which hitherto had been dominated by Protestantism, Founding Fathers, and the rationalism of the Enlightenment, now began to accommodate Catholics, women, and Romantics. As American Catholics received and spread the good news of Mary's triumph over sin, they took part in a movement that resonated far beyond their church. Such eminent Protestant figures as Hawthorne and Longfellow, Lowell and Stowe, Bushnell and Adams would join in a chorus of praise for the Virgin that would have made their Puritan forebears blush. In the first decade of the twentieth century, Henry Adams wrote that "the force of the Virgin was still felt at Lourdes, and seemed to be as potent as X-rays." But Adams, the first great medievalist the United States produced, acknowledged no trace of Mary's power in America. In the Virgin of the Middle Ages, Adams believed he had found "the highest energy ever known to man, the creator of four-fifths of his noblest art, exercising vastly more attraction over the mind of man than all the steam-engines and dynamos ever dreamed of"; and yet, he concluded, "All this was to American thought as though it had never existed."[28]

What Adams failed to see was that he, a descendant of two American presidents and the son of Lincoln's ambassador to Britain, himself exemplified the power that Mary exercised in the United States. Adams also failed to notice that he was not alone in succumbing to her power. He died in 1918—too early to see *The Song of Bernadette*, or to see Walt Disney's *Fantasia* conclude with an animated version of the "Ave Maria." Apparently, Adams ascribed no historical significance to the carols and nativity scenes that proliferated during his lifetime in celebration of a holiday his ancestors had rejected. For him, the Virgin served a purely personal function. Adams "turned in desperation" to Mary, as a later historian noted, when he had lost hope for the modern world.[29] In *Mont-Saint-Michel and Chartres*, he made Mary's cathedral at Chartres the symbol of Western civilization. In his autobiography, *The Education of Henry Adams*, he explained all of history as a conflict between the Virgin and the Dynamo. Yet Adams insisted that the Virgin remained unknown to American culture. The fate of his own books, which first became bestsellers and then classics, demonstrated how wrong he was.

Such blindness requires explanation. Henry Adams had reason to resent Catholics. In the 1870s, Irish Catholics assumed the supremacy his family had held since colonial times in Quincy, Massachusetts. Adams knew that America was changing and felt that this change left him an alien in a world he was raised to rule. He therefore not only taught history but also fled into it. Because Adams encountered Mary in the midst of his flight, he could not relate her to his point of departure. The Mary who meant so much to him could not belong also to the Irish of Quincy.

A similar blindness, compounded of attraction and repulsion, afflicts many Americans today. Divinity students who cheerfully speculate about the sexuality of Jesus are offended and embarrassed by discussion of Mary's relationship to God. Feminists interrupt their search for female symbols to find reasons for rejecting the woman called Queen of Heaven. Protestants who express respect for the pope as a traditional leader fall silent when conversation turns to Mary. Many modern Catholics would also like to forget her. The intensity of these reactions reveals Mary's power. To accept Mary seems to involve acceptance of something primitive, childish, and superstitious about oneself, something especially shameful in a culture so concerned with reform, liberation, and enlightenment. Discussion of Mary can evoke more resistance from students in a college religion course than such predictable sources of controversy as Islam, psychoanalysis, and liberation theology.

The generation that brought Romanticism to America knew Mary's ambiguous power. For Nathaniel Hawthorne in *The Marble Faun* (1860), for example, Mary stood at the center of conflict between past and future, nature and civilization, innocence and experience. Hawthorne placed his heroine Hilda, a "daughter of the Puritans," in Rome; he gave her an apartment in a tower, with a shrine of the Virgin outside one window. Then Hilda witnessed two of her friends committing a murder. She did not trust the government of Pius IX; she had no sympathy for the victim, an apparent blackmailer, but she could not keep silent and so become an accomplice in the crime. Returning to the tower, Hilda looked to Mary for help.

> When she trimmed the lamp before the Virgin's shrine, Hilda gazed at the sacred image, and, rude as was the workmanship, beheld . . . a woman's tenderness responding to her gaze. If she knelt, if she prayed, . . . was Hilda to be blamed? It was not a Catholic kneeling at an idolatrous shrine, but a child lifting its tear-stained face to seek comfort from a mother.[30]

Hawthorne explored the tension between Hilda and Catholic idolatry. When Hilda left her apartment to pray at St. Peter's, she went on what the omniscient narrator of *The Marble Faun* called "a dangerous errand." Nearly "ensnared" by the "gaudy superstitions" of saint worship and holy water, Hilda searched for another place to pray to the Virgin. She succumbed at last to the confessional, where she unburdened herself of the story of the murder. Her actions showed "how closely and comfortingly the popish faith applied itself to all human occasions."[31] Hilda, and America, stood on the side of nature, innocence, and the future; but Rome had all the seductions of civilization, refined by infinite experience. Rome made the Virgin one of the attractions of a sensual religion. The altars at St. Peter's disturbed Hilda, because she found Mary there represented by "the flattered portrait of an earthly beauty."[32]

Despite all these suspicions, however, *The Marble Faun* finally presented Mary in a positive light. Even Hilda's fiancé Kenyon, the most anti-Catholic character in the novel, could accept this one aspect of Catholic piety. "It soothes me inexplicably to think of you in your tower," he told Hilda, "with the Virgin for your household friend. You know not how far it throws its light, that lamp which you keep burning at her shrine."[33] By associating his heroine with Mary, Hawthorne adapted Mary to American tastes. The novel's conclusion identified both Hilda and Mary as innocent powers. When Kenyon proposed that sin, such as the murder around which the story revolved, may finally ennoble human nature, Hilda rejected the suggestion as "a mockery ... of all religious sentiments." She took a stance worthy of the Immaculate Conception. Kenyon accepted her as such, disowning his opinion about sin and begging her to share with him "that white wisdom which clothes you as a celestial garment." Hawthorne completed the parallel:

> Another hand must henceforth trim the lamp before the Virgin's shrine; for Hilda was coming down from her old tower, to be herself enshrined and worshipped as a household saint, in the light of her husband's fireside.[34]

Thus easily did Mary merge into the Romantic vision of marriage. She took her place in a world in which wives served their husbands as spiritual guides.

Certainly, *The Marble Faun* contains more than the story of innocent womanhood finding its way to domestic bliss. But Hilda and Kenyon were the only fully realized characters, and their only believable antagonist was Rome. It does not belittle *The Marble Faun* to say that Hawthorne used the novel to explore his own reactions to Rome; the author admitted as much in the preface. And in the midst of the struggle, Hawthorne accepted the Virgin. She was the only Catholic element he could bring back to America. In return he gave a daughter, Rose Hawthorne Lathrop, who lived with him in Rome while he wrote *The Marble Faun*, and who became a Catholic and founded an order of sisters.[35] Few novels have represented such a substantial exchange of values.

Among the first generation of American Romantics, other artists responded to the power of Mary. Edgar Allen Poe composed a prayer to Mary in verse:

> At morn—at noon—at twilight dim—
> Maria! thou hast heard my hymn!
> In joy and woe—in good and ill—
> Mother of God, be with me still![36]

Henry Wadsworth Longfellow made the Catholic heroine of *Evangeline* (1847) an embodiment of the ideal Romantic woman; and in *Christus* (1872), Longfellow repeated what many Catholics were preaching about Mary:

> If our faith had given us nothing more
> Than this example of all womanhood,
> So mild, so merciful, so strong, so good,
> So patient, peaceful, loyal, loving, pure,
> This were enough to prove it higher and truer
> Than all the creeds the world had known before.[37]

Visiting Mary's cathedral at Chartres, James Russell Lowell found "Imagination's very self in stone."[38] Lowell had received his nurture, as had most American Romantics, within the Unitarian rationalism of New England, but he sought inspiration from the Virgin and the Catholic past. The most powerful moment of "The Cathedral" (1870), a poem describing Lowell's visit to Chartres, was inspired by the poet's encounter with a woman saying the rosary.

> I turned and saw a beldame on her knees;
> With eyes astray, she told mechanic beads
> Before some shrine of saintly womanhood,
> Bribed intercessor with the far-off Judge:
> Such my first thought, by kindlier soon rebuked,
> ... My lids were moistened as the woman knelt,
> And—was it will, or some vibration faint
> Of sacred Nature, deeper than the will?—
> My heart occultly felt itself in hers,
> Through mutual intercession gently leagued.[39]

Quickly regaining his normal frame of mind, Lowell went on to denounce Catholic ritual as a collection of "superannuate forms and mumping shams."[40] But prayer to Mary had made him waver, and throughout "The Cathedral," all sources of inspiration, including Lowell's mother, the Muses, and the soul, were feminine. For Lowell, as for Hawthorne, the Virgin remained attractive in spite of his inbred antipathy to the Catholic system.

Working at the heart of American mass culture, Harriet Beecher Stowe integrated Romantic sentiments into novels and religious books that attained vast sales. Stowe felt less discomfort with things Catholic

than her male contemporaries. Her works advanced Protestant appropria-
tion of Mary beyond admissions of mysterious attraction, to the brink of
explicit doctrine.

In *Agnes of Sorrento* (1862), Stowe drew parallels between Mary and the
heroine Agnes, an Italian peasant of the sixteenth century who was caught
up in the struggles for power within the Catholic Church. For a moment
all hope for reform in the Catholic Church depended on Agnes, because
her lover Agostino led men who would fight for reform, but Agostino himself would not return to religion except through Agnes. If Stowe could
have rewritten history, Agostino and Agnes would have led a Catholic reformation, in the spirit of the Florentine monk Savonarola. Since history
stood as it did, the couple shared exile, clinging to their vision of the "True
Church" as "a veiled bride, a dove that is in the cleft of the rocks, whose
voice is known only to the Beloved."[41]

The church as an innocent woman, and Agnes the symbol of the
church, both depended on Mary as their original model. Agostino courted
the peasant girl by offering her a lily, "such as one sees in a thousand
pictures of the Annunciation." He arrived at the moment when Brother
Antonio, the uncle of Agnes, was painting her as the Virgin, to decorate
the page of his breviary containing the "Ave Maria." Lest the parallel be
missed, Brother Antonio explained the situation to Agnes:

> It is evident that our Lady hath endowed thee with the great grace
> of beauty which draws the soul upward toward the angels, instead
> of downward to sensual things, like the beauty of worldly women.[42]

Even the illicit desire that Father Francesco, Agnes's confessor, conceived
for her had an uplifting effect. According to Stowe, "it was only in the heart
of a lowly maiden that Christ had been made manifest" to Francesco, "as
of old he was revealed to the world through a virgin."[43] The priest harbored
the same hope expressed by Agostino, that Agnes would "lead me to our
Mother's throne in heaven, and pray her to tolerate me for your sake."[44]

Stowe interrupted her narrative to explain why these men should
attach such hopes to Agnes. Those accustomed to thinking "entirely from
a worldly and philosophical standpoint" would find her influence improb-
able. They would also be "utterly at a loss to account for the power which
certain Italian women of obscure birth came to exercise in the councils
of nations merely by the force of a mystical piety." Their inability to understand was related to race: "the Northern mind of Europe is entirely

unfitted to read and appreciate the psychological religious phenomena of Southern races."[45] For men like Agostino and Francesco, Agnes was "not merely Agnes," but a symbol of "life-peace" and "rest of soul." Harriet Beecher Stowe, who had seen through *Uncle Tom's Cabin* something of the power that female piety could generate, undertook in most of her later novels and essays to make women's influence comprehensible to the Northern mind. Stowe knew the complexity of her subject. In *Women in Sacred History* (1874), she described the biblical ideal of woman as "at once wife, mother, poetess, leader, inspirer, prophetess."[46] And Mary, the greatest expression of female influence in Christendom, offered the most basic and most powerful form of ideal womanhood:

> Exalted above earth, she has been shown to us as a goddess, yet a goddess of a type wholly new. . . . Other goddesses have been worshipped for beauty, for grace, for power. . . . In Mary, womanhood, in its highest and tenderest development of the MOTHER, has been the object of worship. Motherhood with large capacities of sorrow, with the memory of bitter sufferings, with sympathies large enough to embrace every aspect of humanity!—such an object of veneration has inconceivable power.[47]

In *Agnes of Sorrento, Women in Sacred History,* and her other articles and books dealing with Mary, Stowe found a middle way between Protestant rejection of the Virgin and Catholic devotion. The prayers and bows and signs of the Cross that Agnes performed at Mary's shrine were "somewhat mechanical," Stowe admitted, but they were also "redeemed by the earnest fervor which inspired each action."[48] After citing Protestants from Martin Luther to Edward Bouverie Pusey on the lack of ancient support for the cult of Mary, Stowe undercut these authorities by referring to "a tendency to the side of unjust depreciation" of Mary among Protestants, "to make up for the unscriptural excesses" of Catholics. The Reformation represented an "opposite extreme" that had obscured the truth.[49] Stowe herself criticized the notion that Jesus could deny Mary nothing—which was a message of several nineteenth-century apparitions—but she believed that Heaven would disclose a relationship between Jesus and Mary that resembled the Catholic picture more than the Protestant.

> That Mary is now with Jesus, that there is an intimacy and a sympathy between her soul and his such as belong to no other created

being, seems certain. Nor should we suffer anything to prevent that just love and veneration which will enable us to call her Blessed, and to look forward to meeting her in heaven as one of the brightest joys of that glorious world.[50]

Stowe's brother Henry Ward Beecher, one of the most influential preachers of the Gilded Age, shared her belief that "the Protestant reaction from Mary has gone far enough." Seeking a similar compromise between Protestant and Catholic, Beecher excused the Catholic preference for Mary over Christ as "an error of the heart." He recommended that Protestants look to Mary for "the type of Christian motherhood," a figure from which Protestants could learn to see in motherhood "the nearest image of the divine tenderness which the soul could form."[51]

Many who had religious objections to novels, poems, and other forms of secular culture absorbed Romantic sentiments from hearing Henry Ward Beecher preach or from reading his widely published sermons or his newspaper. And Mary suited Beecher's version of Romanticism. She belonged to the realm of nature and to the religion of the heart. "Have you ever stood in Dresden to watch that matchless picture of Raphael's *Madonna di San Sisto*?" Beecher asked in a published sermon of 1869. He then conveyed the artist's inspiration to those who had never seen a painting of the Virgin:

> In her face there is a mist. It is a wonder, it is love, it is adoration, it is awe, it is all of these mingled, as if she held in her hands her babe, and yet it was God!
>
> That picture means nothing to me as it does to the Roman Church; but it means everything to me, because I believe that every mother should love the God that is in her child.[52]

Horace Bushnell's sermon on "Mary, the Mother of Jesus" gave the Virgin an active role in bringing about the conception of Christ. Picturing Mary reading the prophets and praying for the Messiah, the Congregational pastor of Hartford said that "her opening womanly nature has been stretching itself Messiah-ward." Through her prayers, Mary was "winning such favor, and becoming inwardly akin to him [Christ] in such degree, as elects her to bear the promised child . . . and be set in a properly divine motherhood before the worlds."[53] A Catholic could not have gone further in attributing the Incarnation to Mary's merit. And Bushnell went on to find the origins of six Gospel parables in Mary's domestic teaching, to deny that Jesus rebuked Mary at Cana or at Capernaum, and to suggest that "we could most easily believe" in the Assumption, though "we have no such traditions."[54] To Horace Bushnell, reconciliation with Mary seemed nearly as important as acceptance of Christ.

> Doubtless it must be the first thing with us, after we have entered the great world before us, to get cleared in our relations to the Son of Man himself. After that our next thing, as I think, will be to know our mother, the mother of Jesus; for no other of the kingdom, save the King himself, has a name that signifies more.[55]

If such reconciliation did not occur on earth, it would in heaven. Bushnell described "our final appearing to her [Mary], on a higher plane of life, where she will most assuredly be the center of a higher feeling than many of us have imagined."

> Our pitiful mistraining here is assuredly there to be corrected, as an all but mortal impropriety. And when that correction is made, such flavors of beauty, and sweetness, and true filial reverence will be shed abroad, I can easily believe, ... as will even recast for us Protestants at least, the type and temperament of the heavenly feeling itself.[56]

Protestants needed this transformation because "we are in a prejudice that extirpates right perception" not simply of Mary, but also of "the true relativity of motherhood."[57] The Virgin who conceived the Messiah was also the Mother, the ideal woman who stood at the heart of the religion Bushnell preached—a religion in which sentiment ruled intellect and nurture replaced conversion.

No nineteenth-century American surpassed Mary Baker Eddy (1821–1910), the founder of Christian Science, in promoting female symbolism. Eddy taught her followers to pray to "our Father/Mother God" instead of to "Our Father" in the Lord's Prayer.[58] Because Eddy denied the power of matter to generate human beings, one might expect to find that she downplayed the Virgin. Eddy taught that gestation and birth depended entirely on Spirit, and many theologians have reduced Mary's role in the Incarnation to providing matter. But Eddy's *Science and Health* (1875), the basic text of her new religion, claimed Mary as the first Christian

Scientist, the first to realize that matter was not the Creator, and credited her with conceiving Christ by this insight.

> Those instructed in Christian Science have reached the glorious perception that God is the only author of man. The Virgin-mother conceived this idea of God, and gave her ideal the name of Jesus. . . .
> The illumination of Mary's spiritual sense put to silence material law and its order of generation, . . . Jesus was the offspring of Mary's self-conscious communion with God.[59]

From Hawthorne to Christian Science—or, from the first American Romantics to the beginning of the twentieth century—Protestant Americans thus appropriated the Virgin both in literature and in doctrine. The next section of this chapter will consider what effects this writing and preaching may have had on sexual behavior. For now, it should be noted that Protestant concentration on Mary as mother did not exclude her from the role of spouse. Heroines like Longfellow's Evangeline, Hawthorne's Hilda, and Stowe's Agnes certainly shared the spirit of youthful attractiveness that informed the nineteenth-century appearances of Mary.

Meanwhile, American Catholics went further. They saw Mary not only as mother and spouse but also as a Catholic equivalent to Phoebe Palmer and Aimée Semple McPherson. Mary became a woman who showed that ecstasy could overcome sin. The works of John D. Bryant, a Boston physician and convert to Catholicism, demonstrated that Mary could move a citizen of the United States to ecstatic emotion. Bryant began his book on the Immaculate Conception (1855) with this invocation:

> Procure for me, by Thy powerful prayers, most Potent Virgin, fresh stories of love. . . . Absorb me in this boundless ocean of everlasting bliss. Let this heavenly flame burn within, and consume me with its ravishing delights.[60]

Naming Mary "the Queen of love," Bryant placed her "infinite desire" for God first on his list of her virtues.[61] The Immaculate Conception taught that God had always reciprocated Mary's love. And because those who love God also love their fellow humans, the Christian could trust that "Mary longs for and desires our salvation" more intensely than anyone other than God Himself.[62]

Bryant thus placed the Virgin at the center of a theology of love that began with God's desire and ended with human desire for God: "The King of love descended from heaven [into Mary] that He might enkindle this divine flame in every heart; and how deeply must it have penetrated Hers, who bore Him."[63] Bryant's book appeared with approbation from the Catholic bishops of Boston and Philadelphia.

Four years later, Bryant produced *Redemption*, an epic poem modeled on *Paradise Lost*, comprising ten books and more than three hundred pages. Here Mary's role rivaled that of Christ. Bryant represented God the Father and the Son looking down from heaven to see whether Mary would fall into sin: "Should she succumb," decreed the Father, "No more my justice waits; man's doom is fixed; His free probation o'er, the world is lost."[64] With everything depending on her choice, the Second Eve stood firm, and so Bryant proceeded to the incarnation, which he represented as a marriage of Heaven and Earth, with as much feeling as propriety allowed.

> When lo, the Holy Ghost, celestial Dove, . . .
> Instant descends with sweet o'erpowering force,
> And in mysterious union with his Spouse,
> The spotless Queen, the Son of God begot.
> Deep in her womb earth felt the thrilling joy;
> The heavens bowing kiss'd the earth redeem'd.[65]

Another American convert, Sister Marie Josephine (born Abby Maria Hemenway), narrated the same story in *The Mystical Rose*, a version of the Gospels in verse published in 1865. The Virgin prepared herself for the Incarnation with passionate reading of messianic prophecies:

> Her rich eye melts, her heart responsive thrills,
> The bright'ning meditation all her spirit fills,
> And fans each ardent breath.[66]

Above the section of her poem called "Annunciation Night," Sister Marie Josephine quoted the second chapter of the *Song of Songs*: "I languish with love, his left hand is under my head and his right hand shall embrace me."

When Bryant and Marie Josephine emphasized the ecstasy of the Incarnation, they were drawing on traditions that dated from the twelfth century. St. Alphonsus Liguori, the same author whose moral theology dominated Catholic teaching on sex, provided the most copious and explicit transmission of these traditions to America. *The Glories of Mary*, Liguori's major work on the Virgin, appeared in nine American editions from five different publishers between 1852 and 1895.

Liguori derived Mary's powers and attributes from her love. That love encompassed God and all humanity, and extended from spiritual devotion to the whole range of human feeling.

> She loved God more, in the first moment of her life, than all the saints and angels have loved him in the whole course of theirs; ... If the love of all mothers for their children, of all husbands for their wives and all saints and angels for their devoted servants, were united, it would not be so great as the love that Mary bears to one soul alone.[67]

At the Annunciation, Mary's love broke forth in her desire to become Christ's mother. The Virgin became "all inflamed ... with the desire of uniting herself thus more closely to God."[68]

God felt a similar desire with regard to Mary, as Liguori pictured the angel Gabriel telling her: "Thy Lord himself, as he is greatly enamored of thy beauty, so much the more desires thy consent."[69] References to God's desire for the Virgin pervaded *The Glories of Mary*. In prayer, St. Alphonsus called Mary the "ravisher of hearts" who "hast enamored a God, and hast drawn him from heaven into thy bosom."[70] Mary's part in the Incarnation began with seduction: God became "so much enamored of her beauty, that with the bands of love she made him a prisoner in her virginal womb."[71]

The Virgin's attractiveness to God resulted from her total abandonment of self, a total consecration that paralleled Methodist formulas for attaining perfect love. In her youth Mary offered to God "all her powers and all her senses, her whole mind and her whole heart, her whole soul and her whole body."[72] Phoebe Palmer would have recognized not only the spirit of this offering but also the very words used by Liguori. Having made her sacrifice, Mary became "wholly annihilated as to self."[73] This annihilation of self had the same effect as it had among Protestant ecstatics: by removing all obstacles to God's love, it made complete union with God automatic. Such love obliterated individuality; God and Mary lost their distinctiveness and flowed together in *ecstasis*.

According to Liguori, the Virgin who entered into union with God became the medium through which others could find a similar love. Liguori asked Mary to abolish the pride and sin that made him unlike her. "I have heard that love makes lovers like things they love ... since thou lovest me, make me like unto thyself."[74] He prayed that writing *The Glories of Mary* would bring him to love the Virgin more, "and that all into whose hands this work shall fall, may be inflamed with thy love, so that immediately their desire shall increase to love thee, and see others love thee also."[75] By praising Mary, St. Alphonsus set her forth as a model of spiritual life for all Christians. *The Glories of Mary* served the same purpose for Catholics that Palmer's *Way of Holiness* served for Methodists, and McPherson's *This Is That* served for Pentecostals.

Nothing less than perfection, complete freedom from sin, satisfied Liguori as a result of his spiritual way, and he made the Virgin indispensable to any who sought perfection. As Liguori wrote in another devotional work, "it is morally impossible, that a soul progress much in perfection, without a particular and tender devotion toward the most holy Mother of God."[76] The dogma of the Immaculate Conception strengthened this association of Mary with freedom from sin.

Catholic theologians in America continued Liguori's use of the Virgin. Adolphe Tanquerey, a professor at St. Mary's Seminary in Baltimore, told those who sought perfection to become "slaves" of Mary. Describing an "act of entire consecration to Mary," Tanquerey pictured the slave giving up "all that he is and has," and first of all, "*his body* with all its senses," into Mary's keeping.[77] Tanquerey warned against the emphasis on feeling that prevailed in nineteenth-century devotional works; he castigated authors who encouraged people to surrender to emotion without first purging themselves through penance; but he applied none of this caution to those who were dedicated to Mary. Although emotional prayer could make "solid piety ... degenerate into sentimental, at times into sensual love, for all violent emotions are fundamentally of the same kind,"[78] wrote Tanquerey, Mary could prevent such degeneration. "Her name breathes forth purity, and, it seems, no sooner do we confidently invoke her, than temptation is put to flight."[79]

From those who vowed entire consecration, Tanquerey required only confidence, a willingness to trust Mary more than themselves, just as Phoebe Palmer required only confidence in God. In *The Spiritual Life*, a textbook used in Catholic seminaries through the 1930s, Tanquerey covered many of the same questions that were debated among Protestant evangelicals during the Holiness movement. He inquired into the necessity for ecstatic experience, whether the senses were destroyed or sanctified by ecstasy, and the role of the will in ecstasy, and he answered the questions in much the same way Phoebe Palmer had. The greatest difference between Protestant and Catholic ecstatics was symbolic: while Protestants followed contemporary women, Catholics followed the Virgin. But this did not prevent a general, if unrecognized, agreement between the Catholic and Methodist schools of piety. Both sought sanctification in addition to justification; both denied the inevitability of remaining in sin throughout life; both expected ecstasy to be part of the process of sanctification; and both described the sanctified soul as feminine in relation to God. The Virgin fostered emotional and doctrinal agreement between some Catholics and some Protestants, even though she maintained a symbolic distance between them.

Mary also had an oppressive side. She could stand for ecstatic union with God, freedom from sin, and female leadership, but she could also reinforce the tendency of Romantic values to congeal into Victorian constraints. The different results of her influence may have related to cultural or, as Harriet Beecher Stowe would have suggested, racial dispositions. To the Italian Liguori or the French-born Tanquerey, Mary was pure inspiration; but to an Irish-American like the Reverend Peter Kenrick, who published *The New Month of Mary* in 1840, the Virgin's holiness rebuked the unworthiness of all other humans.

Peter Kenrick wrote *The New Month of Mary* to introduce in America the custom, recently begun in Italy and France, of dedicating the month of May to the Virgin. According to the usual interpretation, the choice of May reflected Mary's kinship with nature, as a later American bishop preached: "For her, the flowers bloom, for her the children sing, and the birds are glad, and the skipping flocks."[80] But Kenrick saw a darker meaning: "the month of May was selected in preference to any other, from a wish to change a season of dissipation and amusement into one of instruction and devotion."[81] Kenrick prescribed daily devotions for May, based on the titles given to the Virgin in the Litany of Loretto, that would have transformed the month into another Lent. For the sixteenth of May, for example, he offered this reflection on the title, "Cause of Our Joy":

How can we truly call Mary the cause of our joy, when ... we have not permitted its influence to reach our souls; but have preferred the gloom and agitation of a troubled conscience.[82]

His prayer for the sixteenth began, "O Mary! what sentiments shall I have at the hour of death! When I consider my sins, . . . I am seized with fear and trembling."[83] On the eighteenth day, the title of "Mystical Rose" prompted him to mention Mary's beauty, but he tempered this with a lengthy meditation on the "thorns" of affliction that surrounded the Rose.[84] As an edifying example of the attitude toward affliction that devotion to Mary could foster, Kenrick told the story of St. Stanislaus Kostka, a Jesuit novice who had surrendered to a fatal illness with the words, "I shall never more rise from this bed, what a happiness."[85]

No Catholic went further than Orestes Brownson in negating the ecstatic and perfectionist potential of devotion to Mary, or in using the Virgin to inculcate repression of emotions and submission to authority. Brownson began as a friend of the Transcendentalists but turned his back on the Romantic movement when he converted to Catholicism. In 1866, Brownson presented Mary as an antidote "to that Teutonic worship of woman as a goddess to which this age . . . is strongly addicted, to the great detriment of manliness, manners and morals."[86] In other words, Brownson hoped that Mary could preserve his time from Romanticism and sexual immorality. "The predominating sin of our times is that of impurity," Brownson wrote in 1853, "at once the cause and the effect of the modern sentimental philosophy."[87] The impurity of the Romantic era sprang from a philosophy in which "intellect is derided; reason is looked on as superfluous, if not tyrannical; and the heart is extolled as the representative of God on earth."[88] Against the cycle of unbridled action and thought, Brownson pitted the Virgin's power to buttress chastity. Love of Mary "checks all lawlessness of the affections, all turbulence of the passions, all perturbations of the senses."[89] Brownson knew that Mary had become fashionable precisely in and through the Romantic age, but he utterly disowned "those light, frivolous, volatile creatures, who practice, by fits and starts, certain little coquettish devotions to Mary."[90] He preferred a pattern of devotion that would place Mary before children, especially young girls, as "a model which it must be the unremitting labor of her life to copy."[91]

Besides ensuring chastity, the Virgin might also help keep women in their place. "We have no sympathy for those who make woman an idol, and clamor for what they call 'woman's rights,'" wrote Brownson.[92] He believed that this unseemly clamor could be stilled by "having Mary always before the minds and hearts of our daughters, as their model in humility, purity, sweetness, and obedience."[93] Brownson agreed that women had a special mission but argued that this mission was to preserve "Catholic morality in the family," not to advance new types of devotion or political causes. With regard to the young women who saw visions of Mary, Brownson remained cautious, delaying his acceptance of Lourdes until 1874, twenty-six years after the event, and explicitly rejecting the appearance at La Salette.[94]

Isabella Beecher Hooker, the sister of Harriet Beecher Stowe, used Mary in her arguments for women's right to vote;[95] but other advocates of Mary enlisted with Brownson against the women's movement. Horace Bushnell wrote an entire book called *Woman's Suffrage: The Reform Against Nature*. In an address on "The Virgin Mother," the Right Reverend John L. Spalding, Catholic bishop of Peoria, brought repression of sensuality and political repression together in the same passage:

> Sensuality and love, though mysteriously related, are contrary as religion and superstition. The baser passion grows upon the grave of the finer virtue. Woman, like religion, appeals to what is highest in man. Her power over him is that of sentiment, and to seek to place her in rivalry with him in the rude business of life is an aim worthy of an atheistic and material age.[96]

Small wonder that Henry Adams found it difficult to read the signs of his times. Mary could stand for acceptance of emotion or for its repression; the Immaculate Conception reminded some of the promise of perfect freedom from sin but told others that everyone except Mary lived under God's curse; the power women gained through their likeness to the Virgin could sway the councils of nations or justify the exclusion of women from those councils.

Surrounded as he was by Victorians, with ecstatic Methodists and Catholics living on a social plane far beneath his notice, Henry Adams felt constrained to remind his countrymen that Mary's power had always stemmed from sex. The cult of the Virgin arose from the twelfth-century conviction that "religion was love; in no case was it logic." Adams called on Bernard of Clairvaux and Francis of Assisi to witness that the mystics of the high Middle Ages sought to know God "directly; by emotion; by ecstasy; by absorption of our existence in His; by substitution of his spirit for ours."[97] Mary exemplified this experience, as anyone might see "who stops a moment to feel the emotion that lifted her wonderful Chartres spire up to God."[98] For the Virgin of Chartres, "sex was strength.... She was goddess because of her force; she was the animated dynamo; she was reproduction—the greatest and most mysterious of all energies; all she needed was to be fecund."[99] By giving birth to God, the Virgin demonstrated that the same force worked in creation and in procreation. But it seemed to Adams that Americans denied this force: "The trait was notorious, and often humorous, but any one brought up among Puritans knew that sex was sin."[100]

Therefore, America would never feel the power of the Virgin. As Adams put it, "An American Virgin would never dare command; an American Venus would never dare exist."[101] Adams asked himself "whether he knew of any American artist who had ever insisted on the power of sex, as every classic had always done," and he concluded that American art was "used sex for sentiment, never for force...." The descendants of the Puritans worshiped the machine, not the Virgin. Their civilization arose directly from repression.

> American art, like the American language and American education, was as far as possible sexless. Society regarded this victory over sex as its greatest triumph, and the historian readily admitted it, since the moral issue, for the moment, did not concern one who was studying the relations of unmoral force.[102]

But Adams had not seen that some in his culture were carrying sentiment so far as to regain the force he ascribed to sex. The ecstatics found sexual force in spiritual love. Many were learning to deny sensuality while pursuing ecstasy. By 1918, the year of Adams's death, birth control advocates were separating sexual energy from procreation. Psychologists had already found the pathway from sex to the mind, identifying sex with sentiment. The Virgin who commanded in America would subject every physical fact to love. Innocence like hers would become capable of surviving defloration, childbirth, and divorce. Without the sentimental Virgin of the Romantics, the Virgin that Adams discounted, this twentieth-century ideal would not have been possible.

On May 31, 1843, at the commune called Brook Farm, just outside Boston, Isaac Hecker described this vision in his journal:

> About ten months go ... I saw (I cannot say I dreamed; it was quite different from dreaming; I was seated on the side of my bed) a beautiful, angelic being, and myself standing alongside of her, feeling a

most heavenly pure joy. It was as if our bodies were luminous and gave forth a moon-like light which sprang from the joy we experienced. I felt as if we had always lived together, and that our motions, actions, feelings, and thoughts came from one centre.[103]

Hecker did not name this vision Mary. His Methodist background included no devotion to the Virgin. But Hecker did address his "eternal, ever-blooming virgin" in prayer, and he complained that the memory of her beauty prevented him from marrying. Within three years of this experience, Hecker became a Roman Catholic priest. Later, he would found the Paulist Fathers, an order of priests dedicated to the conversion of America. His successor as head of the Paulists interpreted the vision as a sign that God had given Hecker the supernatural virtue of chastity.

Whatever one thinks of supernatural virtues, Isaac Hecker's vision did reorganize his desires. From childhood, severe repression had marked Hecker's character. The Reverend Walter Elliott saw in Hecker a "repugnance to touching or being touched by anyone." "Even his mother refrained from embracing him," wrote Elliott. "She would stroke his face, instead, . . . and say, 'That is my kiss for you, my son.'"[104] His mother's disapproval kept him from using liquor or tobacco. He claimed that he had never masturbated, committed any sin against purity, or fallen into any other mortal sin, even before he considered becoming a Catholic.[105] When Hecker was twenty-three, his conscience drove him out of his family's business, a bakery in New York City, because he could not bear to profit by the labor of employees. He joined the Workingmen's Party and thus met Orestes Brownson, who led him to Brook Farm, where a group of American Romantics, including Nathaniel Hawthorne, were trying to live in harmony with nature. Brook Farm left Hecker unsatisfied, however. When a doctor there advised him to marry for his health, he answered: "Rather than follow this advice, I would die."[106] A month later he complained of loneliness, because he could meet people "only by coming down into my body, of which . . . I am now almost unconscious."[107] Having exhausted the possibilities for self-purification at Brook Farm, Hecker went on to Fruitlands, the vegetarian commune founded by Louisa May Alcott's father, Bronson Alcott. Hecker adopted the diet prescribed by Sylvester Graham. He welcomed hunger and cut his sleep to a minimum. Through self-denial, Hecker sought escape not only from actual sin but also from the knowledge of sin. "The effect of the fall was literally the knowledge of good and evil," Hecker wrote at Brook Farm. "God knows no evil, and when we become one with Him, . . . we shall regain our previous state."[108]

In the midst of Hecker's self-mortification, the celestial bride opened a more positive way to purity. The vision that made Hecker forsake human women also brought a higher joy. "I am charmed by its influence," the young man wrote, "and conscious that, should I accept any other, I should lose the life which would be the only one wherein I could say I live."[109] Praying to the angelic woman in 1844, Hecker expressed his hope that love for her would set him free from sin.

> The grace and beauty I see in thee passes into my soul, and I am all that thou art. I am then wedded to thee, and I would that it were an eternal union. But ah! My eyes, when turned upon myself, lose all sight of thee, and meet nothing but my own spots and blemishes. Flow canst thou love me? I say; and for thy pure love I am melted into thee as one.[110]

Despite the celibacy that Isaac Hecker chose, his pursuit of purity had as much potential for application to sexual life as did the ecstasies of Phoebe Palmer or Aimée Semple McPherson. Palmer and McPherson married God directly, and then reaffirmed their attachments to human spouses. When Palmer strove for sanctification, she feared that affection for her husband might prevent her from reaching perfect love.[111] McPherson did leave her husband for a time to regain the Spirit. But Hecker sought God through union with an ideal woman. His vision connected him with a current of sexual mysticism that had long flowed through Mary, and found new channels during the nineteenth century.

It may seem paradoxical to suggest that yearnings for angelic virgins could help anyone to accept sexuality, but the paradox lessens in light of the medieval assertion that Mary had provoked desire in God and entered into a sexual relation with him sufficiently real to result in a Son. St. Bernard of Clairvaux (*d.* 1153), arguably the most powerful man in twelfth-century Europe, explained the angel Gabriel's salutation of Mary in the Gospel of Luke, "The Lord is with thee," in terms of God's desire. Although Gabriel's mission was to ask Mary's consent for the Incarnation, his words revealed that God was already there. According to Bernard, the greeting showed that God's "excessive desire in its flight" had "preceded His messenger to the Virgin, whom he had loved, whom He had chosen for Himself, whose comeliness He had desired."[112] Bernard's word for "desired," *concupierat*, was the same term theologians used for the essence of original sin: concupiscence, the inordinate desire that caused humanity to prefer the flesh to the spirit. Before St. Augustine's diagnosis of sin as concupiscence took hold, St. Jerome used the term to translate Scriptural passages that the church applied to Mary.[113] Bernard and his followers seized on these passages to support their attribution of concupiscence to God. The new application of the word helped Bernard guide a movement of religious orders that brought adult men and women, rather than children, into monasteries.[114] Among those adults, the problem of what to do with desire presented itself with a new vigor. Contemplation of God's relationship with Mary was one aspect of Bernard's answer. Divine desire fit into his whole approach to spiritual life, in which the monk recognized desire to redirect it rather than trying to extirpate concupiscence through ascetic practice.

As other monks developed Bernard's insight, they also developed his illustrative use of the Virgin. St. Amadeus of Lausanne (*d.* 1154), who trained as a novice under St. Bernard, spoke of divine passion in a sermon in which he addressed Mary: "He has longed for [*concupivit*] your beauty. . . . Impatient of delay, he hastens to come to you."[115] Amadeus then questioned the Virgin about her feelings:

> By what affection were you moved, by what love were you held, by what stimuli were you touched, when . . . the Word took flesh from you? . . . You were burning, dissolved by heavenly fires; having dissolved in fire, you took strength from the fire, that you might always burn, and once again dissolve.[116]

Contemplatives needed to know how Mary felt because they were attempting to emulate her. Retiring to their cells and pondering the Scriptures, they would draw divine desire upon themselves. As a Yorkshire abbot, Aelred of Rievaulx, advised in a letter to a group of sisters, they would develop a chastity that "makes the King, your Lord God himself, desire [*concupiscat*] your beauty."[117] Guerric of Igny called the male monks in his charge "blessed mothers" and warned them against the perils of pregnancy. "Attend to yourselves," he advised, "until Christ is formed in you. Be careful lest any violent blow coming from without should injure the tender foetus." Spiritual gestation would yield physical redemption: "He who is now conceived as God in our spirits, conforming them to the Spirit of his charity, will then be born as a man in our bodies, conforming them to his glorified body."[118] Sex became the model of salvation, and sexual desire, far from being despised, was the "fire" from which the contemplative drew strength. According to Isaac of Stella (*d.* 1169), the capacity for desire (*concupiscibilitas*) was one of the powers by which people came to know God. Isaac advanced this idea in his sermons on the Assumption of Mary.[119]

Sometimes the association of Mary with redemption through sex grew incredibly explicit. Godfrey of Admont (*d.* 1165), a Benedictine abbot, compared the Virgin to the biblical harlot Rahab:

> Rahab had lovers like herself, unjust men and sinners to whom she prostituted her body; Mary also had lovers, the Father and the Son and the Holy Spirit, ... just as Rahab among her lovers earned the price which was suitable for her, thus the blessed Virgin Mary by the incorruption of her body merited from her lovers, Father and Son and Holy Spirit, that price by which the human race, sold under sin, was to be restored to life.[120]

With even greater specificity, Richard of St. Laurent (*d.* 1245) recommended meditation on the loins of Mary, "which she girded ... with a vow of virginity, strongly binding in herself the flow of carnal pleasure," so that she might provoke "that same concupiscence in the eyes of God."[121] Augustine had located the root of sin in his disobedient member, his penis; but for the high Middle Ages, every part of the body, at least of the Virgin, could be holy. It was no accident that Bernard and his followers taught that the happiness of the saints would not be complete until they received glorified bodies at the Resurrection.[122]

The medieval model had one serious flaw: it was one-sided. Bernard and his followers ascribed concupiscence to God, but they denied concupiscence to Mary. Some argued that the Virgin had pleasure (*delectatio*) in the conception of Jesus; some denied even this; and none went so far as to endow Mary with a positive *concupiscentia*. In recent discussions of the Immaculate Conception, theologians have continued this theme, claiming that Mary's exemption from original sin implied an exemption from concupiscence.[123] The same exemption has extended to other feminine ideals. When Isaac of Stella represented desire in the relations between God and the soul, he reversed usual gender to picture the soul as a male with its concupiscence directed toward a strangely female Jesus. Whether the sacred marriage joined God and Mary or God and the soul, the Middle

Ages saw redemptive power only in the active, self-moved desire associated with males, and ultimately with God, who alone could claim to be Pure Act. By denying Mary's desire, the monks also denied the type of desire they attributed to women: the reactive, receptive aspect of desire. They therefore left at least half of concupiscence unredeemed. In our own time, the Catholic theologian Karl Rahner has defined concupiscence as the resistance or inertia of nature.[124] If God really felt concupiscence, God could not be Pure Act; the Incarnation should have taught Christians this. If human concupiscence had redemptive force, that force had to appear in the passionate reactions of humans, not simply in the active desire that medieval mystics exalted.

The nineteenth century began to redress this imbalance. "Man requires a new birth—the birth of the feminine in him," wrote Isaac Hecker. Hecker's biographer dismissed the statement as "an odd echo from a certain school of mysticism," probably referring to Swedenborg, but Hecker was simply repeating a commonplace of his age.[125] Female desire broke through the patriarchal bias of all Western cultures. In modern appearances of Mary, her desires and her emotions, the needs of her Immaculate Heart, eclipsed the feelings of the Father and the Son. Girls and women, from Bernadette Soubirous to Phoebe Palmer to Harriet Beecher Stowe, taught the way to God through feeling. And when Romantic writers presented redemption in sexual terms, they shifted their focus from the infinite desires of God to the infinity of human desires.

Alongside Mary, the Virgin who mediated the redemption of sex to St. Bernard, the nineteenth century ranked myriads of virgins whose feelings were themselves redemptive. Let the reader suppress laughter for a moment while considering Babette, heroine of *The New Psyche* (1895), a novel set in Catholic Canada, written by Lucy Irwin Huntington of New Orleans.

> The mouth has the pure curves of the race, with the coy kisses bursting through, as a bruised field flower. . . . The mouth of this little maid is tender with her unawakened power of love; full—nay, one does not think of such things when one sees Babette; somehow one never looks at her but through her to the Truth beyond; . . . One feels the God within; . . . one with the eternal beauty which permeates and moves all life. The village folk are vaguely conscious of this.[126]

The "vague" sense of sacredness surrounding this nymph of fourteen had sufficient force to cause people to cross themselves when Babette walked by. According to Huntington, the girl was "a fire-woven veil of the Holy of Holies, half-revealing the Perfect; a virgin Prophet of the Beautiful; a consecrated Priestess of the Word; at once a mystery, a solitude, and a light." But this walking sacrament thought of nothing but marriage. Babette readied her trousseau, and spent her time "dreaming by night, and singing by day, with a voice that sounds like a little mass bell, of the true love she knows 'is coming, is coming.' "[127] For her, desire and holiness merged into a single, natural response—just as they did for Mary, the mother of Jesus, as imagined by theologians like St. Alphonsus Liguori and the Reverend Horace Bushnell.

John D. Bryant, the Boston doctor who wrote so vividly on the Annunciation and the Immaculate Conception, also used the fictional virgin of his novel, *Pauline Seward* (1847), to depict the sacredness of desire. Raised a Presbyterian, Pauline searched Catholic books to satisfy her yearning for a closer walk with God. Every step that Pauline took into the Roman fold revealed how thoroughly passion mixed with her devotion. Attending a confirmation, "Pauline's breast heaved with uncontrollable emotion."[128] At the home of the bishop who received her into the church, the heroine met her best friend Isabel, who had secretly prepared to profess Catholicism on the same day. Instantly, "Pauline and Isabel were clasped in each other's arms, mingling their tears, their hearts beating in unison of fond affection, and their burning lips again and again meeting in the simultaneous gush of purest love, of sympathy, and joyful surprise."[129] The masses that sustained Pauline's Catholic life evoked enough emotion to prostrate a less capacious nature. While she sang the "Sanctus," Bryant marveled: "With what delicious fervor beat the warm heart of Pauline; what exulting rapture tuned her notes of praise." A hymn floated through Pauline's mind as she awaited Communion: "O King of love, thy blessed fire/Does such sweet flames excite,/That first it raises the desire,/Then fills it with delight." Having received the Host, Pauline prayed to God to "fire my soul with infinite desire." She quoted the Song of Songs to declare, "Now, my well-beloved is mine." Bryant made every mass into Pauline's wedding day: "Ardent love swelled her throbbing bosom in an effort to make some faint return for that of her amiable spouse."[130] Before the novel ended, Bryant also gave Pauline a human husband, worthy of "that love, which her heart had taught her to cherish as the holiest of passions."[131] Whether her heart throbbed in response to Catholic ceremony or to her husband, Pauline's feelings always had a sacramental quality.

If a woman's feelings were to convey spiritual meaning, it helped for the woman to be beautiful. The prolific Catholic writer Anna Hanson Dorsey (1815–1896) followed this rule in her novel *The Sister of Charity* (1846). "Long black eyelashes fell like two brooding shadows on her white cheeks," Dorsey wrote, introducing the sister who was her main character. After a shipwreck left her habit in disarray, the nun "revealed a neck and shoulders of exquisite fairness and delicacy of mould."[132] The conversion of two daughters, their father, and one fiancé naturally followed when such a representative of Catholic faith found refuge in a Protestant home.

Scores of Catholic novelists dramatized the redemptive power of the desires of beautiful women. By 1850, more than fifty publishers of Catholic literature were doing business in the United States; by 1900, more than one hundred American Catholic novelists had published at least one book.[133] Most of the writers were women, and most of their fictions mingled Christian aspiration with the romantic life of the heroine. Orestes Brownson protested: "the ... novel which aims to explain and defend Catholic faith and morals in connection with a story of love and marriage, strikes us as a literary monstrosity, ... equally indefensible under the relation of religion and that of art."[134] In an article entitled "Religious Novels, or Woman versus Woman," which appeared in *Brownson's Quarterly Review* in January 1873, Brownson blamed these novels for supporting the sensual tendencies of the age. By mixing responses of the senses with Christian love, which Brownson insisted "always means an affection of the rational soul," the women who wrote religious novels encouraged men to regard a woman "as an instrument of pleasure."[135] Because religious novels led women to trust their feelings, they also created believers in women's rights, free love, and easy divorce. The danger seemed to justify comparison of these authors to prostitutes:

> The Holy Scriptures are full of warnings against "strange women" .... It is hardly less necessary to warn women, and men, too, enfeebled as they are by the feminine literature and perverted female influence of the day, against "strong-minded" women who are even more dangerous, and in heart equally impure, and whose influence, if not resisted in season will precipitate society, the nation, into hell.[136]

But Brownson spoke too late. Fourteen years earlier, in 1859, his own daughter Sarah had published *Marian Ellwood: or How Girls Live, by One of Themselves*, in which the heroine returned to God through her love for a certain Mr. King.[137]

Behind such fiction stood the lives of real American women who sought sanctity and rapture in the Roman Catholic Church. Thousands formed the pattern of their religious emotions in schools run by sisters, where they learned prayers like this evening exercise, recommended in *The Ursuline Manual* (1851):

> O my God and my All! I most ardently desire, by every breath I draw, by every thought, word, and action, by every movement of body and soul, to tell thee a thousand and a thousand times, that I love thee.[138]

The prayer reflected the spirit of some of the sisters themselves. Cornelia Connelly (1809–1879), founder of the Society of the Holy Child Jesus, became an ecstatic through personal experience of the interaction of sexual and religious desires. Born Cornelia Peacock, she married an Episcopal priest named Pierce Connelly, who decided to enter the Catholic priesthood after Cornelia had already borne three children by him, with another on the way.[139] Pope Gregory XVI granted his request in 1843, with the condition that Cornelia also take the vow of chastity and found a teaching order. Two years later she sang in the choir while Pierce was ordained. As a sister, Connelly faced a struggle to get the rule of her order approved and a conflict with her ex-husband, who left the priesthood and brought suit to regain his wife. But her heart was buoyed by the new outlet she found for desire. "She suffered from the ardors of love," wrote a member of her order, "and would heap affectionate epithets on our Lord and His Mother, in a way which sometimes astonished people unused to such exuberant devotion."[140] According to another sister, Connelly's success as a founder stemmed partly from her physical endowments:

> Her beauty was striking. No one could pass her without being struck by her appearance. Her complexion was pale and her eyes dark, if not black. She impressed me at once with her deep spirituality and her power of attracting hearts to herself in order to lead them on to God.[141]

Cornelia Connelly entered upon the same quest for perfection that was putting the consciousness of sin to flight across America. A sister who knew her for thirty-one years said that Connelly had "obtained permission to make the vow to do always what was most perfect."[142] The schools of her order emphasized freedom, play, and happiness, with the aim of fostering "a sunny, sinless childhood."[143] Like the Protestant perfectionists of her own time and since, Cornelia Connelly taught the duty of happiness: "even in sickness and in sorrow there should always be joy in the heart, and . . . a smile should show the sunshine of the soul."[144]

Probably, few of the sisters matched Connelly's ideal, a novice she had known "who was favored with frequent ecstasies in her work of sweeping the cloister."[145] Certainly there were few whose experience of the vicissitudes of love could match Mother Connelly's own. But the influence of sisters like Connelly has been vastly underestimated. A single book, the Reverend Joseph B. Code's *Great American Foundresses*, gave brief biographies of more than a dozen American women who started orders during the nineteenth century. Mother Connelly's Society of the Holy Child Jesus operated schools in Portland, Cheyenne, Chicago, New York, Massachusetts, and Pennsylvania, including Rosemont College outside Philadelphia.[146] Other sisters also helped to spread the fervent style of nineteenth-century devotion to every group within Catholic America. Among Italian immigrants, St. Frances Xavier Cabrini (1850–1917), the first saint to adopt American citizenship, labored with a spirit "on fire from her constant union with the divine Heart."[147] Not all of the sisters had raptures; not all of them taught the way to God through ecstasy. But the nun inevitably became a figure of romance to Catholic and non-Catholic Americans. A culture addicted to sacramental women would not rest until it saw Audrey Hepburn playing the lead in *The Nun's Story*.

Meanwhile, the male approach to God through woman elicited more of the Romantic feelings that Orestes Brownson feared. Union with an ideal woman made Isaac Hecker into an apostle of nature. He contrasted himself to Irish Catholics, whom he blamed for overemphasizing penance and for placing the supernatural too far above the natural: "I am a Saxon and cling to the earth," said Hecker, and, incredibly, for one whose mother refrained from kissing him: "I want an explicit and satisfactory reason why any innocent pleasure should not be enjoyed."[148] After attending an opera about nuns, Auber's *The Black Domino*, Hecker reflected that "the Church does not provide religious gratifications for the true wants of humanity," and therefore must not protest if people gratified their desires in opera houses. "The Church has provided for the salvation of the sinner's soul," he pronounced; "now she must provide terrestrial sacraments for the salvation and transfiguration of the body."[149]

From the pulpit, Hecker assaulted Protestant theology for being too pessimistic about human nature. His most popular sermon, "The Church and the Republic," marshaled quotes from the Reformers on original sin to prove that only Catholics could consistently hold "that man is naturally virtuous enough to be capable of self-government."[150] Within his adopted church, Hecker pressed for acceptance of modern culture, sensitivity to the presence of the Holy Spirit in all nature, and recognition that many Christians lived in freedom from sin.[151] In 1899, ten years after Hecker's death, his views had come to seem so threatening to the authority of the church and to its traditional teaching that Pope Leo XIII cited Walter Elliott's biography of Hecker as the source of a modern heresy, "Americanism."[152] The papal censure released a conservative reaction throughout the Roman Catholic Church in the United States. Yet the Paulist order remained, and still remains, on the liberal edge of Catholic thinking, especially with regard to sexuality and ecumenism. In recent years, Paulists have operated missions to divorced Catholics and published the Reverend Anthony Kosnik's *Human Sexuality*, a moral text tolerant enough to provoke new censures from the Vatican. The major project of the Paulist Press today is a series of volumes of spiritual writings in which Jews, Muslims, Native Americans, and Protestants appear alongside St. Theresa of Avila and St. Bonaventure.

Hecker's life, his doctrine, and his heritage showed that American Catholic and Protestant piety were coming together. At the age of ten, Hecker had set type for a Methodist newspaper, *Zion's Herald*, which provided his first exposure to the idea of complete freedom from sin.[153] Hecker's mother, with whom he professed himself to be in constant spiritual communion, remained a Methodist until her death in 1876 and attended the "love-feasts" at which Phoebe Palmer's followers sought perfect love.[154] When Hecker wrote that the grace God gave to the saints was "not a miraculous power, specially bestowed upon some men, but merely a higher degree of ordinary divine guidance,"[155] he asserted the same doctrine of "free grace," always available to those who accepted it, that had marked John Wesley's break from Reformed tradition.

Many Protestants who were too genteel or too inhibited to join either the Catholics or the evangelicals also accepted a gospel of desire embodied in female figures. For Charles Beecher, another minister sprung from the family of Harriet Beecher Stowe and Henry Ward Beecher, it was

unsatisfying to see the Virgin Mary depicted as "merely the embodiment
... of saintly purity and grace." Instead, Beecher portrayed an "artless
Jewish girl," endowed with "a beauty, glorious in its glossy raven locks,
lustrous hazel eye, full red lip, aquiline nose, finely arched eyebrow, and
the rich, deep complexion of the East."[156] He wanted Mary to possess what
his culture would have called a sensual beauty. This Virgin prefigured the
redemption of humanity, which was "predestined to become spiritually
feminine in relation to Christ," and ultimately "to preside maternally over
an endlessly increasing universe."[157] The prophecy of the Woman Clothed
with the Sun, in the New Testament book of Revelation, Chapter 12, signified that portion of humanity that would become the Bride of Christ.
When this woman appeared, Beecher expected a world in which "all
bodily appetites and passions" would become "sinless and sanctifying."[158]

In the last quarter of the nineteenth century, as Romanticism occupied the center of American religion, some Protestants seemed already to
be living in Beecher's promised land. Ella Wheeler Wilcox, the religious
writer who coined the phrase "Laugh and the world laughs with you,/Cry
and you cry alone," believed that a woman needed passion to avoid falling
into sin.

> It is impossible for an absolutely passionless woman to be either just
> or generous in her judgements of humanity at large. It is a strange
> fact that she needs an admixture of the baser physical element, to
> broaden her spiritual vision, and quicken her sympathies.[159]

A century earlier, these thoughts would have put Wilcox on the leading
edge of the Romantic movement, but by 1893 they were platitudes.

Henry Adams, who thought that the medieval gospel of love he described would be news to America, concluded a prayer to the Virgin of
Chartres with this petition:

> Help me to feel!—not with my insect sense,—
> with yours that felt all life alive in you;
> Infinite heart beating at your expense;
> Infinite passion breathing the breath you drew![160]

There was envy in these lines: envy of Mary, envy of those who had loved
her in the past, and envy of the women who bore her likeness in the present. Adams wanted passion. He feared that the grandson of John Quincy

Adams and the great-grandson of John Adams must be doomed to a life of repressed feeling. He sought release from that damnation through the ideal woman, who had not lost the power to feel. In all these things Adams prophesied to Victorian America, but he was not a lonely prophet. His condition more closely resembled that of most of the biblical prophets—which is to say that he taught in a school, consulted other prophets, and wove his message out of the unconscious fears and needs of his time, with whatever spirit God granted him. The envy of Adams, the yearnings of Hecker, and the warnings of Brownson all signified the advent of redemption through sex. The woman who conquered sin through desire would teach the race to desire without sin.

7

Redemption through Sex

Margaret Sanger and the Gospel of Birth Control

On November 19, 1921, fifteen hundred people came to the Park Theatre in New York to hear a nurse lecture on birth control. She disputed those who would limit sex to procreation, pointing out that this might mean that intercourse could take place only a few times during a marriage. Then, speaking "in a low, intense voice," she gave her reason for rejecting such restraint.

> I contend that it is just as sacred and beautiful for two people to express their love when they have no intention of being parents, and that they can go into that relationship with the same beauty and the same holiness with which they go into music or to prayer. I believe that it is the right understanding of our sexual power and of its creative energy that gives us spiritual illumination.[1]

The speaker was Margaret Sanger (1879–1966), inventor of the term "birth control" and evangelist of sexual pleasure to the nation. She repeated her message again and again, in person and in books that sold in the hundreds of thousands. And she left behind a network of clinics known as Planned Parenthood to teach people how to control the creative power of sex.

Sanger's background combined Methodist and Catholic influences. Born in Corning, New York, into the family of an Irish-American stone-cutter, Michael Higgins, she received Catholic baptism and confirmation. As a child she "stole money to buy flowers to put at the feet of the Virgin Mary."[2] In her autobiography she admitted preferring Mary to Christ: "I much preferred the Virgin Mary; she was beautiful, smiling—the way

I should like to look when I had a baby."[3] But Margaret's free-thinking father disrupted this early piety. When he heard Margaret pray for her daily bread, Michael Higgins asked if she thought of God as a baker.[4] He collected money to bring Robert Ingersoll, a famous atheist, to speak in Corning, with the result that the local priests told Catholics not to go to Mr. Higgins for tombstones, and the Higgins children were taunted in the streets as "children of the devil."[5] Persecuted in her native church and city, Margaret fled a hundred miles from Corning to attend Claverack College, on the Hudson River between New York and Albany.

Claverack was founded by ministers of the Dutch Reformed church, but Methodists had taken over long before Margaret's arrival in the fall of 1895. The college was coeducational, with slightly more males than females, and always produced many candidates for the Methodist ministry.[6] The religious freedom exhilarated Margaret. "Chapel never bored me," she reported, because "in a Methodist chapel anyone could get up and express an opinion."[7] John Wesley's decision to permit lay teaching thus encouraged another woman, whose influence would far exceed that of Phoebe Palmer. In chapel, Margaret gave her first speech for women's rights. All her life she would believe that Claverack stood for enlightenment, despite the college requirements of daily morning prayers, Sunday attendance at one of three local Protestant churches, Sunday evening Bible classes, and "social religious" meetings twice a week.[8]

At Claverack, Margaret encountered the Holiness movement. The January 15, 1896, issue of *The Vidette*, a student newspaper, routinely noted that a recently deceased professor "had the baptism of fire."[9] Also in evidence at the college was the Holiness doctrine that passions could be sanctified. The Reverend Arthur H. Flack, president of Claverack from 1886 to 1900, regularly taught Francis Wayland's *Elements of Moral Science*, a text that presented sexual pleasure as the will of God.

> The very fact that our Creator has constituted us with a capacity for a particular kind of happiness, and has provided means for the gratification of that desire, is in itself an intimation that he intended that this desire should be gratified.[10]

According to Wayland, passion, self-love, and conscience normally fit together to produce human actions. In cases of conflict, he taught that conscience and self-love should both have priority over passion, but nothing in Wayland's text suggested that passion was tainted by any corruption, or unnaturally strengthened by sin. He believed that the Bible could appeal to human reason with sufficient power to keep passion from getting the upper hand.[11]

Apparently, President Flack loved to teach the proper management of passion, because the other course for which he was remembered also dealt with that subject. An alumnus recalled Flack teaching the *Elements of Criticism*, by Henry Home, Lord Kames.[12] The first chapter of this text was entitled "Emotions and Passions." Home described both emotions and passions as reactions of the mind to external objects; he distinguished between them by defining emotion as reaction without desire and passion as reaction with desire.[13] According to the alumnus, President Flack enjoyed teaching the *Elements of Criticism* because the book "encouraged free discussion," and "the sessions of his class always became delightfully controversial."[14]

After three years of honesty on the Hudson, Margaret Higgins found her father's house and Corning too confining. She moved to White Plains and enrolled in a hospital to train as a nurse. There she met and married William Sanger, an architect with whom she went to live in New York City. While working among the urban poor, Mrs. Sanger discovered the need for contraception. She ascribed her adoption of this cause to a single dramatic case.

In July 1912, Sanger answered a call for help from a Grand Street tenement. There Mrs. Sachs, "a small, slight Russian Jewess" with "a madonna-like expression," lay close to death from a self-induced abortion.[15] For three weeks, Sanger and the doctor she called battled the bleeding and infection. Having barely survived, Mrs. Sachs asked how she could prevent another pregnancy. "You want to have your cake and eat it too?" said the doctor. "Well, it can't be done." His only advice was, "Tell Jake to sleep on the roof." The woman turned to the nurse, certain that she knew some secret the doctor would not share. Sanger promised to return to speak with her, but she broke that promise, because in fact she had no answer to give. Three months later, Mr. Sachs called her again to save his wife from the effects of an abortion. This time Mrs. Sachs died within ten minutes of Sanger's arrival.

Biographers of Margaret Sanger have downplayed this story, attributing it to her penchant for dramatizing herself and her cause.[16] They have traced her crusade for contraception to her association with Emma Goldman and other socialists. But whatever caused Sanger's conversion, it revolutionized her life. Leaving her husband and two children, she traveled to England and France in search of knowledge about methods of contraception. She became the student and the sometime lover of Havelock Ellis.[17] She smuggled diaphragms into America; recruited others to keep up the supply; and lectured, wrote, and solicited funds to inform the public. She even went to prison for the cause.

Though others advocated some of what Margaret Sanger wanted, none duplicated either her message or her success. Victoria Woodhull (1838–1927) spoke out for free love, which Sanger practiced but never preached, throughout the Gilded Age. Emma Goldman (1869–1940) wanted women to enjoy sex and to know how to prevent conception. Certainly Havelock Ellis (1859–1939), who devoted his life to exploring the psychology of sex, offered as much mysticism on the subject as Sanger could digest. But only Sanger saw the potential of contraception to bring all the debate on sex into focus. And only Sanger began and remained close enough to the center of American culture to use the heritage of American religion to advance her movement. By renaming contraception "birth control," she presented herself as a reformer, working with natural law rather than against conception. By associating birth control with happy marriage and healthy motherhood, she appropriated the ideals of wife and mother. By applying the most Romantic stereotype of women to her advice on sexual practice, she turned the cultural tendency to regard women's desires as sacred into an argument for birth control. By exalting sex as a redemptive force, she addressed the yearning for freedom from sin. Her message suited Americans so well that her ideas triumphed long before her death. What Margaret Sanger published as radical doctrine in the 1920s became standard advice to married couples during the thirties, forties, and fifties.

For Sanger, good sex was always sacramental. As she wrote in *Happiness in Marriage*, "Sex expression is not merely a propagative function, nor the satisfaction of an animal appetite." Rather, "Sex expression, rightly understood, is the consummation of love, its completion and its consecration."[18] To understand sex correctly meant knowing that it should control every aspect of married life:

All the everyday relations between husband and wife in reality constitute the prelude for the ritual of sexual communion. They are likewise also indications of the success or failure in the attainment of mutual ecstasy.[19]

Therefore, a couple should approach sex carefully. Sanger's chapter on foreplay prescribed at least twenty minutes to half an hour of preparation for intercourse, so that the husband could bring his wife "into a mysterious realm of enchantment, of poetry and adoration."[20] The wife's regard for her husband after successful foreplay revealed the religious dimension of sex: "In leading her successfully, nay triumphantly, through this mysterious initiation he becomes for her a veritable god—worthy of her profoundest worship."[21]

The chapter on intercourse, entitled "Sex Communion," urged wives to express their adoration with an active passivity reminiscent of the states attained by Aimée Semple McPherson, Phoebe Palmer, and other female ecstatics. To be able to let go, women had to overcome a certain mistrust that Sanger, like Palmer's Methodists, blamed on the Puritans. "Here is the crux of the marital problem," Sanger warned. Women had been trained, "especially in countries in which the Puritanic tradition dominates, . . . to submit but not to participate."[22] Instead, Sanger taught participation *through* submission. "She must not seek to crush down the passion which wells up from her deepest nature. On the contrary: she should and must abandon herself to it *utterly*."[23] The wife who followed Sanger's directions would not actively stimulate her husband, but she had to let herself feel, to be active in her response.

Meanwhile, wrote Sanger, "The husband should aim to control his emotions."[24] As foreplay ended and intercourse began, his role changed from that of the divine source of love to that of a participant in the rapture of the woman. This required shifting concentration from the physical to the spiritual, from the details of foreplay to the meaning of intercourse.

> Rather than to permit purely physical impulses to dominate, he may master the strong current of passion . . . by dwelling on the inner harmony, the spiritual mystery of this communion of two natures.[25]

But the husband was not to stray so far into the spiritual realm that he lost track of his wife's condition. His sublimation would enable him to "attune his own desire to hers and aim to reach a climax simultaneously with that of his beloved."[26]

By prescribing simultaneous orgasm, Sanger advanced an ideal that marriage manuals would commonly endorse from the 1930s to the present.[27] She must therefore share some of the blame for generations

of husbands gritting their teeth and striving for discipline, and generations of wives feigning orgasm to fulfill the ideal. Instead of relying on
the capacity of women to have orgasm before, and therefore during, male
ejaculation—a capacity well known to eighteenth- and nineteenth-century
writers on sex—Sanger's instructions led couples into obsession with the
single moment of perfect union. Yet she did intend to foster sexual pleasure, and some of the sex that resulted from her work doubtless represented an improvement over what had gone before. For the couple who
achieved simultaneous orgasm, Sanger promised: "This joy is the finest
fruit of monogamy; and the miracle of undying love is the fruit of such
experience."[28] They would find "a true union of souls" because their sex
"takes on the nature of a sacrament."[29] Simultaneous orgasm would be
truly ecstatic, carrying each partner out of self and obliterating the distinctions between them, between sex and religion, and between sex and love.

Of course, sacramental sex required practice, and freedom to practice
required contraception. Margaret Sanger's primary argument for birth
control was that it would enable "woman," the generic woman of whom
she wrote with the ease of a Romantic, "to develop her love nature separate from and independent of her maternal nature."[30] Only with security
from unwanted pregnancies could married women learn to enjoy sex. The
argument appealed to husbands as much as to wives, to monogamists as
much as to partisans of free love.

Once woman's "love nature" had developed, Sanger prophesied the
redemption of motherhood. "Maternal love, which usually follows upon
a happy, satisfying mate love, becomes a strong and urgent craving,"
she wrote, describing the future in *Woman and the New Race* (1920).[31]
Abortion, infanticide, child neglect, and child labor all would disappear
before the "passionate intensity" of mothers' love.[32] Ultimately, this new
mother love would redeem humanity.

> Great beings come forth at the call of high desire.... When the
> womb becomes fruitful through the desire of an aspiring love, an-
> other Newton will come forth.... There will come a Plato who will
> be understood, a Socrates who will drink no hemlock, a Jesus who
> will not die upon the cross.[33]

This vision of a womanhood that could make the crucifixion unnecessary had major consequences for Sanger's idea of original sin, and for her
reformulation of the relation between sex and sin. Sanger acknowledged

that there was a danger in sex; indeed, she rejected Marx for his failure to recognize the need to control human sexuality. In *The Pivot of Civilization* (1923), she condemned "those pretentious but fundamentally fallacious social philosophies which place the blame for contemporary world misery upon anybody or anything except the indomitable but uncontrolled instincts of living organisms."[34] Here Sanger spoke the language of evangelicals, making individual regeneration the prerequisite for social reform. But Margaret Sanger also blamed Christians for perpetuating the evil they abhorred. Churchmen who taught "that the sex life itself is unclean" obstructed redemption because they made people feel that "all knowledge of the sex functions" was "unclean and taboo."[35] Ignorance fostered the real sin, the uncontrolled use of sex that made women the enslaved producers of unwanted children. It was shame, not concupiscence, that transmitted sin; but the remedy lay at hand.

> The great central problem is ... the abolition of the shame and fear of sex. We must teach men the overwhelming power of this radiant force. We must make them understand that uncontrolled, it is a cruel tyrant, but that controlled and directed, it may be used to transmute and sublimate the everyday world into a realm of beauty and joy. Through sex, mankind may attain the great spiritual illumination which will transform the world.[36]

Sanger's critique of Christianity included a new version of the Protestant charge that Roman Catholic sexual doctrine colluded with human depravity. *Woman and the New Race* represented Catholic authorities deliberately changing their teaching to augment their power, first preaching celibacy because the church needed missionaries, then emphasizing the duty of procreation "to provide laymen to support" an "increasingly expensive organization."[37] Always the Catholics encouraged shame and restricted sexual knowledge, to keep women under control. Catholic doctrine on sex and sin "created about the whole love life of woman an atmosphere of degradation," while at the same time denying women the right "to refuse to submit to the marital embrace, no matter how filthy, drunken, diseased, or otherwise repulsive the man might be."[38] According to Sanger, the men of her day had won freedom from the church in many fields, and the women had made strides into public life, but people still derived most of their ideas about sex from the heritage of the Roman Catholic Church. She argued that the church relied on sexual repression as the key to its survival. "It clings to this last stronghold of ignorance, knowing that woman free from sexual domination would produce a race spiritually free and strong enough to break the last of the bonds of intellectual darkness."[39] Other enemies of birth control would fight harder in the open, Sanger predicted, but "the ecclesiastic will fight longest in the dark."[40] The priest understood how quickly his empire would crumble if women deserted. "For, be it repeated, the church has always known and feared the spiritual potentialities of woman's freedom."[41]

Sanger had some cause to feel this way. Catholics were urging the police to break up birth control meetings, denying support to hospitals that taught birth control, and speaking out in public against her.[42] In view of Rome's modification of its doctrine in 1930 to allow one form of contraception, the rhythm method, one scholar has blamed Sanger's strident anti-Catholic attitude for damaging any possibility of further accommodation on the part of the church.[43] But by taking up the stance of the Protestant hero, crusading to break the tyranny of Rome, Sanger tapped deep sources of support in American culture. The sexually charged antagonism between Protestant and Catholic in the United States, which had begun with Protestant austerity and Catholic sensuality in the 1830s, and then resolved itself into a Victorian consensus, now assumed the modern form of Protestant objection to Catholic repression.

After pronouncing doom upon Rome, Sanger described her positive goals in terms familiar to evangelical Christians. The conquest of shame and the spread of birth control would reverse the effects of sin on sex:

> When women have . . . purged the human mind of its unclean conception of sex, the fountain of the race will have been cleansed. Mothers will bring forth, in purity and joy, a race that is morally and spiritually free.[44]

Morality and instinct would work together in the harmony of which perfectionists dreamed. "We will then instinctively idealize and keep holy that physical-spiritual expression which is the foundation of all human life."[45] When every human being was the result of a desired pregnancy, "the inner energies of a redeemed humanity" would recreate the world.[46] "Life for them would be enriched, intensified, and ennobled in a fashion that it is difficult for us in our spiritual and physical squalor even to imagine. . . . The children of that age would . . . produce a terrestrial paradise."[47] Horace Bushnell's dream of regeneration in the womb, the apogee of the

Victorian religion of health, would come to pass without repression. Once sex became pure and ecstatic, children would inherit sanctification. And the one thing needful was faith in the promise. "Let us look forward to this great release of creative and constructive energy, not as an idle, vacuous mirage, but as a promise which we ... have it in our power ... to transmute into a glorious reality."[48] Phoebe Palmer had offered perfection in exchange for trust in the promises of the Bible; Margaret Sanger offered perfection to those who could trust the power of nature in sex.

Sanger did not limit her involvement with religion to borrowing concepts and rhetoric. She courted the Protestant churches, sent representatives to annual meetings, and gradually won the support of churchmen for birth control. By 1931, the General Council of the Congregational and Christian Churches was ready to declare, "We favor the principle of voluntary child bearing, believing that it sacramentalizes physical union."[49] In the same year, the Federal Council of Churches of Christ endorsed birth control, in part because it encouraged "sex union ... as an expression of mutual affection."[50] Other groups moved more slowly, but all major Protestant denominations moved into Sanger's camp during her lifetime.[51]

Under Margaret Sanger's guidance, contraception shook off the associations with free love, socialism, and radical medicine that would have barred it from the American mainstream. Sanger made birth control part of the perfectionist program of American Christianity. In the process, she reinforced some aspects of Christian culture that had no necessary relation to her cause.

Besides reviving the opposition between Protestant and Catholic on sexual doctrine and presenting orgasm as an experience analogous to reception of the Holy Spirit, Sanger translated the sex roles of Romantic religion directly into her crusade. Only women's desires had redemptive power; male sexuality remained, as one biographer of Sanger has written, "bestial, selfish, and dangerous."[52] In *What Every Girl and Boy Should Know* (1927), Sanger told adolescents that biology made women want to embrace and to caress, while male biology demanded penetration and release of sperm.[53] A trauma Sanger described in *My Fight for Birth Control* (1931) suggested that her fear of male sexuality dated from her eighth or ninth year.

> The only memory I have of any sex awakening or sex consciousness was when I was ill with typhoid fever. . . . I awakened in the

night.... I felt around me and knew I was in ... mother's bed....
Then I heard heavy breathing beside me. It was Father. I was terrified. I wanted to scream out to Mother to beg her to come and take
him away.... I dared not move, fearing he might awaken and move
toward me.... I was petrified; but he only turned over on his other
side ... then I felt I was falling, falling—and knew no more.[54]

As one of eleven children borne by an invalid mother who died at forty-
eight, Sanger had already learned to distrust what Father did in bed. In one
sense, the birth control movement was an attempt to protect women from
men. Sanger approved of diaphragms more than of condoms, because she
wanted to put protection from pregnancy into the hands of women. Forty
years after being terrified by her father, she had a dream that seemed to
cast her relation to male sexuality into biblical terms. She dreamed "that
a large, glossy, spotted snake lay full length in my bed, head up, looking
defiantly at me." Sanger attacked the snake with a saw, but accidentally
struck a baby who was also in her bed. Then the snake "glided away," leaving her with the infant "cut and in a fever."[55]

The archetypes that informed Sanger's thinking on sex included
another theme of her childhood: her devotion to Mary, the "beautiful,
smiling" woman who looked "the way I should like to look when I had a
baby," and whom Catholic iconography depicted treading the serpent of
sin underfoot.[56] A dream recorded in 1930 showed that Mary still lived in
Sanger's subconscious mind.

I dreamed that like a flash of light came a picture of the Madonna
and Child on a wall in front of me, a beautiful painting filling all
the side of the wall.... When the flash came I made the sign of the
cross on myself as the Catholic children are taught to do.... It was
a nice dream so full of color and motion.[57]

Before seeing the Virgin that night, Sanger had dreamt of herself in bed
with George Bernard Shaw. She felt that there was some connection between the two dreams. "All because I started to dream of Shaw," Sanger
wrote, concluding her account of the dream of Mary in a letter to Havelock
Ellis.[58] Her campaign for the sexual pleasure and freedom of women had
not really left Mary behind. Sanger projected onto all women the beauty
and rapture and innocence that she had first encountered in the Virgin.
Her message never challenged the limits of Mary's role, within which the

fulfillment of women came through marriage and motherhood. Instead, Sanger used that role as she used other religious traditions, as resources for her cause. Surely Pope Pius IX, who had declared Mary's freedom from sin, would not have approved of Sanger's work; nor would her teachers at Claverack College have endorsed her translation of Christian perfection into sexual practice. Nevertheless, it was Sanger's Christian background that gave her the vision she followed in transforming American sexual ethics.

Although contemporary feminists have seen Sanger's limitations, they have also been nurtured in a world of small families made possible by her achievement. Her attempt to set women free *through* sex had immeasurably greater impact on American life than the work of more respectable feminists like Charlotte Perkins Gilman, who sought to free women *from* sex. In the wake of Margaret Sanger's crusade, Americans found the old association of sex and original sin almost impossible to maintain.

G. Stanley Hall and Adolescence

Even those who rejected birth control could not escape psychology. Sigmund Freud has unquestionably received more praise and more blame for influencing American thinking on sex than any other individual. With Freud's concepts of repression and sublimation, every human action could be made to disclose a sexual meaning. Freud forced parents to acknowledge infantile sexuality. His impact on marital advice initiated a controversy on clitoral and vaginal orgasm that has continued into the twenty-first century. And nowhere did Freud find a more receptive audience than in America. Psychoanalysis remained an esoteric specialty in Europe, while the United States not only produced analysts and patients in the tens of thousands but also welcomed Freud into popular culture.[59] Montgomery Clift played the lead in his film biography. Despite assaults by other psychologists, by feminists, and by critics of the therapeutic value of his method, Freudian theory pervaded the advice of newspaper columnists, the creation of advertising campaigns, the training of social workers, and the everyday lives of millions who came to know an unresolved Oedipus complex, a "Freudian slip," or an anal character when they saw one.

Yet many of Freud's conclusions did not survive the transatlantic crossing. For example, his belief in a death instinct, his diagnosis of religion as illusion, and his tragic view of progress gained few adherents in America. What really won popularity was Freud's pansexualism, translated into religious terms by Americans like G. Stanley Hall (1844–1924).

Hall began his career as a pious young man of the New England type, a graduate of Williams College who naturally aspired to the Congregational ministry. His mother was caught up in the Holiness movement, recording her desire "for more entire consecration" in her journal.[60] And her grandfather's "ecstatic piety and unwavering faith" had been a byword among his neighbors.[61] But Hall came to reconsider his vocation after conferring with the Reverend Henry Ward Beecher, who always had a keen sense for the signs of the times.[62] Instead of entering the ministry, he went to Germany to study psychology. He would return to found psychology departments at Johns Hopkins and at Clark University. His *Adolescence*, a pair of huge volumes completed in 1904, inaugurated the twentieth-century obsession with that time of life. And in 1909, as president of Clark University, Hall instigated and hosted Freud's only visit to America.[63] No one did more to establish the new science of psychology in this country.

But G. Stanley Hall did not need Freud to teach him the meaning of sex. Hall had his own ideas on that subject, some of which appeared in the description of intercourse he wrote for *Adolescence*.

> In the most unitary of all acts, which is the epitome and pleroma of life, we have the most intense of all affirmations of the will to live and realize that the only true God is love, and the center of life is worship.... This sacrament is the annunciation hour, with hosannas that the whole world reflects. Communion is fusion and beatitude. It is the supreme hedonic narcosis, a holy intoxication, the chief ecstasy, because the most intense of experiences.[64]

In intercourse passion and holiness, sex and love all coalesced and reinforced each other. As Hall told his readers, "this act can never be normally passionate unless it is pure."[65] His evocation of the effects of intercourse left no distinction between sex and sanctification.

> Now the race is incarnated in the individual and remembers its lost paradise.... Now the soul realizes the possibility of a new heaven and a new earth; ... It pants for more and fuller life.... The flesh and the spirit are mated, and now for the first time an apperception organ is molted forth.... Nature, as hitherto conceived,

is transcended ... and the extra and supernatural organ of faith comes into possession of its kingdom.[66]

Intercourse as described here comprehended every aspect of the Christianity Hall had inherited. After glimpsing the "lost paradise" of Eden, lovers entered upon the prophecies of a renewal of the earth; they received the more abundant life that Christ had promised. They obtained the "supernatural organ" or capacity that Jonathan Edwards discerned in the elect, that evangelicals promised to those reaching perfect love, and that Catholics attributed to contemplatives. Having relived the Annunciation, the couple might also recapitulate the Passion, since "reproduction is always sacrificial."[67] If their sex achieved its full potential, they would not bring forth their children in sin. As Hall put it, "Each personality is a god to the other and every such conception is immaculate for both."[68]

Of course, evil continued in the world, and sometimes appeared to increase. This was precisely because of the misuse of sex: "all sin either is, or is measured by, the degradation of this function."[69] Hall took the medical reduction of original sin to sex for granted. In a paper presented to the American Society of Sanitary and Moral Prophylaxis and published in 1908, Hall referred to this reduction as if to a common postulate: "Now the aberrant fallen aspect of man, wherein he differs from all animals, is rooted in the excessive development of the sex functions."[70] Like Margaret Sanger, Hall faced the problem of accepting the reduction of sin to sex while rejecting the repression prescribed by Victorian doctors and theologians. For Hall as for Sanger, the solution was to direct sexual energy into the right channels. But Hall went further than anyone in translating into sexual terms the whole process of rebirth, the central image of deliverance from sin for American Protestants.

> The chief sin of the world is in the sphere of sex, and the youthful struggle with temptation here is the only field where the hackneyed expressions of being corrupt, polluted, lost, and then rejuvenated, of being in the hands of a power stronger than human will become literally true.[71]

The paper concluded with a call for a "revival," to bring about "a new dispensation of sexual theory and practice."[72]

Although this same address went on to praise Freud for his contributions to the increasing knowledge of sex, Hall entirely denied Freud's

concept of infantile sexuality. "Our life fortunately begins with a sexually neuter period during which no sex consciousness exists," he asserted.
Imagining that this "age of primeval innocence" normally continued
past the fourth year, he recommended that ignorance of sex "should be
prolonged by every possible means."[73] Hall did not see sex as central to
human life because he had read Freud's *Three Essays on Sexuality* (1905);
instead, he had inherited the idea that sex was central from the Victorian
religion of health.

No doctor amalgamated religion and health more thoroughly than
G. Stanley Hall. In a lecture at a YMCA meeting in 1901, Hall said that
health expressed the entire biblical meaning of holiness. He suggested
retranslating Scriptural texts: "worship the Lord in the beauty of healthfulness" and "what shall it profit a man if he gain the whole world ...
and lose his own health?"[74] He spoke of "the healthful Scriptures" and
inserted "the healthful Spirit" into the Trinity.[75] Health became the criterion for determining the value of religion: "religious systems are thus
measured by the health, wholeness, and holiness they can produce."[76] And
because health brought "abounding joy or euphoria," like the joy people
sought in sex, religion should promote sexual pleasure. Hall had affinities
to radical healers of the nineteenth century like Andrew Ingersoll and
Edward Bliss Foote, but he went further in reconstructing religion, and
he commanded an audience that was both broader than theirs and better
prepared to receive his message.

The psychologist explained that all religion, and especially Christianity,
arose from sex. According to Hall, prehistoric humanity had practiced
a sexual cult, which fell away gradually as tribes migrated northward.
A stage of rejection of sex ensued. Yet "the elect pressed on, yearning
for the reincarnation of love in its primitive, high, holy, and wholesome
sense in their midst."[77] In the Scriptures of ancient Israel, sex regained its
rightful prominence: "The story of creation is full of ancient and subtle
symbols of divine generation. The tale of Eden and the fall, whatever historical validity it may or may not have, is a masterly allegory of the first
stage in the decadence of love."[78] Christianity accelerated the return of sex
to religion, beginning "with the annunciation and conception from on
high."[79] The sexual meaning of the New Testament appeared distinctly in
the persons of Jesus, Mary, the Father, and the Spirit.

We glimpse the hero, at the dawn of puberty, in the temple, turning, as is germane to gifted souls at this stage, to the great themes

of religion. One at least of his temptations was probably fleshly, but gloriously overcome. He dies at the acme of prolonged adolescence, nubility, and ideal perfection. Motherhood is idealized in the adoration of Mary, who has lost none of the charm of virginity, but combines the two into unique glory. God is our Father and heavenly Parent, and the Gospel is through and through a literal deification of love.... The logos or spirit of wisdom, which made the world, was spermatic; ... Thus the great work of Jesus was, when all else save love alone was dead, to create the world from this vital germ.[80]

So Christianity proved that "psychologically, religion and love rise and degenerate together."[81] If any took offense at this assertion, Hall said that they must "either think vilely about sex or ... lack insight into its real psychic nature."[82] Between sex and love Hall saw no difference at all. He did not prescribe a return to erotic rituals, but he did recommend an attitude of worship in sexual activity, with the recognition that God "is the most immanent of things, and that the higher monotheism is not altogether separable from the higher pantheism."[83] Sex joined humanity to the force that created the world, and revealed God through the ideals held by people in love. "The supernatural in religion, therefore, is the homologue of the idealization of the mistress in whom ... the lover sees all perfection."[84]

Of course, Freud also described religion as derived from sex. But Freud told a story of tragic conflict, beginning with the desire of sons for mothers and the inevitable mixture of hatred, love, and fear between sons and fathers.[85] In primitive tribes, sons murdered fathers, and they still wanted to murder them in modern families, so that they could marry their mothers. Racked by their guilt over this Oedipal wish, sons exalted the fathers they loved and hated to the skies, thus creating the gods. All subsequent religion expressed this continuing tension. To Freud, Christ was the symbolic Son who died for his drive to supplant the Father, and whose execution paid for the guilt of all sons. But in contrast to this tragedy, G. Stanley Hall offered a romance of God and the world. The Hebrew Scriptures told the story of hereditary redemption, showing that "Jehovah could breed men"; the New Testament showed that people could breed gods.[86] A glance at the works of Erich Fromm, Norman O. Brown, Rollo May, and Herbert Marcuse will confirm that Hall's romance found many exponents in the United States who bypassed Freud's tragedy with regard to applying psychology to religion.

Romantic, religious love called for control in the service of pleasure. "The most rigid chastity of fancy, heart, and body is physiologically and psychologically as well as ethically imperative till maturity is complete on into the twenties," Hall declared in *Adolescence*.[87] Premature indulgence in sex would injure young people, making them incapable of genuine passion. "Alas for those . . . mutilated by premature or excessive experience in Venusberg," lamented Hall, "for these can never know the highest, largest, and deepest things of life!"[88] Even after maturity, married men should take care to curb their tendency to ejaculate too quickly. "Explosive and instantaneous" pleasure was one of the symptoms of "natures weakened by venery."[89] Hall rejected the notion, held by Freud among others, that the basic purpose of sexual activity was the release of tension. He advocated sexual practice that increased tension to the highest possible level, in the interests of women and of any children conceived.

> The motive of merely relieving organic pressure tends to degrade the act to its very lowest possible level, seen in masturbation; it also involves the most degrading view of woman and ignores the fact of the necessity and high developmental power of control and of maintained sex tension.[90]

This reference to a "developmental" power in sexual tension implied yet another connection between sex and the religion of health. Like Margaret Sanger, who predicted that sexually satisfied women would give birth to a redeemed race, Hall stressed the hereditary effects of sexual behavior. "To . . . give an inheritance that is all-sided and total, nature seems to require . . . special prenuptial activities known as courtship, wooing, falling in love, etc." All animals exhibited some courting behavior, but humanity required more elaborate and prolonged stimulation, "for the most effective propagation of the higher mental, moral, and esthetic qualities."[91] From such biology, sexual ethics took its primary law: "the act of impregnating the ovum is the most important act of life."[92] Intercourse had to be undertaken with consciousness that success or failure in the ritual of sex would bring down a blessing or curse on all posterity.

Part of Hall's intention in prescribing this approach to intercourse was to increase women's sexual pleasure; but Hall endorsed this pleasure only in the name of the most restrictive, Romantic ideal of woman. He disagreed with the charge that Eve fell first into sin: "The contrary seems true, that . . . woman is normally and constitutionally more unfallen

than man."[93] By their natural modesty, women gained the power to pro-
long courtship and to select the best men, thus contributing to hereditary advance. Each woman also elevated the man who loved her. Because
"woman is a more generic being than man, closer to the race, and less
mutilated by specializations or by deformities of body or of soul," man
could find the whole universe in her. "She becomes for him the flower
in the crannied wall, by knowing and loving which he knows God and
man."[94] To keep women this way, Hall called for a drastic reinforcement
of sex roles. Schools should educate girls "with the proper presupposi-
tion of motherhood." Sports for girls should have "the competition element sedulously reduced." Even academic subjects should be tailored to
accentuate sexual stereotypes. Hall suggested "a woman's botany," which
would teach English rather than scientific names for plants and would
emphasize "the moral value" of each plant.[95] Intensifying the differences
between men and women would foster racial progress. "Every man should
be just as manly and every woman just as womanly as possible," Hall said
in 1913, addressing the Fourth International Congress on School Hygiene.
"It is vital to the race that sex distinctions . . . should be pushed to their ut-
termost. The highly civilized woman and man differ more and more from
each other in bodily dimensions, in life occupation, in mental, moral,
social traits."[96] To build civilization, parents and teachers should instill
submission or aggression depending on the gender of the child.

The Virgin Mary exemplified the role Hall assigned to women. In
the chapter on "Adolescent Girls and Their Education" in *Adolescence*,
he wrote:

> I keenly envy my Catholic friends their Maryolatry [*sic*]. Who ever
> asked if the holy mother . . . knew the astronomy of the Chaldees or
> had studied Egyptian or Babylonian, or even whether she knew how
> to read and write in her own tongue, and who has ever thought of
> caring? We can not conceive that she bemoaned any limitations of
> her sex, but she has been an object of adoration all these centuries
> because she glorified womanhood by being more generic, closer
> to the race, and richer in love, pity, unselfish devotion and intu-
> ition than man. The glorified madonna ideal shows us how much
> more whole and holy it is to be a woman than to be artist, orator,
> professor, or expert, and suggests to our own sex that to be a man
> is larger than to be gentleman, philosopher, general, president, or
> millionaire.[97]

Hall did not seem to know the Catholic legends of Mary as a mystic vowed to virginity, who brought about the Incarnation by meditating on the prophecies. Nor did he acknowledge the medieval Queen of Heaven who had inspired Chartres, or the debates as to whether Mary's Immaculate Conception meant that she possessed the same gift of unimpaired intellect that Adam and Eve enjoyed before the Fall. Hall found the Mary he wanted in the childlike, sentimental Virgin of the nineteenth century. Linking "the eternally womanly ... to the eternally childlike, the best of which in each are so closely related,"[98] Hall brought the modern Mary into his vision of redemption through sex.

The limits of American sexual ethics also appeared in Hall's recommendations on infant care. By 1913, Hall had adopted Freudian views of infantile sexuality. His paper at the school hygiene conference reproduced, without attribution, Freud's description of oral, anal, and phallic stages in sexual development. But where Freud saw an inevitable, biologically determined process, Hall found opportunities for prophylaxis and improvement. Considering the oral stage prompted Hall to warn against the pacifier as a possible source of "passionate hysterical impulsions";[99] only breast feeding could safely gratify the urge to suck. Careful training of the bowels at the anal stage would "erect ... efficient barriers against a trope of bad traits and even diseases later."[100] At the phallic stage, when the child discovered the difference between the sexes and began to explore the genitals, parents should limit the child's "exposure to sex phenomena"; they should avoid handling the child with "intimacy so close or prolonged" that it might inhibit the transfer of affection from the parents to a mate; and yet they should take care to present the child, through their own example and those of other adults, with images of the opposite sex that would later "spring up and take control in the phenomenon known as falling in love."[101] For Freud, sublimation, repression, and aim-inhibited gratification were unconscious, involuntary reactions. For Hall, these psychological mechanisms were so many tools that parents and teachers could and should use to shape the development of the child.

With regard to gender, both Freud and Hall saw anatomy as psychological destiny, but Freud regretted at least part of the destiny allotted to women.[102] Hall felt no such regrets. The whole sexual life, from infancy through senescence, would be "controlled by judicious insight and regimen"[103] so that humanity would fulfill natural law. Hall thus participated in the American transformation of psychoanalysis into a method for social control and self-improvement, which would foster adjustment at the expense of Freud's critical perspective on nature and culture. Christian perfectionism, with its conviction that no basic flaw in human nature prevented perfect adjustment, had prepared the way for this use of psychoanalysis.

Ultimately, G. Stanley Hall saw himself more as the heir of Jonathan Edwards than as the colleague of Sigmund Freud. He focused on adolescence because he identified that period as the most likely time for conversion experiences.[104] In *Adolescence*, Hall acknowledged that all religions marked puberty with some rite, but he argued that only the Puritans had grasped the whole significance of puberty. "It was reserved for ultra and especially American Protestantism ... to enter the soul at pubescence and attempt to prescribe and normalize its states and changes."[105] This Puritan achievement in psychology seemed so important to Hall that he offered a brief history of New England religion, following an orthodox evangelical line, within the pages of *Adolescence*.

According to Hall, the Pilgrim Fathers knew the importance of conversion, for they had experienced its power themselves. But with their passing, "piety declined"; "men never converted ... entered the ministry."[106] Then came Jonathan Edwards, who "alone grasped the whole situation." Edwards revived "the modern idea of re-birth as essential to the salvation of the soul."[107] Along with the Methodists, to whom Hall allowed some credit although they "came in a little later," Edwards inspired the adolescents of New England. The result was the Great Awakening of the 1730s and 1740s, the birth of revivalism in America. Though another decline in conversions ensued, the Second Great Awakening then continued Edwards's work through the nineteenth century. The conclusion of all this history was clear: Hall, the psychologist who interpreted the story, had inherited the role of the minister as a guide to rebirth. But the psychologist could go further than the evangelist. He could "enter the soul," not only of adolescence but also of infancy, adulthood, and old age, and "prescribe and normalize" the soul's "states and changes." Because the psychologist understood the sexual source of those changes, he could lead people more surely through the crises of life. The goal Hall set forth resembled what Edwards had called "true virtue," or "love to Being in general," but with a biological twist:

> The final stage is the love of being or of all that exists, visible and invisible. The ontological passion culminates thus in a mystic

devotion to the absolute in which self is forever merged and swallowed up, and the mind and life find their supreme value in anticipating, and accepting with joy their inevitable final fate.[108]

For Edwards, this final stage, "the love of being or of all that exists," was the special gift of God to the elect, a new power that enabled them to love each thing according to its being and to love God supremely as the source and perfection of being. But Hall added the loss of self to the description of true virtue. He identified the love of all being with an experience of self-obliteration resembling the sanctification experience that nineteenth-century ecstatics had praised, and which Hall himself and Margaret Sanger had located in intercourse. Thus, G. Stanley Hall smothered the noblest ideal of Reformed Christianity in a religion of health that centered on sex and culminated in death.

Religion now seemed only a fable useful for teaching the significance of sex and heredity. As Hall said, "If religion were known to be a myth and a superstition by cultured adults, it would have to be kept and its function modified for the young because of its prophylactic value for this [sexual] function."[109] Because "God himself when biologically interpreted is simply posterity personified,"[110] it followed that anyone who had a redemptive marriage and family life would need nothing more from religion. Redemption through sex had become capable of leaving Christianity behind.

Conclusion: History
and Theology (1985)

Pastor, I never dreamed when I accepted Christ that He
would invade our sex life, but we had never been able to
make my wife's bells ring until after we were converted.
Now she has a climax most of the time.[1]

THE CLAIM THAT redemption improved sex—here reported by the
Reverend Tim LaHaye, a founder of the Moral Majority—emerged from a
long evolution. Eighteenth-century Catholic moralists made orgasm obligatory, but they never entirely cleared sex of its association with original
sin. Then Victorian physicians and theologians diagnosed original sin as
a sexual disorder. Their work enabled medical and religious perfectionists
to redeem sex by showing people how to overcome sin. Psychologists and
birth control crusaders took the next logical step when they taught that sin
could be overcome *through* sex.

By the 1970s, many Christians in America actually identified the power
of salvation with the force of sexual desire. To Marabel Morgan, conversion meant the fulfillment of the female sex role. "God is waiting and
wanting to fill your vacuum, to make you complete," she wrote, urging
her readers to accept Jesus. "Right now you can become a Total Woman."[2]
Father Andrew Greeley ended his *Bottom Line Catechism for Contemporary
Catholics* (1982) with a comparison of the attractiveness of God to the attractiveness of actress Jessica Lange in the film *All That Jazz*. "The difference between God and Jessica Lange," according to Greeley, "is not that
God is less sensuous (less attractive to the human senses) but more. Ms.

Lange's appeal, impressive as it is, is but a hint of the appeal of Ultimate Grace."[3] A Catholic charismatic who took my course on sexuality and religion described God as One who, by virtue of the divine presence in all things, was "always having sexual intercourse." At Indiana University in 1980, another student gave me the text of a purported revelation by God to an Episcopal priest, who wrote down God's words in a trance:

> I have built into all creatures that move a desire for the pleasure of sexual union.... I linked love with pleasure with procreation, so that you cannot escape the presence of my holiness in natural life. In moments of your desire, I am stirring my love in you. In moments of your passion, I am flooding you with the power. In moments of your ecstasy, I am drawing you into my holiness. In moments of procreation, I am binding you into my eternal life. In moments of your bliss, I am holding you in my perfection. Please enjoy what I am doing in your sexual love and refuse to pollute it with the perverse idea that it is evil and bad.

The student who showed this to me wanted to become an Episcopal priest herself, but she had no idea what her tradition taught about sex and sin. She had never read the statement of the ninth Article of Religion that original sin was an "infection of nature," manifest in concupiscence. When I pointed out that this description of sin would rule out any simple identification of human passion with the power of God, she looked for a way around tradition, which was easy enough to find, since the last edition of the Book of Common Prayer segregated the Articles of Religion in a section reserved for "Historical Documents." She was nearly as unlikely to accept the ninth article on sex and original sin as she was to accept the tenth article on the inability of the human will to choose the good.

Such attitudes first became dominant in the 1920s, when advocates of a positive approach to sex dismissed the whole doctrine of original sin. As Ben B. Lindsey, a Denver judge who won fame by writing *The Companionate Marriage* (1927), commented, "if some of our theologians want to call this wonderful thing [sex] the result of the 'Fall,' and if they want contemptuously to dub it 'Carnal Appetite,' they are at liberty to do so. The words no longer mean anything."[4] Most American theologians had no intention of saying anything that Judge Lindsey would find meaningless. In 1929, the Federal Council of Churches reported with approval that American young people normally "entered into a relationship in marriage which to them has been deeply and consciously rooted in sex experiences and which they have thought of as natural but at the same time as spiritual."[5] The council did not suggest that original sin disrupted the harmony between nature and spirit. Both Lindsey and the theologians were entering an age in which sin meant crime, or conscious violation of divine law, not a state of being into which people were born. A school of neo-orthodox thinkers arose in the twenties and thirties to remind Americans of original sin, but the neo-orthodox message never reached beyond the seminaries into popular culture.

Reacting against liberal theology and against the social disruptions of the twenties, evangelicals entered a phase that historians have named "the Great Reversal."[6] They left the center of the American culture they had helped to create and abandoned any effort to exert social or political influence. From the repeal of Prohibition to the rise of the New Right, Christians who preached the necessity of rebirth maintained an attitude of hostility toward modern culture and modern sexual ethics. Catholics also encountered much that they could not accept in American life from 1920 through 1960, and they also responded by concentrating on discipline. Meanwhile, the Protestant majority gradually accepted birth control, remarriage after divorce, and some sexual experimentation before marriage, because mainstream Protestants had become convinced of the sacredness of sex and the moral obligation to sexual pleasure. Some customs changed with startling rapidity. For example, when Judge Lindsey suggested that legal provisions be made for a new type of marriage, a "companionate marriage" in which the parties would contract to live as man and wife without any intention to have children, and concede to each other the right to dissolve the relationship, the idea shocked the public. Yet this was exactly what marriage became for many Americans within fifty years. Motion pictures, the radio, the automobile, and television continued the process that the steam press and the radio had begun, making basic patterns of attitude and behavior more and more susceptible to cultural influence and more and more uniform across the whole country.

When evangelicals and Catholics rejoined the American mainstream during the sixties and seventies, they revealed that they had just as little sense of original sin as liberal Protestants. *Intended for Pleasure* (1977), an evangelical marriage manual by Ed Wheat, MD, and his wife, Gaye, admitted that "sin did enter the human race in the Garden and brought with it the possibility of perversion of every good thing (including sex)"; but the Wheats saw this perversion only in overt actions, not in the being of humanity. "Sex apart from marriage is spelled out as obviously wrong. Sex in marriage is wonderfully right," they concluded.[7] In *Human Sexuality* (1977), a study commissioned by the Catholic Theological Society of America and produced by a committee under the direction of Father Anthony Kosnik, the chapter on the theology of sex mentioned sin on the first page: "Another influence that Christians should never lose sight of is the reality of sin and the role it plays in keeping persons from both appreciating and realizing the ideal in their lives."[8] The study then proceeded to lose sight of sin, characterizing sex as "the concrete manifestation of the divine call to completion" and as "the Creator's ingenious way of calling people constantly out of themselves into relationship with others."[9] Though Kosnik and his collaborators noted that some events made it appear that "God's ingenious gift ... has been seriously abused,"[10] they rejected any assertion of an inherent tendency toward abuse in human sexuality, and they supplied no explanation for sexual evil.

Always without peer for cheerfulness, Marabel Morgan briskly denied any connection between sex and original sin. "Sex was not the first sin," she wrote; disobedience was. "Sex was going strong before sin ever entered the world."[11] And to judge from her encouragement of modern men and women to free themselves from shame, it seemed that sex today could still proceed in the spirit of Eden.

> There they were, men and women before each other, naked and beautiful. They had no shame. . . . This was God's idea. What a great romantic. After all, He could have had them reproduce by rubbing noses. With no marriage manuals and no doctors to consult, can't you imagine their fun and games experimenting with their new-fangled parts? . . . The Creator of sex intended for His creatures to enjoy it. We need never be ashamed to talk about what God was not ashamed to create.[12]

Morgan placed the responsibility on women to make their homes new Edens, and in this she continued the project of all generations of American sexual reformers. Concentration on women united nearly everyone who wrote about sex from 1830 to the 1980s. The redemption of sex came through women and the self-appointed friends of women. When health experts reduced original sin to sex and suggested cures for sin, they were seeking to protect women. Women led the evangelicals who found holiness through ecstasy. Ideal women inspired Roman Catholics and Romantic

Protestants with visions of sacramental emotion. When prophets of sexual pleasure arose, they preached control to men in service of the pleasure of women. And today the association of women with sexual redemption goes on. Feminist theology, from the biblical scholarship of Phyllis Trible to the Christology of Rosemary Ruether and the post-Christian radicalism of Mary Daly, carries on the Victorian feminist crusade to sanctify the body, to establish a religion of health, and finally to abolish the disharmony between body and soul, or nature and God.[13] Such reconciliation is the goal of all theology, and feminist theologians have thus had some justification for seeing their movement as the ultimate cause, the cause of causes. But modern feminist theology also has asserted that recognition of any inherent sin, or acknowledgment of any distance between nature and God, itself perpetuates disharmony. In *Christian Feminism* (1984), an anthology that includes Beverly Wildung Harrison's article, "Human Sexuality and Mutuality," the index contains no entries under "sin" or "original sin."[14]

Because the redemption of sex came to American culture through women, Americans have learned to see only female sexuality as redeemed. Judge Lindsey demonstrated this selective vision in his description of innocent sexual appeal:

> Young girls, clad in one-piece bathing suits, now swarm our beaches, glowing with health, brown from the sun, lovely in their unhampered grace; chaste in the unashamed and unafraid uses of their fine, strong bodies ... they swim and dive in a way that should bring clean delight to the heart and mind of any healthy-minded person.[15]

Here was the style, of perception more than of dress, that informed the ethic of innocent ecstasy. The boys who swam and dived beside the girls did not convey the same message to Lindsey. Women regained the innocence of Eden; men followed, and adjusted, and admired. According to Lindsey, the "flapper" of the twenties was the "major determining factor" in the liberation of sex.[16] It never occurred to him to ask how the patriarchal, Christian, and Victorian culture he denounced had produced the flapper.

Alongside changes in style came changes in sexual behavior, for which the crucial decade was the twenties. Kinsey found that thirty-six percent of women born between 1900 and 1909 had intercourse before marriage, as opposed to fourteen percent of those born before 1900. The women who came of age in the twenties also had more orgasms after marriage, and later generations "accepted the new pattern and maintained or extended it."[17] By 1975, when *Redbook* magazine surveyed one hundred thousand married women, the percentage reporting orgasm in most of their sexual acts had risen from Kinsey's forty-seven percent to sixty-three percent.[18] The relation between orgasm and religion also changed. Though Kinsey found that in 1953, the more religious a woman was the less likely she was to have orgasm in marital sex, *Redbook* reported that in 1975, seventy-two percent of "strongly religious" women were "almost always orgasmic," as opposed to sixty-two percent of "non-religious" women.[19] The editors of the *Redbook* study identified religion and communication as the two factors most conducive to "good sex" in marriage.

More selective surveys have yielded higher correlations of faith and sexual pleasure. According to the Reverend Tim LaHaye and his wife, Beverly, who questioned 3,377 evangelicals from the lists of participants in their Family Life Seminars, seventy-seven percent of the wives in their group reached orgasm "frequently or always."[20] The LaHayes also found that eighty-eight percent of the wives who described themselves as "Spirit-filled" said they were "very happy" with their sex lives, as opposed to seventy-eight percent of those in the sample who were not "Spirit-filled."[21] To the LaHayes the lessons seemed clear: "Christians are considerably more satisfied with their love life than non-Christians, and Spirit-filled Christians tend to record a somewhat higher degree of enjoyment than even the average believer."[22]

Further correlations between belief and sexual activity have appeared in surveys taken at the beginning of my own courses on sexuality and religion, which I have taught at three different colleges since the spring of 1980. Although forty-one percent of my 155 students have called themselves regular churchgoers, and seventy-two percent have affirmed belief in the virgin conception of Jesus Christ, sixty-one percent of these students, including more than half of the regular churchgoers, have also admitted to oral-genital experience. Fifty-seven percent have had some sexual intercourse. Not a single student has ever answered "no" to the question "Do you expect to have a satisfactory sex life, by your own standards of pleasure?" And the usual formulations of original sin have provoked disbelief nearly as universal as the expectation of sexual satisfaction. When I have asked whether children are born innocent of any moral guilt, fewer than ten percent have answered "no" or "probably not"; sixty-seven percent checked "yes" or "probably," affirming the innocence of newborns; and twenty-three percent checked "undecided." On the question of whether seeking sexual pleasure was always somewhat sinful, even for the married, eighty-six percent have answered "no" or "probably not," and only five percent have said "yes" or "probably."

Yet the feeling that religious belief must correspond with sexual repression persists, and there may be one sense in which that feeling represents the truth: in the matter of sexual lifestyles. My surveys have shown that Roman Catholics are dramatically less likely than Protestants to admit homosexual activity, for example. In a study of eight sexual styles published in *Parade* magazine in 1984,[23] people who described themselves as "very devout" made up seventy-four percent of the group called "satisfied sensualists"—those who, on the one hand, expressed satisfaction with their lives in general and said they found kissing, hugging, and manual stimulation of breasts and genitals to be sexually arousing, but scored low in responses to questions about oral-genital activity, pornography, sexual fantasy, masturbation, and other actions that the survey used as criteria for the "erotic" sexual style. Less religious people made up a majority of those in all three "erotic" lifestyles: the "satisfied erotic," the "unsatisfied erotic," and the "lonely erotic."

Evangelical sexual advice has certainly borne out the image of people for whom sex is highly important but who restrict their actions within very specific boundaries. The LaHayes have insisted on orgasm, and they have given directions for obtaining it, even interpreting the Song of Solomon 2:6, "Let his left hand be under my head and his right hand embrace me," as a reference to manual stimulation of the clitoris.[24] But they omitted oral sex entirely from their chapter on "The Art of Lovemaking," and they suggested in another context that oral-genital contact might have some special role in the spread of herpes. Their warning had the ring of hope: "It may well be that additional research will ... expose oral sex, which some already find repugnant, as being extremely dangerous to the health."[25] Although Dr. Ed Wheat raised no health questions about oral sex, he did argue that the practice could not provide the same "unity and oneness" as genital intercourse, and he expressed concern that husbands who relied on oral stimulation to bring their wives to orgasm might fail to develop "the discipline and skillful control" they would need to produce an orgasm through intercourse. Apparently grasping for any objection he could find, Dr. Wheat concluded his discussion by pointing out that "oral-genital sex definitely limits the amount of loving verbal communication that husband and wife can have as they make love."[26]

With regard to homosexuality, pornography, masturbation, or any sexual activity other than genital intercourse between married partners, evangelical Christians have maintained a hard line. Their position has paralleled that of the Catholic moralists who made orgasm obligatory in marital sex but condemned it as "pollution" in any other context.

Meanwhile, other believers of all denominations have come to accept the erotic in many forms. The sexual style that *Parade* called "pansexual," exponents of which had high scores in the three categories of life satisfaction, traditional sexuality, *and* erotic experimentation, included 19.8 percent of the adult population—more than any other single style— and fifty-five percent of pansexuals described themselves as devout.[27] Among my college students, fewer have admitted to alternative forms of erotic expression than to the more standard interpersonal activities (only thirty-five percent have admitted masturbation, for example, as opposed to the fifty-seven percent admitting intercourse), but the students have also shown no great willingness to condemn particular actions as sin. Only thirty-three percent, for example, have answered "yes" or "probably" when asked whether homosexual relations are sinful; nineteen percent have said that masturbation is at least probably sinful. Some tolerance of variations, coupled with pride in their own normality and prowess, would appear to be the ideal for these students. The older sense in which religion once meant repression, not with regard to sexual style but with regard to sex in general, has nearly disappeared.

How closely surveys reflect behavior remains questionable. But experts have certainly encouraged the increasing orgasmic activity that surveys recorded. In the thirties, expert opinion made orgasm obligatory for married women. One scholar has described the marital advice of that decade as a "cult of mutual orgasm."[28] Promotion of mutual orgasm extended during the forties and fifties to concern for vaginal, rather than clitoral, orgasm; then concern for multiple orgasm arose after Masters and Johnson published their research in the sixties. Experts rediscovered the clitoris in the seventies, and some have sent husbands and wives searching for the "G-spot" in the eighties.[29] Every step in the development of sexual advice has increased pressure on men to be skillful and on women to be responsive.

Meanwhile, no challenge to the roles of men and women in sex has altered the pattern that emerged sixty years ago. As Germaine Greer lamented in 1970, "Lovemaking has become another male skill, of which women are the judges."[30] The moral supremacy Victorians attributed to women carried over into modern sexual practice, and so, according to Greer, did the woman's detachment from sensuality. "He labors for her pleasure like a eunuch in a harem.... She is still alone, egotistical, without libido to desire him or bring him to new pleasure in her."[31] Yet Greer's remedy revealed her own captivity to the ethic she condemned. "If women are to avoid this last reduction of their humanity," she warned, "they must hold out not just for orgasm but for ecstasy."[32] Holding out would never change the passive/receptive model that sexual ethics inherited from religion. Forces comparable to those that arose in the 1830s—industrialization, massive immigration, and a cultural movement as popular as Romanticism—may have to intervene before a challenge to the model of the female ecstatic can succeed.

To consider the relation of social forces to the idea of sexual redemption is to confront once again the problem of historical causality. The modern attitude toward sex did not result from any single cause. The fact that roles in sexual practice have not really changed since 1830 does suggest a social context, however. As Barbara Welter, Ann Douglas, and many others have pointed out, the "cult of true womanhood" that emerged in the nineteenth century was directly related to the rise of capitalism and industry.[33] The male who entered the new world of commerce "left behind a hostage ... to all the values which he held so dear and treated so lightly."[34] At home, the wife of the manager or entrepreneur, relieved of the duties of production, would concentrate on beauty, children, religion, art, and sex. The ethic of sexual pleasure that suited this situation was analogous to Max Weber's Protestant Ethic in economic life.[35] Condemning sensuality, just as the capitalist condemned idle wealth, men would work to make sex serve the glory of God. At first this meant repression. Eventually the men who learned to work in business for work's sake, with quantitative standards for success, also learned to work for a quantitative standard in sex, counting female orgasms after the modern fashion. Women showed men how to work at sex, just as nature disclosed her secrets to engineers.

When Weber described the Protestant Ethic, he was recovering from a depression that had nearly destroyed his capacity for work. Weber wondered who would live in "this iron cage" in the future. Mechanical sex can inspire similar feelings. But there was a truly redemptive side to redemptive sex; just as the work ethic really helped to produce abundance, so modern sexual ethics have fostered real freedom and real pleasure. From a psychological standpoint, the ideal woman who haunted Victorians compensated for the Victorians' manipulative, exploitative attitude toward the world.

Actual women also rebelled against the concept that nature was fallen, and against the God who expelled humanity from Eden. Harriet Beecher Stowe and Phoebe Palmer, Mary Baker Eddy and Margaret Sanger united in rejecting the God of their fathers, and their rebellion succeeded. Even if their success, as Ann Douglas wrote, amounted to "a complicated mass dream-life in the busiest, most wide-awake society in the world,"[36] it was still the dream that made life bearable for many. The earnest, innocent, self-consciously healthy sex of the American middle class, protected from procreative consequences, became the most important spiritual practice in American life. To reject redemption through sex altogether would be to reject the best part of ourselves. It should be possible to mitigate modern problems without any such rejection, by recovering traditional wisdom.

The pressure to practice sex well would decrease if Christianity recovered the doctrine of original sin. Promises of freedom from sin, the recapture of Eden, or millennial harmony may be inspiring, and probably were necessary to the success of causes like birth control and to one phase of the struggle for women's rights. But perfectionism also exacts a price. Correctly understood, the idea that human beings will always be imperfect offers consolation. Original sin does not have to mean a positive force for evil, a curse of God, or an aspect of sexual desire. It can be simply the absence of harmony between human consciousness and nature. The Book of Genesis tells us that at some point human beings began to judge good and evil, usurping the place of God.[37] Having gained this capacity to judge, people could not get rid of it; to judge became an imperative of human nature. But because people were not omniscient, their judgments of good and evil were wrong. The world became a field of labor, suffering, and death because humans no longer lived in the world God made but in a world shaped by their judgments. Those judgments continue to be as mistaken as the decision of Adam and Eve to be ashamed of their bodies. Meanwhile, the body came to seem rebellious, because human consciousness had detached itself from the physical world to sit in judgment upon it. The ancient perception of an "infection of nature" expressed how prideful, judgmental, sinning spirits have experienced the physical world.

In a world torn by sin, sex will also be sinful, though no more so than business or scholarship. The history of Catholic doctrine on marriage showed that people can accept sexual pleasure without denying the consciousness of sin. Before the nineteenth century, many Catholics accepted sexual pleasure as the fulfillment of natural law while admitting that sex as they knew it also expressed the distortion of human nature by original

sin. The problem with natural law was its tendency toward tyrannical cer-
tainty. A return to this attitude, incorporating Reformation skepticism
about the human ability to know natural law completely, would reduce the
pressure on sexual performance today.

Acknowledgment of sin should include the roles we adopt in sexual activity. Although many evangelicals and Catholics support the roles of men
and women as part of a divine plan, the Scriptures present those roles as a
consequence of sin. "Your desire will be toward your husband, and he will
rule over you," was part of God's description of the life of fallen woman in
Genesis, no more a subject of rejoicing than death, the need to work, or
suffering in childbirth.[38] Just as we strive to mitigate the other effects of
sin, so should we struggle against the evil inherent in sex roles, for even
if sex roles are beneficial in some ways, as Krister Stendahl has observed,
they are contrary to justice, and we must be willing to forgo benefits to do
justice.[39]

The history of modern sexual ethics discloses a possible trajectory for
development beyond sex roles. When American culture defined women
as more religious than men, a process began that has led, in our time, to
large enrollments of women in theological schools. Most of these women
subscribe to the perfectionist creed of Victorian feminism. But at the
same time, there are many women in America who have explored, and
begun to describe, their own passions. One day a female Augustine may
arise, admitting her own experience in the "cauldron of lust," to provide
Christendom with an account of female sexuality under fallen conditions.
Simultaneously, men may find in themselves some of the innocence, emotional sensitivity, and beauty that they have projected onto women.

Pleasure remains the most unqualified good promoted by the last
century and a half of development in sexual ethics. It seems beyond reasonable doubt that Americans today experience pleasure that reaches the
limits of physical capacity more often than Americans of 1830, 1880, or
1930. Now there is need to recover the capacity for sensual celebration
that has been forgotten in the quest for a moment of ecstasy; and again, a
renewed sense of sin might actually facilitate this recovery.

The religion of health became ascetic through misguided perfectionism. We have treated the body as a thing to be sanctified, controlled,
and directed toward a transcendent goal. But human beings can neither
sanctify nor escape from their bodies. We began to regard the body as
inferior when we began to sin; yet the capacity for passion may be the
means of salvation. Thomas Aquinas taught that humans will attain

supreme happiness by receiving the direct impression of the action of God.[40] Perhaps God created the material world to enjoy this relationship, to become incarnate, to fill the passive, passionate capacity of matter with the power of spirit. In Christian terms, this would mean that sin did not cause the Incarnation, but only the Crucifixion. The Resurrection testifies that the physical and the spiritual will still attain harmony, with the senses intact. In true perfection, the difference between matter and spirit would be resolved in communion rather than strife.

The Scriptures represent humanity not as a compound of body and soul, but as living matter or embodied spirit, living in a disharmony that makes us ashamed of our natural state. Hope for the resurrection of the body provides hope that this disharmony will end; but disharmony cannot be abolished by flight from the body. It is the hope for abolition of the body that leads us to transform sexual pleasure into a search for ecstatic religious experience. Because humans cannot stand outside their bodies, they can never really be ecstatic except by a special grace of God. Orgasm is not the ecstasy of the mystics, but a physical event. And we should rejoice that this is the case. How would two souls united in ecstasy express affection? If we will always be bodies, always separated from each other and from God by irreducible physical being, then we will always be able to love.

Since 1985: Redeeming the Body

Evangelicals, Blacks, and Ecstasy in Music

In January of 1986, eight months after *Innocent Ecstasy* was published, evidence that the American ethic of sexual pleasure could redeem the body came in the first induction ceremony of the Rock and Roll Hall of Fame. Ten performers were inducted: Elvis Presley, Buddy Holly, Chuck Berry, Fats Domino, James Brown, Jerry Lee Lewis, Ray Charles, Sam Cooke, the Everly Brothers, and Little Richard.[1] Nine of ten came from evangelical Protestant families. The only nonevangelical, Fats Domino, was a serious Roman Catholic. Six of ten were black, and the whites also took much of their music from black church traditions.

Elvis Presley and Jerry Lee Lewis, two of the white rock stars, were raised Pentecostal. Pentecostals (as Chapter 5 indicated) are evangelical Christians whose worship centers on the experience of the Holy Spirit through the practice of entering into ecstatic states. In ecstasy, Pentecostals speak in tongues and receive deliverance from original sin, including bodily effects of sin such as disordered lust. Presley and Lewis both said that when they sang rock-and-roll songs (which often concerned sex), they moved their bodies in the way they had learned at services of worship. According to a memoir by Presley's barber, Larry Geller, the singer resented "preachers tryin' to make people feel guilty for things they never done" (the effects of original sin), but the energy of the congregation made a more positive impression. "All that dancin' and the free movement, it taught me that God is natural, and to move my body was natural," said Elvis. Although some ministers denounced Elvis and even held bonfires to burn his records, he argued that he was only doing "what I learned when I was a little kid in church, movin' my body to the music."[2]

And Pentecostal church music included a much wider repertoire than traditional hymns. Instruments used in Pentecostal churches included banjos and fiddles played in fast tempos, producing "music geared to bring the congregants to an ecstatic state."[3] Besides congregational singing and choir performances, Pentecostal services often featured solos, offertory songs as people got up from their seats and came forward with their gifts, and even spontaneous singing by people seized by the Spirit. A biography of Jerry Lee Lewis and his cousins, preacher Jimmy Swaggart and country singer Mickey Gilley, who grew up in the Assembly of God Pentecostal church of Ferriday, Louisiana, pointed out that their church devoted more than half of its ninety-minute services to music with "a hard beat, a fast rhythm," suited to "an ecstatic, lively worship style."

Non-Pentecostal evangelicals were less exuberant in their music, but the era that began in the 1930s, when those first Rock and Roll Hall of Famers were born, had seen the church music of black Baptists also moving in the direction of rock. Thomas A. Dorsey (1899–1993) became known as "the father of black gospel music" after shuttling between dance halls and churches for much of the 1920s and 1930s. Dorsey transplanted syncopation and the eight-bar chord progression from blues into gospel, and so increased gospel music's popular appeal.[4] At a meeting in Chicago in 1930, the National Baptist Convention, the largest organization of black Baptists, heard two examples of Dorsey's new gospel music and endorsed them for use in churches, two decades before rock broke through in the secular world.[5]

Elvis always acknowledged these connections. Twenty minutes into his longest television appearance, a mostly live "comeback" concert in 1968, he explained that rock and roll had come from gospel. He then performed three gospel songs on a churchlike set with groups of black and white dancers, ending with a song that had "I'm Saved" as its refrain. In fact, the whole arc of the 1968 show was a story of redemption, starting with Elvis dressed in black and claiming to be "evil," but ending with Elvis in a white suit singing "If I Can Dream," an anthem affirming that a man can "redeem his soul and fly."[6] He continued to record gospel albums throughout his career.

Before gospel and rock came the spirituals and "shouts" of slave religion, and before spirituals and shouts had come the music of the Yoruba people of West Africa. Yoruba drums, dancing, and spirit possession rituals gave rise to religions called Voudou, Santeria, and Condomblé in the African diaspora to the Americas.[7] Pentecostalism in the United States grew from revival meetings where evangelical preachers, both white and black, drew crowds of white and black people to camp meetings that might go on for several days and nights.

From Cane Ridge, Kentucky, in 1801 through the protracted revivals at Topeka, Kansas, in 1901 and at Azusa Street, Los Angeles, in 1906, the Pentecostal movement remained racially integrated, in contrast to much of American life.[8] By the 1920s, however, when Elvis Presley's great-uncle built the Pentecostal First Assembly of God in Tupelo, Mississippi—a tiny wooden building with a capacity of forty-eight worshippers—most churches in the South, including Pentecostal churches, had become segregated.[9] A general movement of segregation afflicted American culture in the era after 1876, and segregation increased after World War I, when racial theories of social development reached their height. Still, the music and dancing of Pentecostal churches remained rooted in the African heritage that had been transmitted by slaves and free black people during more than a century of integrated revivalism.

Music began to break all barriers in the 1950s. When Sam Cooke went straight from being lead singer of the Soul Stirrers, the most important gospel quartet in black churches, to singing rock classics like "You Send Me," "Bring It on Home to Me," and "Another Saturday Night," he shocked the gospel music world. But for millions, black and white, Cooke's smooth voice and optimism conveyed a sense that sexual pleasure could not only be free from sin, but might even be a means of liberation.

Ray Charles "soaked up gospel music at the Shiloh Baptist Church" in the segregated Florida of the 1930s,[10] then broke through to popular culture in 1957 with "I Got a Woman," a rock translation of the gospel tune "It Must Be Jesus." As columnist Bob Herbert reflected in the *New York Times* after Charles died in 2004, this first popular hit from Ray Charles "had an irresistible gospel feeling that moved with tremendous power toward a culmination that couldn't be anything but sexual." Herbert also noted that Charles always had "a shamanistic quality," that his music "was both spiritual and profane," and that he scandalized both the "white-bread mass culture that was on its guard against sexuality of any kind" and the "black religious community, which felt that gospel was the Lord's music, and thus should be off-limits" to secular use. Instead of conforming to these categories, Charles made music that moved people "precisely because it is religious." He transformed "America the Beautiful" into a hymn, and used the rock classic "What'd I Say?" (1959) to bring listeners into the call-and-response rhythms of the black church, while singing about sex rather than God. According to Herbert, this music brought people to spiritual transcendence: "it envelops the willing listener in a glorious ritualistic expression . . . without the coercion, hypocrisy, or intolerance that is so frequently a part of organized religion."[11]

Of course, everyone did not accept rock music. Before Jerry Lee Lewis would agree to record his second hit, "Great Balls of Fire," he had to be convinced by Sam Phillips, the owner of Sun Studios in Memphis, that he was not leading people to Hell.[12] Religious leaders often denounced rock and roll. But no one could deny that the rhythms and climaxes of rock echoed the music of evangelical and Pentecostal churches, or that rock lyrics encouraged people to seek sexual pleasure.

And the first generation of rock stars was succeeded by others, for example, Aretha Franklin (the daughter of a famed minister who sang gospel, and the first woman in the Rock and Roll Hall of Fame), Stevie Wonder, Marvin Gaye, Michael Jackson, and Prince, all of whom emerged from evangelical backgrounds to deliver musical messages of redemptive sex. Some singers fared badly in life because of tension between the Christian fervor of their families and the sexual fervor of their songs. Marvin Gaye was shot and killed by his father, a Pentecostal preacher, two years after he won a Grammy for "Sexual Healing." The saga of the Jackson Five and Michael Jackson, who grew up going door to door as Jehovah's Witnesses, grew darker as Michael moved from pop toward rock and sex with "Billie Jean" and "Thriller." The story turned to farce with the Janet Jackson "wardrobe malfunction" at the 2004 Super Bowl, and finally to tragedy as Michael Jackson was tried for child molestation in 2005 and died from a drug overdose in 2009. Prince had no public tragedies before his death, but his identity followed a stressful path from an Adventist childhood to hypersexual rocker to fervent Jehovah's Witness, with an odd moment in the middle, when he renounced his name in favor of an androgynous symbol.[13]

As rock and soul gave rise to hip-hop in the 1990s, the merger of religious and sexual messages in the lives of performers reached new heights. Tupac Shakur (1971–1996), among the greatest hip-hop artists, identified with Jesus so much that the last album he released before his death (from a shooting in Las Vegas) featured a crucifixion of his own body on the CD cover and the hit song "Hail Mary," referencing his mother. Kanye West, a hip-hop star of 2015, calls himself "Yeezus," which is also the title of his 2013 album, featuring lyrics of dialogue between West and Jesus. In 2005, West won the Grammy for Best Rap Song for "Jesus Walks," an unambiguous assertion of faith that in a world "at war," God stays with convicts, sinners, and rap artists.

Strong and continuing connections with Christianity distinguished American popular music from British or other versions of rock that emerged in the 1960s and after. The Beatles evoked Indian religion, and the Stones appropriated the Devil, but neither the Beatles nor the Stones had the deep Christian roots of American rock.

Madonna and Catholic Redemption through Ecstasy

From the 1980s through the Grammy Awards show of 2015, innocent ecstasy found a dramatic proponent in Madonna Louise Veronica (her Confirmation name) Ciccone, popularly known only as Madonna. She merged the rock derived from gospel music with dance music, visual art, and explicit theology to express her own messages about sin, redemption, and sexual ecstasy. As Madonna told an interviewer in 1989, "Once you're a Catholic, you're always a Catholic." By that she meant a struggle with original sin, "because in Catholicism you are born a sinner and you are a sinner all of your life. No matter how you try to get away from it, the sin is within you all the time." As Madonna said of her childhood, which was scarred by the loss of her mother to breast cancer when she was five years old, the consciousness of sin "taunted and pained me every moment. My music was probably the only distraction I had."[14] Madonna's music dramatized the struggle to affirm the body and sexuality despite sin, or perhaps even through what the church called sin, leaving any sense of guilt behind. And her music helped others to reach the same goal. As a professor of gender studies wrote, "It was also Madonna, leading her own sexual revolution, who made me realize that sex was not a sin, nor was it a bad thing, in spite of what the Catholic Church and my family thought."[15]

Madonna dramatized her struggle with sin by mixing religious imagery with sex. She became a cultural phenomenon, frequently scorned by religious leaders and music critics but also called the most famous woman in the world by a journalist in 1998.[16] In the first decades of the music video she was the queen, a dancer, choreographer, and actress as much as a singer and songwriter.

Her first number one hit, "Like a Virgin," came out in November of 1984, and it used Madonna's music and dance to claim rebirth through sex. "I made it through the wilderness," the song began, "Somehow I made it through/Didn't know how lost I was/Until I found you." In the video, Madonna dances through Venice, flirting with a huge male lion. She wears a black top with a huge crucifix, then changes into a short white wedding dress with a buckle spelling "BOY TOY." The song celebrates a feeling of innocence inspired by sex: "Yeah, you made me feel shiny and new/Like a virgin/Touched for the very first time." Over the next thirty years, Madonna reinvented the song often.[17] One notable version came during the Blond Ambition World Tour of 1990, when Madonna slowed the song's tempo and gave it a Middle Eastern feeling, writhing on a bed covered in red velvet and simulating masturbation. This led to a police threat to close down the show in Toronto and a clash with Vatican spokesmen in Italy.

In *Truth or Dare*, a documentary of this tour, Madonna recorded herself telling journalists that she was an "Italian-American," proud to be a citizen of a country that values "freedom of speech and artistic expression."[18] She said that the masturbation scene was part of a drama that dealt with "redemption and salvation." She also claimed to be a prayerful person, and *Truth or Dare* showed Madonna praying with her dancers five times, examples of a ritual that occurred before every show. Nevertheless, the reaction of the church was so negative and so influential that she did not sell out her theater in Rome and canceled the show in Turin.

Immediately after the scene miming masturbation in the Blond Ambition show, sex flowed into salvation as Madonna said the word "God," and the stage went silent. The red velvet bed was replaced by hundreds of candles, and Madonna sang her most directly religious song, "Like a Prayer," which had been released in 1989.[19] This song was also the subject of her most artistic video.

The "Like a Prayer" video begins with sirens and dissonant guitar chords as Madonna runs down a hill, wearing a coat over a slip, and falls. Lifting her head, she sees a burning cross. Quick clips show a white woman stabbed by a white man, Madonna witnessing the crime, and a black man being arrested. Madonna enters a small church that has a statue of Saint Martin de Porres, a black Catholic saint, behind bars (as if the saint is in a cell) on a side altar. As the lyrics assert that "Life is a mystery/Everyone must stand alone," then "I hear you call my name,/And it feels like home," Madonna kneels, now in her slip without the coat, and sees the saint cry blood. She opens the cell and kisses the saint's feet. The saint kisses her on the cheek and forehead, in a gesture of blessing, then walks out.

Now the video enters a dizzying succession of scenes. It shows the crime in more detail, then Madonna dancing outdoors in front of five burning crosses. Suddenly back in the church, she picks up a knife and gets wounds (stigmata) on both of her palms. She then dances with a choir, whose voices came from a real black Pentecostal church, singing

"Just like a prayer, your voice will take me there." When the choir leader, a tall black woman, puts her hand on Madonna's head, Madonna falls, dancing, to the floor as if "slain by the Spirit," a frequent occurrence in Pentecostal services. As Madonna lies on the floor, the black saint appears on top of her and kisses her, gently but sexually. The saint then returns to the altar, and the choir and Madonna sing with building speed and power: "Just like a muse to me, you are a mystery/Just like a dream, you are not what you seem/Just like a prayer, your voice (no choice) will take me there." The video cuts to a police station, with the black man behind bars. Madonna tells the desk sergeant the man is innocent, and he is released. Finally, everyone appears on a stage and takes a bow before a red curtain closes, and the words "The End" appear in script across the screen.

Pepsi-Cola canceled an endorsement contract with Madonna, even though they still had to pay her $5 million, because of this video.[20] Many were outraged by the burning crosses, by Madonna dancing in her slip in a church, by the use of stigmata, by the participation of the Pentecostal choir, and by the sexual moment with the black saint (who is identified as Jesus in many accounts of the video). Often, Madonna was called an exploiter of religious imagery for money and fame.

But others, including Andrew Greeley, a priest/sociologist and author of the novel *The Cardinal Sins* (1981), saw how the video grew out of Catholic teaching on sex and sin. Greeley wrote that "Like a Prayer" showed how "Catholicism . . . passes on to its children both obsessive and imprisoning guilt and a liberating sense of God's love as sacramentalized . . . in human love."[21] The courage Madonna drew from her ecstasies in the church showed that "sexual passion may be revelatory," he concluded.

Of course, Madonna's most important audience was not liberal priests, but the girls and young women who were her most ardent fans. A generation of girls imitated Madonna's clothing and hairstyles, accessories and makeup and dance moves, and opinions. In 2012, thirty-nine of these women contributed to a book, *Madonna and Me*. An editor at Penguin recalled that "Like a Prayer" had freed her, at ten years old, from compulsive praying of the Rosary and given her the confidence to join girls jumping rope.[22] A vice president of the Women's Media Center wrote that she didn't know what a virgin was when she first heard "Like a Virgin," but then came to see that "Madonna equated holy redemption with the freedom of sexual ecstasy."[23] Inspired by Madonna, she took up dance and experienced "transcendent spirituality through movement."[24]

Through the 1990s, Madonna pushed sex further, sometimes too quickly for most of her audience. The gay and transgender and sadomasochistic themes of her shows became mainstream, but not until the early twenty-first century. In "Justify My Love," the video that immediately succeeded "Like a Prayer," she depicted cross-dressing by both sexes, a threesome, and gay sex between women, while hinting at bondage, with plenty of crucifixes dangling from necks and hanging on walls. MTV refused to show that video, but people bought "Justify My Love" and rented it from video stores.

This was followed by an infamous book called *Sex*, perhaps the most upscale soft porn in history, a 134-page coffee table book with an aluminum cover and spiral binding. Priced at $49.95 and enclosed in a Mylar sheet so that it could not be examined before purchase, the book sold out its entire print run of a million copies on the first day (October 22, 1992) it became available in seven different countries.[25] *Sex* featured nude and partially clothed shots of Madonna in situations from the mundane (eating in a pizza parlor or walking down the street) to extremes like being bound to a chair, threatened with a knife, and fondled by butch lesbians. She was pictured being gang raped by men in a high school gym (while laughing) and having her foot licked through dominatrix boots. Many, even among the models, called the book exploitative.

The Madonna of *Sex* was losing touch with the innocent dimension of innocent ecstasy. But ten years after the *Sex* debacle, in 2002, she won her first Grammy Award for an album with a collection called *Ray of Light* (influenced by Kabbalah) and then won another Grammy in 2007 for *Confessions on a Dance Floor*. In the *Confessions* World Tour of 2006, she wore dominatrix leather and rode a man with a bit between his teeth, but these scenes did not provoke the negative reactions that had accompanied *Sex*.

In the same *Confessions* show, Madonna acted out a crucifixion, mounting a cross made of disco black mirrors with a platform to stand on and hooks for her wrists. She wore a crown of thorns along with a cheery smile, modest pants, and boots while singing one of her older ballads, "Live to Tell." When Bill Donohoe, the president of the Catholic League, demanded that the scene be cut on NBC's broadcast, Madonna responded that her performance was "neither anti-Christian nor sacrilegious nor blasphemous."[26] On the wall behind Madonna's cross were projected pictures of African children orphaned by AIDS, with the words "In Africa 12 million children are orphaned by AIDS."[27] She insisted that "if Jesus were alive today, he would be doing the same thing." NBC did cut the crucifix, but it kept the pictures of orphans and the words.[28]

A late peak of Madonna's career came at halftime during the 2012 Super Bowl. Madonna ended the show with "Like a Prayer." As the song ended, all stage and stadium lighting went dark, and "World Peace" appeared in a script of light across the football field and across the screens of 114 million viewers in their homes.

Later in 2012, controversy surrounded Madonna's MDNA World Tour. MDNA was said to mean several things, including a shortening of Madonna's name and the idea that the show expressed her heritage or DNA, but it also suggested the drug called Ecstasy, often associated with electronic dance music and called MDMA because its chemical name is 3,4-methylenedioxy-methamphetamine. Ecstasy acquired a nickname, "Molly" for "molecule," in 2008, and Madonna enraged some leaders of the electronic music movement by asking about Molly when she appeared as a guest at an electronic music festival. Seeking to evoke ecstasy, Madonna had again lost touch with innocence.

But by 2012, Madonna had many successors. The most famous was Stefani Joanne Angelina (her Confirmation name) Germanotta, an Italian-American woman who stayed in her parents' New York apartment when she performed in New York[29] as Lady Gaga. In the 2011 videos "Born This Way," an anthem of sexual tolerance, and "Judas," which focused on Lady Gaga as the woman in a motorcycle club composed of Jesus and the apostles, she built upon Madonna's combination of sex, sin, and redemption. And in November of 2014, a Sicilian nun named Sister Christina released her own video of "Like a Virgin," using the song to describe her romance with God.[30] Lady Gaga and Sister Christina made it clear that Madonna and innocent ecstasy had triumphed, both in American music and in at least one subculture within the Roman Catholic Church.

AIDS and the Gay Revolution

As the 1985 edition of *Innocent Ecstasy* appeared in bookstores, the crisis of AIDS, or acquired immune deficiency syndrome, began a new stage in the triumph of sex over sin. AIDS had entered the news on July 3, 1981, when the *New York Times* reported that forty-one cases of a rare cancer, Kaposi's sarcoma, had occurred among gay men in New York and California.[31] Kaposi's manifested itself as purple blotches on the skin, so that it made AIDS visually horrifying, and this was only the most obvious effect of a collapse of the immune system that left victims susceptible to Pneumocystis pneumonia and other infections. Many went from health to critical illness within months and became living skeletons, dying after great distress in a year or so. At first there was no clear cause of the syndrome, which was called GRID, or gay-related immune deficiency. Because no one knew how it was transmitted, the afflicted were often shunned, even by medical personnel and undertakers. By May of 1985, the month when *Innocent Ecstasy* was published, the Centers for Disease Control and Prevention reported that ten thousand cases of AIDS had been identified in the United States, and that 4,942 of those who had been diagnosed with AIDS were already dead.[32]

On July 25, 1985, Rock Hudson announced that he had developed AIDS. A leading man of movies from the 1960s and of television in the 1970s, Hudson was the first major public figure to have AIDS. After a dramatic trip to Paris for treatment,[33] Hudson died on October 2. During the same summer and fall, thirteen-year-old Ryan White became nationally known when his parents fought against his being barred from school in Kokomo, Indiana, because he had developed AIDS. White was a hemophiliac, and he had developed AIDS after being infected through blood-based treatments.[34] In 1987, the first drug that slowed the HIV virus that caused AIDS was approved by the Food and Drug Administration, but this drug (azidothymidine, or AZT) also had poisonous effects on bone marrow, especially in the high doses at which it was first prescribed. Not until 1996 did a combination of AZT with two other drugs begin to turn HIV infection from a nearly one hundred percent fatal condition into a manageable but serious chronic disease.[35]

The terror associated with AIDS in the 1980s and early 1990s redirected the sexual revolution. For a few decades after the conquest of syphilis by penicillin in the 1940s, it had seemed that there were no longer any life-threatening sexually transmitted diseases. AIDS challenged a way of life premised on sex without consequences that had become especially prevalent in the gay community. Gays began to indulge in public or near-public sex, often anonymously, in enclaves such as dance clubs, bath houses, and resorts like Fire Island in New York and Key West in Florida during the 1970s. As Larry Kramer wrote in his 1985 play, *The Normal Heart*, millions of gay men had "singled out promiscuity to be their principal political agenda, the one they'd die [from] before abandoning."[36] For such gay men, free sex meant redemption. These gay men were among the prime practitioners of the sexual ethic of innocent ecstasy.

Fear of AIDS quickly spread to the heterosexual world, especially after 1991, when basketball star Earvin (Magic) Johnson announced that he had become infected with HIV. As Magic Johnson was forced into a premature retirement from basketball by the threat of contagion, but then did not develop AIDS and survived, another and more sober phase of the crisis began. Monogamy, or at least serial monogamy with safe sex, began to displace free love as the cultural ideal, among both straight and gay people.

The sudden, horrible deaths brought by AIDS led some Christians to interpret the disease as a curse of God. A widely reported (but possibly inaccurate) story quoted Jerry Falwell, a televangelist who founded the Moral Majority political organization and Liberty University, declaring that "AIDS is a lethal judgment of God on the sin of homosexuality and it is also the judgment of God on America for endorsing this vulgar, perverted and reprobate lifestyle."[37] In 1986, Catholic conservative William F. Buckley called (on the op-ed page of the *New York Times*) for tattooing everyone with the HIV virus on the buttocks and forearms, "to protect" drug users and homosexuals.[38] Others argued that such tattoos should be visible to all. According to another Catholic, writing under a pseudonym about her dying brother in 1992, it seemed that "the loss of his immune system is the symbol of the loss of his true spiritual center."[39]

But in the longer term, AIDS contributed to the victory of innocent ecstasy. A holocaust of disease and death, blame and stigma, yielded to rebirth. Gay rights gained a religious affirmation with Tony Kushner's *Angels in America*, a play (really two plays, often performed consecutively) that grew from the AIDS crisis. The logic of innocent ecstasy had always implied that gay sex might be as redemptive as any other ecstatic experience, and *Angels in America* claimed that redemption. Beginning on stage in 1992 in San Francisco and then in New York, *Angels* toured the country in the 1990s and came to the whole nation as an HBO movie in 2003.

At the heart of the play is a man dying of AIDS named Prior Walter, who is the heir of Englishmen (ghostly ancestors appear). Prior has been abandoned by his Jewish lover, Louis. He is visited by the Principality of America, the angel in charge of the United States, who crashes through the ceiling above his sickbed to give him a prophecy to proclaim. This angel wants humanity to stop changing, because human history has drawn God to leave heaven, leaving the angels alone.

Sex is central to the plot of *Angels*. Whenever the angel appears, Walter has an orgasm, although illness had made him impotent. These angels

are hermaphroditic, with eight vaginas and a "bouquet of phalli." Their intercourse creates "protomatter, which fuels the Engine of Creation."[40] But
their happiness was disturbed by humans, who are "Unigenitaled: Female.
Male." As a result of this genital imbalance, humans disrupt the heavenly
balance, causing change, random events, and motion forward in time.

On one visit of the angel to Prior Walter, a Mormon woman who knows
her Bible is with him in his hospital room, and she advises the hero to
seize the angel and to demand a blessing, as Jacob did in Genesis 32.
By wrestling with the angel, Prior Walter wins the right to return the
scroll demanding that history stop to heaven. After he climbs the ladder
and disappears, the Mormon woman and the angel share an orgasm. The
woman's daughter-in-law, recovering from being abandoned by her gay
Mormon husband, leaves New York on an airliner to San Francisco, and
sees the spirits of AIDS victims rising into the atmosphere and joining
hands to heal the ozone layer.[41] Later, at the angel of Bethesda fountain
in Central Park, the Mormon mother predicts that when the Millennium
comes, the Bethesda fountain will flow, and everyone will be bathed
clean.[42] Prior Walter declares, "We won't die secret deaths anymore. The
world only spins forward. We will be citizens. The time has come."[43]

These words proved prophetic. Many attempts were made to stop the
change that *Angels in America* predicted, yet momentum toward gay rights
continued to build. President Clinton's 1993 rule of "Don't ask, don't tell"
for gay members of the military was intended to help gays to serve, but
the rule made discrimination worse by allowing gays to be dismissed
for "telling."[44] Another set of steps forward and back began in New York
City, where schools chancellor Jose Fernandez lost his post in 1993 because of reactions against the condom distribution program he started
and the "Children of the Rainbow" curriculum he introduced.[45] That
curriculum included two books, *Heather Has Two Mommies* (1989) and
Daddy's Roommate (1991), that represented same-sex domestic partners.
In 1994, Republican Senators Jesse Helms and Bob Smith read the entire
text of *Heather* into the Congressional Record as part of their argument
for denying federal aid to any school district that ran programs supporting homosexuality. Their amendment passed the Senate but failed in the
Democratic House.[46] Then Republicans took Congress, and they passed
the 1996 Defense of Marriage Act to forbid the federal government from
granting benefits to same-sex spouses. Meanwhile, popular culture witnessed the success of *Will & Grace*, a sitcom featuring upscale gay men,
that ran from 1998 to 2006. In *Lawrence v. Texas* (2003), the Supreme

Court struck down a Texas law forbidding sodomy, and with that ruling eliminated all state antisodomy laws. Many such laws had been upheld by the Court as recently as 1986.[47]

Sometimes, it seemed that a backlash against gay rights was gaining strength. George W. Bush won re-election against John Kerry in 2004, partly because a referendum on gay marriage brought out the evangelical vote in Ohio.[48] California passed Proposition 8, ending that state's recognition of gay marriage, in 2008, with support from Mormons and Roman Catholics and evangelicals.[49]

But the shift in gay culture from dance clubs and bath houses to life partners was eroding opposition to homosexual rights. Demographics moved toward acceptance: the generation called millennial, born in 1980 and later, proved more likely to oppose abortion than equality for gays.[50] Barack Obama did not support gay marriage in 2008, but his campaign in that year was covered by the first openly gay news anchor on a national television network, Rachel Maddow. For the next few years, she publicized the plight of those driven from the military for being gay, and the policy of "Don't ask, don't tell" was overturned in 2011. In May of 2012, as President Obama campaigned for re-election, Vice President Biden announced his support for gay marriage and forced Obama to admit that he also had "evolved" on the issue. The Supreme Court ruled the Defense of Marriage Act unconstitutional in June of 2013. At the time of that ruling, twelve states sanctioned gay marriage. A year and a half later, in January of 2015, the number had grown to thirty-six states, encompassing seventy percent of the US population.[51] Six months later, *Obergefell v. Rogers* made gay marriage legal in all fifty states.

Although many Christians resisted these changes, some churches contributed to the acceptance of gay equality. In 2003, the Episcopalians of New Hampshire, members of the worldwide Anglican Communion, voted to consecrate Gene Robinson as their bishop, despite the fact that Robinson was living in a sexual relationship with another man. The consecration of Robinson provoked a split by some Episcopal churches in the United States and a threat of secession by evangelical Anglicans in Africa. In 2006, American Episcopalians elected their first female presiding bishop, Katherine Jefferts Schori, who vigorously pursued an agenda of gay equality.[52] Bishop Schori participated in consecrating a female gay bishop in Los Angeles, and she used every legal means to retain control of church buildings and property claimed by conservatives seeking to leave the larger church. Meanwhile, in 2005, the General Synod of the United Church of Christ, the Protestant denomination most directly descended from New England's Puritans, voted to endorse full marriage equality for gays and lesbians.[53] The largest body of Presbyterians accepted gay marriage in 2015, and Methodists seemed likely to follow.

Even the most formidable and conservative Christian institutions that still opposed gay rights were shifting their positions. In the summer of 2013, the recently elected Pope Francis said in an interview that if a gay person "is searching for the Lord and has good will, who am I to judge him?" The pope followed up with a resolution at a Synod of Bishops in 2014, as the Afterword will discuss. In January 2015, the Public Affairs Committee of the Mormon Church announced that Mormons would no longer fight gay marriage in an organized way, as in the campaign for Proposition 8 in 2008.[54]

The cause of gay liberation has also been furthered by opinion leaders with Christian backgrounds who have become spokespeople for innocent ecstasy. Among the most important moments in this history was the coming out of Ellen DeGeneres, which took place in 1997, in the context of a situation comedy centered on Ellen's life as a single woman. DeGeneres was raised a devout Christian Scientist in Louisiana. When her parents divorced, Ellen went to Texas with her mother and stopped participating in the church, but faith remained important to her. "I believe in God," she told *Entertainment Weekly* in 1998. "I think that God is everywhere. Every morning I look outside, and I say, 'Hi God.' Because I think that the trees are God. I think that our whole experience is God."[55] DeGeneres made her first hit as a comedian with a routine about a phone call with God. This routine, developed after a female lover died in an automobile accident in 1980, resulted in her being the first female comedian called to sit next to Johnny Carson on the *Tonight Show* couch. She began to host a daily talk show in September of 2003. By the spring of 2014, DeGeneres was regarded as a safe choice to host the Academy Awards, a relief from the edgier humor of *Family Guy* cartoonist Seth McFarlane, who had hosted in 2013.

Ellen's image of youthful, innocent good humor helped to make being gay acceptable everywhere. On the other hand, Ellen gives no sexual advice, nor does her show feature sex or relationship experts. Her studio audience is overwhelmingly female, but her clothing, dancing, overall message and persona are almost asexual.

Meanwhile, in the second decade of the twenty-first century, the role of sex advisor to the nation, once held by figures like Abigail Van Buren and Ann Landers, who provided no physical counseling, and then by the more specific Dr. Ruth Westheimer, has passed to a gay man, Dan Savage, who answers questions for gays and straights. Born in 1964 as one of four children of a Chicago policeman (and Catholic deacon) in an Irish-American family, Savage served as an altar boy and started high school in a Roman Catholic seminary. He left the seminary when he discovered his sexual orientation and came out as gay, in the early years of the AIDS crisis. Although he became an agnostic with regard to God, he is still inclined to cross himself on airplanes and seeks to commune with the spirit of his dead mother in Roman Catholic churches.[56] His deep familiarity with Catholicism has led him to use Christian arguments against opponents of gay rights. In one of his books, *American Savage* (2013), he pictured Jesus urging an intolerant follower to "go worship Thor or Quetzalcoatl or Isis" and to stop calling himself a Christian.[57] Later in the same book, he described hosting Brian Brown, head of the National Organization for Marriage (an organization dedicated to fighting gay marriage), at dinner in his home with his male spouse and their child. Savage ended that night offering to send Brown tickets for the hit musical *The Book of Mormon*, so that Brown might see that he stands "on the wrong side of history."[58]

The popularity of Dan Savage and of *The Book of Mormon* (which has been running on Broadway since 2011) both show the extent to which the ethic of innocent ecstasy has been extended to include formerly marginal sexual and religious positions and practices. During the 2012 presidential campaign, Savage damaged the ability of Republican Rick Santorum to use the Internet by promoting an online association of the word "santorum" with the mix of lubrication, sperm, and fecal matter that commonly results from anal intercourse. Establishing this definition on search engines seemed to Savage a fitting punishment for Santorum likening gay marriage to marriage between men and dogs. For most of Savage's readers and followers, doing this to Santorum's name did not seem to transgress any boundary of taste. At the same time, *The Book of Mormon* featured humor regarding AIDS in Africa, female genital mutilation, and being cast into Hell for homosexuality—remarkable subjects for a Broadway musical comedy—alongside more gentle mockery of Mormon missionaries.

As an extension of this revolution in sensibilities, transgendered people broke into televised situation comedy, a stronghold of normalcy, with *Transparent* in 2014. In *Orange Is the New Black*, transgendered actress Laverne Cox had already become a dramatic costar playing a prisoner in 2013, and Cox was poised in 2015 to star in her own series as a heroic lawyer. On April 24, 2015, 16.8 million Americans watched a news program on a

Friday night to see 1976 Olympic decathlon gold medalist Bruce Jenner an-
nounce his own transition from male to female, at age sixty-five.[59]

By 2015, the right of anyone, regardless of sexual orientation, to seek
and to speak out for innocent ecstasy was firmly established in the culture
of the United States.

Innocence and Recovery

The freedom from guilt celebrated in innocent ecstasy has always resulted
from redemption. Unlike the innocence ascribed by some to infancy or to
Eden, prior to the judgment of good and evil and the discovery of nakedness
and gender roles, American innocence has been attained through liberation
from sin. Ecstatic experience has been both the means of that recovery and a
capacity celebrated and increased after recovery.

No one has been more influential in spreading a gospel of recovery
than Oprah Winfrey, who preceded Ellen DeGeneres as the leading voice
in afternoon television talk. In the television episode in which Ellen's
character came out as lesbian in 1997, Oprah played Ellen's therapist.
Winfrey had an intensely religious childhood, speaking in Baptist
churches of Mississippi from the age of three, when she lived on her
grandmother's farm. After moving at twelve to the home of her father,
Vernon, in Nashville, she recited James Weldon Johnson's sermons in
verse, "God's Trombones," in "churches all over the city."[60] Then, while
living with her mother in Milwaukee, she was sexually abused by male
relatives. She responded by acting out with sex and drugs, and gave birth
at age fourteen to a premature baby boy who did not survive. She recovered back in Nashville with her father, whose strictness she credited with
saving her life.[61] Winfrey went to college in Tennessee, became a television news anchor, then moved to Chicago to host a talk show in 1984. Her
profile was raised by her role as Sofia, for which she was nominated for
an Oscar, in the Steven Spielberg film *The Color Purple* (1985), based on
Alice Walker's Pulitzer Prize-winning novel of 1982.

The Color Purple revolves around recovery from abuse and redemption
through sex. It is an epistolary novel, beginning with letters to God from
the main character, a black woman named Celie, who rises from an abu-
sive marriage to peace and prosperity and family unity. The first element
of redemption in *The Color Purple* is Celie's relationship with Shug Avery,
a glamorous singer. Shug teaches Celie about sex and God at the same
moment in the novel.

Shug tells Celie (in the same language that Ellen DeGeneres would later use with *Entertainment Weekly*), "I believe God is everything."[62] She goes on to say (again as Ellen said, perhaps with *The Color Purple* as her source), "My first step from the old white man [as God] was trees." Shug identifies God with other elements: "Then air. Then birds. Then other people." A crucial step was taken, Shug said, when she felt that she herself was really "part of everything." That moment gave her a sexual feeling: "sort of like you know what, she say, grinning and rubbing high up on my thigh." When Celie protests her sexual touch, Shug assures her that "God love all them feelings. That's some of the best stuff God did." Celie wonders, "God don't think it dirty?" But Shug replies, "Naw ... God made it." The idea of original sin making sex animalistic or shameful or sick was dismissed as an invention of "man" who "corrupt everything."[63] Celia should "just relax, go with everything that's going, and praise God by liking what you like."

For Oprah Winfrey, *The Color Purple* was a revelatory text.[64] When she heard that it would be made into a movie, she became obsessed with playing Sofia, a big woman who fought back against her husband when he tried to beat her.[65] Winfrey had never acted, but she went to an audition, waited for months, then called a casting agent who dismissed her chances of getting the role because Alfre Woodard, "a real actress," was also auditioning. Thinking that she might be too fat for movies, Winfrey went to a "fat farm" to lose weight, praying that she would either get the role or become reconciled to seeing someone else get it. At the moment she found peace, imagining herself happy to watch Alfre Woodard playing Sofia, Steven Spielberg called. Reflecting on this twenty years later, Winfrey said that it taught her the spiritual principle of surrender, to do everything one can for a goal and then to let go.[66]

Oprah, Ellen, and Madonna—the single-named women who did so much to shape American attitudes toward religion, spirituality, and sex around the turn of the twenty-first century—each had a story of abuse and recovery. Madonna was raped shortly after she had come to the city to dance in 1978. That incident, which happened when she was nineteen, marked the end of the extremely difficult childhood in which she lost her mother to cancer at five years old, then had to fight her father to leave Michigan for New York without finishing college.[67] In 2005, Ellen DeGeneres revealed that after her father and mother divorced when she was in her teens, and she left her Christian Science church and hometown in Louisiana and moved with her mother and stepfather to Texas, her stepfather abused her. She recalled having to kick out a window in her bedroom and sleep all night in a hospital to escape.[68] So Ellen lost her biological father and her first religion, as Madonna and Oprah had lost their mothers, and as Oprah had lost her baby. All three women had lost at least some of their sexual innocence to abuse and assault in their teens. But all of them recovered to affirm their sexuality and to become guides, examples, and inspirations.

Redeeming Dark Sex: Angels, Witches, Vampires, and Sadomasochists

Beyond personal recovery, the American ethic of sexual pleasure expanded to encompass the redemption of figures and actions associated with cosmic, spiritual evil. This meant overcoming not just the effects of original sin on humans, but the causes of sin itself. As has been said earlier, in Tony Kushner's play *Angels in America*, disorder arose with "unigenitaled" humanity, according to the polymorphous angels. Healing began when angels and humans came together. And that play was one of many examples of an angel craze that ran from the 1930s through the turn of the century. The craze often included stories of humans having sex with angels.

Sex between angels and humans has been regarded as taboo through most of Western history. In Genesis 6, the Flood story begins with a statement that "the sons of God saw that they [the daughters of men] were fair; and they took wives for themselves of all that they chose." The chapter implies that these marriages resulted in the birth of "Nephilim," or "fallen ones," and that these children of angels and humans filled the earth with wickedness and so brought on the Flood.

Theologians argued. Many, including Augustine, John Calvin, and Jonathan Edwards, insisted that the "daughters of men" in Genesis were descendants of the murderous Cain, while the *bene elohim* or "sons of God" were sons of Adam's good son Seth, so that sex between good and evil branches of humanity rather than between angels and humans was the problem.[69] St. Thomas Aquinas reasoned that angels had no bodies and could not have sex.[70] Still, the phrase *bene elohim* normally meant angels in the Bible, for example, in Job 1:6. Artists of the Renaissance loved to portray angels with human bodies, as did Victorians. Swedish mystic Emanuel Swedenborg wrote accounts of meeting angels that helped to humanize the "sons of God."[71] Books about visits to heaven became popular in the late nineteenth century and continued the trend.

A breakthrough occurred in 1923, the dawn of the era of innocent ecstasy. The sculptor Daniel Chester French, creator of the Minuteman statue at Concord and the Lincoln of the Lincoln Memorial, made a genitally complete male angel over six feet tall, lifting a nude human female by one arm as his hand cradled her head. French called this white marble group "The Sons of God Saw the Daughters of Men That They Were Fair," quoting the King James Version translation of Genesis 6:2.[72] It is an image of angelic rape, and it stands today at the center of the Corcoran Gallery in Washington, DC.

Over the ensuing eight decades, plays and movies with titles like *I Married an Angel, The Bishop's Wife, Down to Earth, Barbarella, Date with an Angel, Michael*, and *City of Angels* (the last based on the German *Wings of Desire*) played with the theme of romantic attraction, and sometimes sex, between angels and humans. Even *Touched by an Angel*, the theologically careful, wildly popular television series that was broadcast from 1994 to 2003, once (on May 6, 2001) featured a story in which the angel Monica was tempted by sex with a human male. Songs by artists from Madonna to the Goo Goo Dolls, Sarah McLachlan, and U2 celebrated love between humans and angels.[73] As the ethic of innocent ecstasy grew in strength, sex between angels and humans turned out not to result in disasters like Noah's Flood, but rather in redemption.

In several novels—John Updike's *The Witches of Eastwick* (1984), Andrew Greeley's *Angel Fire* (1988), and Anne Rice's *Memnoch the Devil* (1995)—Satan himself was redeemed. Updike (a theologically preoccupied Episcopalian) brought Satan to Rhode Island to seduce a group of three women who were practicing black magic. In Andrew Greeley's novel of angelic sex, Lucifer figured as the deceased, misunderstood husband of Gabriella (the biblical Gabriel), who defended Lucifer as she had sex with a human scientist to heal his perspective on women. Anne Rice (a Catholic born in New Orleans) portrayed the fall of Satan as the result of his attraction to a woman. Rice's Devil was not destructive; he ruled the land of the dead as a school where people could learn to understand and to forgive. Each of these novels celebrated sexual ecstasy as a transformative experience, both for humans and for angels.[74]

In the age of innocent ecstasy, witches could also be redeemed through sex. Witches became witches by copulating with the cold phallus of Satan, according to the most famous handbook for witch hunters, the *Malleus Maleficarum* (or "Hammer of Evil-Doing Women"), which was written by Dominican fathers Heinrich Kramer and Jacob Sprenger in 1486.[75] But in the 1980s and 1990s, witches became proto-feminists. American witches gathered, not in secret covens but in public groups such as the Covenant of the Goddess and the Covenant of Unitarian Universalist Pagans. They met at festivals to dance around bonfires, and they ran stores selling books and candles and ritual equipment. Acceptance of sex as redemptive was critical to this positive approach to witchcraft. American witches including Zsuzsanna Budapest, Starhawk, and Luisah Teish criticized traditional Christianity for its association of women and sex with original sin and integrated erotic energy into their rituals. The positive sexual message about witches appeared in popular culture between 1998 and 2006 in *Charmed*, a television series that focused on young and beautiful sisters who discover that their deceased mother was a witch and that they have inherited her powers.

Meanwhile, from 1997 to 2003, a show called *Buffy the Vampire Slayer* featured another young woman with supernatural powers. In Buffy's case, the male vampires she fought (one appropriately named Angel, another named Spike) also fought for her love. Fallen angels, witches, and vampires all could be redeemed by ecstatic experience.

Anne Rice became famous writing about vampires before she wrote about angels, and she also contributed to the redemption of vampires through sex. Medieval vampires were "bloated, red-faced" monsters.[76] In *Dracula* by Bram Stoker from 1897, and in the movies of the 1930s, vampires became suave and handsome, but they still did not promise sexual pleasure. But for Anne Rice, in novels about the vampire Lestat and his family and friends, vampirism became erotic. Still, Rice's vampires remained dark, not innocent, and their human partners did not lead them.

With the *Twilight* series of four vampire novels for young adults by Stephenie Meyer, published between 2005 and 2008, vampires came into daylight, where they began to sparkle like diamonds (this was Meyer's take on the effect of sunlight on vampire skin). The sexual attraction between vampire Edward Cullen and human Bella Swan was innocent, and it was also unconsummated for three of the four books. Meyer is a Mormon, and some liberal critics accused her of harming young readers by putting them under a spell of "abstinence porn."[77] Her books and the movies made from them presented their young lovers as exponents of innocent ecstasy.

The *Twilight* series also had an American focus on original sin and redemption. Before meeting the vampire, the heroine was not only a virgin but also a girl alienated from the physical world, uncomfortable in her body, dangerously clumsy in high school gym, and incapable of dancing. Because of the sweet smell of her blood, she became the medium of temptation who led the hero to transgress boundaries. The first book began with a quote of God's warning to Adam, before the creation of Eve, in Genesis 2:17: "But of the tree of the knowledge of good and evil, thou shalt not eat of it; for in the day that thou eatest thereof thou shalt surely die." When Bella was seated next to Edward in Biology, she noticed him becoming tense, and she thought: "It couldn't have anything to do with me. He didn't know me from Eve." The cover of the first novel bore a picture of two female hands cupping a red apple. By the end of the fourth novel, Bella has become a new Eve, the founding mother of a new race formed by vampires and humans.

Although sex was never explicitly described in the *Twilight* novels, and only briefly evoked in the movies, all two thousand pages of the four books amounted to an account of the heroine's loss of virginity. Bella intrigued Edward because he could not read her thoughts, which made her different from other humans. On the last page of the fourth book, she has learned to let him read her by making a bubble of energy around them.

Like all compelling fictions in American popular culture, *Twilight* generated fan fiction, alternative stories created by readers who shared with each other. The most commercially significant fan fiction of all history to date, *Fifty Shades of Grey*, emerged in 2009 among *Twilight* readers as an alternative story about Bella and Edward called *Master of the Universe*, written by an Englishwoman named Erika Leonard who had worked on a TV biography of Madonna. Leonard's story evolved after many readings and reviews and rewritings, and then a final scrubbing of all explicit links to *Twilight*, into *Fifty Shades of Grey*, which was published under the pseudonym E. L. James in 2011.[78] In *Fifty Shades*, the original power dynamic of the virginal woman transforming the powerful man remained, but the vampire had become a billionaire and the high school senior a woman about to graduate from college. The setting of the US Pacific Northwest carried over from *Twilight*, as did the heroine's response of feeling something like an electric shock from any contact with the hands of the male.

More significantly, vampirism had become sexual sadomasochism. At the start of relations with her hero, Christian Grey, the heroine Anastasia Steele was asked to accept a contract to live as his submissive—to do any sex he wanted, to kneel naked in his lair, to accept handcuffs and blindfolds, spankings and whippings. Where Bella had awakened covered in bruises after her first (never described) night with her vampire Edward, Ana was described in great detail being dominated and possessed, many times being brought to orgasm, and being marked by her billionaire's leather strap.

At the end of *Fifty Shades of Grey*, Ana refused the contract. In the second novel, *Fifty Shades Darker*, she found herself back in Grey's realm. She ultimately brought him into a life beyond compulsions in the third book, *Fifty Shades Freed*. The need for recovery from abuse—in this case Christian Grey's history of being abused, as the son of a "crack whore" who had been abandoned, then adopted, and later made into a male sub- missive by an older woman—gave Anastasia the same role in the redemp- tive arc of *Fifty Shades* that Bella had in *Twilight*. And as in *Twilight*, the triumph of the heroine of *Fifty Shades* came through bearing a child of the dominant male.

This theme of innocence triumphant helped to make *Fifty Shades of Grey* the first mainstream pornographic novel, sold in drugstores and supermarkets. Its appearance in those settings formed part of a process that included the marketing of vibrators and lubricants, and of sexual medicines like Viagra and Cialis, on the shelves of the same stores. It was not the first pornography written by and for women—Anne Rice had published a quartet of fantasies beginning with *The Claiming of Sleeping Beauty* in 1983, and Anais Nin had published *Delta of Venus* in 1977 and *Little Birds* in 1979. But *Fifty Shades* was the first fiction written to arouse sexual desire in women that conformed to a particular version of innocent ecstasy, the male redeemed by the innocent female.

Years before *Fifty Shades*, evangelical Christians had already wit- nessed some attempts to integrate sadomasochism (without using that name) into their spiritual lives. A movement called Christian Domestic Discipline, focused on submission to spanking as a spiritual experi- ence for women, blossomed on Yahoo groups in 2006. Leah Kelley, a Kentucky housewife, launched a career publishing advice and fictions focused on the theme of Christian women being spanked by Christian husbands.[79] In Seattle, the homeland of *Twilight* and *Fifty Shades*, found- ing Pastor Mark Driscoll of the Mars Hill megachurch and his wife, Grace Driscoll, preached a gospel of biblical manhood and womanhood that stressed the need for male leadership. Driscoll's abrasive personal- ity eventually led to the dissolution of his church in December of 2014, but Mars Hill did not dissolve before the book of sexual advice written by the Driscolls, *Real Marriage*, had a good run on the bestseller lists.[80]

The Driscolls's book allowed for sex toys and role playing, anal sex, oral sex, and masturbation as means of maintaining sex in marriage.[81] Both advocates of Christian Domestic Discipline and the Driscolls stressed acceptance of male authority as a way of overcoming the "sin nature" of women after the Fall.

Meanwhile, the liberating aspect of innocent ecstasy was still expanding its influence. Addressing women raised in the black evangelical world, journalist Cora Daniels wrote a chapter, "Let's Pray for Sexually Active Daughters," in a book called *Impolite Conversations* (2014). Daniels recalled the advice of Dr. Jocelyn Elders, President Clinton's Surgeon General, who lost her job for advocating masturbation.[82] Kathryn Lofton, a professor at Yale Divinity School and biographer of Oprah Winfrey, concluded a volume on *Queer Christianities: Lived Religion in Transgressive Forms* (2015), by asking, "Is it possible to be Christian *without* being queer?" Her answer was no, but that queer Christians must not become complacent. "Christianity could be queer, but only and ever if it is a protest and not the rule."[83]

At the Grammy Awards show of 2015, the durable Madonna was still acting out redemption through sex. Dancing with a crew of men in horns and bull masks, costumes denounced by some evangelicals as Satanic symbols, she sang "Living for Love," about a woman who was taken to heaven, then betrayed by a lover who "fired a shot in my heart." She was still determined to live for love, asking God to forgive her and to lift her up. At the end of the video, Madonna had this passage from Nietzsche displayed: "Man is the cruelest animal. At tragedies, bullfights, and crucifixions he has so far felt best on earth; and when he invented hell for himself, behold, that was his very heaven."

The flag of innocent ecstasy waved more boldly, over the body and over more dimensions of sex and of life, in 2015 than it had in 1985.

Afterword: Projecting the Future

THE FIRST DECADES of the twenty-first century have seen an apocalyptic mood in American culture. With regard to sex and religion, the real outlook has remained bright. Advances in sex and gender equality, freedom, safety, and pleasure are proceeding, but these are frequently missed because of a pessimism that pervades all public discourse.

The millennial generation, composed of those born after 1980, has adopted a new pattern of mating that many writers call "hookup culture." Often presented in negative terms, this new way of socializing is a natural outgrowth of more egalitarian gender roles and other social changes, including the rise of innocent ecstasy. Instead of courting by visiting a potential girlfriend at her home and meeting her parents, or by dating as couples, millennials have grown up "hanging out," and sometimes talking about sex, in mixed-sex groups of friends who are not sexual or romantic partners. This pattern may have been initiated or encouraged by higher rates of attendance at college and by mixed-sex dormitories, but it now begins in middle school or before. Electronic social media has enabled millennials to hang out with their mixed-sex circles of friends even while staying at home. Growing up with the Internet, millennials have often seen and shared sexual images with each other without having to go to a store and purchase pornography. Electronics have become increasingly important for singles seeking prospects. According to *Modern Romance*, a recent book by millennial comedian Aziz Ansari and NYU sociologist Eric Klinenberg, online dating sites now result in more marriages than introductions by friends, meetings in school, and meetings at work *combined*.[1]

When millennials seek sexual partners in person, they tend to go with friends into larger contexts like parties, dances, or concerts and to try for some sexual interaction as a spontaneous experiment, not as the deliberate step in the direction of marriage that courtship and dating were. The sexual "hookup" may take place between two old friends, inspired by the new context, or with a stranger, under the cover provided by the presence of friends. Rarely does the first hookup proceed to genital intercourse, though it usually includes intimate kissing and may involve orgasm or oral sex.

Hookup culture has been denounced in many sociological studies, such as *Sex and the Soul: Juggling Sexuality, Spirituality, Romance, and Religion on America's College Campuses* by Donna Freitas (2008) and *Lost in Transition: The Dark Side of Emerging Adulthood* by Christian Smith (2011). One of America's greatest novelists, Tom Wolfe, portrayed the damage that this culture inflicts on some young women in vivid, thankfully fictional, detail in *I Am Charlotte Simmons* (2004). As a college professor, I have been filled with disapproval as a witness to the theme parties and dances that my own college has sponsored. At such parties, millennials gather in the dark and grind against each other (dancing becomes twerking, an upright version of a lap dance) while hip-hop music blasts from speakers. To prepare to hook up, students too young to drink legally in public often "pregame," or binge drink with their friends in their rooms. With inhibitions reduced and misbehavior excused by intoxication, a culture of acquaintance rape has become the dark side of the hookup scene.

According to Donna Freitas, who teaches at Boston University but who studied sexual and religious attitudes at seven other colleges for the results reported in *Sex and the Soul*, this hookup culture prevails at all colleges other than those with explicitly evangelical identities.[2] Freitas says that hookups foster sex but prevent romance. She recommends that parents and students looking at colleges ask schools to develop explicit programs to discuss the spiritual dimensions of sex.[3] For Christian Smith, a sociologist at Notre Dame, the millennials seem to be living out the dark side of a sexual revolution their parents began. Smith found that, based on a "nationally representative survey" of more than three thousand people over ten years, an average unmarried young American had about three oral sex partners and three partners for genital intercourse before age twenty-three.[4] He concluded that, although most of the young people he and his colleagues interviewed said that they were happy with their sexual experiences, many were not: *"not far beneath the surface appearance of happy, liberated emerging adult sexual adventure and pleasure lies a world of hurt, insecurity, confusion, inequality, shame, and regret"*[5] (italics his).

But it may be well to remember that date rape also happened in the dating culture, when young couples went alone in a car to deserted country roads and drive-in theaters. Even courtship at the home of parents was not without sexual activity, because the parents often discreetly withdrew for a time to let the young couple have privacy. In colonial New England, courting couples bundled together overnight in bed.

The latest way of socializing has its advantages. Probably, more short-term sexual partners and more sexual activity result from hookup culture, but there may be fewer cases of young women strung along for months or years as steady dates by young men with no intention of marrying them. Females have more chance to take the initiative at today's dark parties than they had at traditional dances, or when they had to wait at home for someone to call for a date.[6] Both males and females with social anxiety have a better chance of enjoying themselves by "hanging out" and attending parties in groups than they had under the cultures of courtship and dating. Friendships between males and females were once thought to be impossible—the premise of *When Harry Met Sally* (1989), representing baby boomers who had graduated from college in 1977—but such friendships actually flourish among those groups who "hang out" and find sex partners in the maligned "hookup culture." Friendships between gay and straight people, which were almost unthinkable during the sexual revolution of the 1960s and 1970s, are normal on college campuses and among high school students today.

In fact, it has sometimes been suggested that the hookup culture itself may represent the influence of gays on straight behavior. Gay men have long found sexual partners in that way. A telephone app for gay men seeking hookups, Grindr, came before its straight (and more detailed) counterpart, Tinder. Gay influence may have also appeared in the increasing acceptance of oral and anal sex and even in clothing styles. Leggings and sweatshirts, a key fashion element for women from the 1990s through the present, began with gay men in tights in Greenwich Village in the 1980s.

The gay revolution continues, and Christians are engaging with it in several ways. In 2013, Pope Francis, returning from his first trip as pope, famously remarked to a journalist that if a gay person was sincerely seeking God, even if that person was a priest, "Who am I to judge?"[7] This brought consternation in conservative Catholic circles, and a quip from a talk show host that the pope must have had quite a time in Brazil, but it also reflected a deeper tendency. At a synod of bishops in 2014, the pope

2 votes short

pushed for a statement that welcomed gay people to take part in Catholic life.[8] The draft first proposed won 118 of 180 ballots, failing by two votes to get the two thirds needed for passage, but Pope Francis said that he would try again at the next synod.[9]

Evangelicals have also taken new positions on gays. In May of 2015, the Intervarsity Press, a major evangelical publishing house, published *Redeeming Sex: Naked Conversations about Sexuality and Spirituality*, by Debra Hirsch, an Australian-American evangelist. Hirsch identified herself at the beginning of the book as someone who once lived as a lesbian, though she has been married to a man for twenty years. She presented sexuality and spirituality as parallel efforts to seek intimacy, with sexuality directed toward other people and spirituality to God. Like Pope Francis, Hirsch urged Christians to respond to homosexuals in the same way they would to anyone else. She tried to reset the whole discussion of sex, teaching that greed and hatred were far more serious sins than sexual misbehavior, and pointing out that some evangelicals are participating in the gay marriage movement. A group called the Gay Christian Network (GCN), founded in Raleigh, North Carolina, in 2001, accommodates both evangelicals who believe that gay Christians should be celibate and those who think that they can live in monogamous relationships.[10]

What seems increasingly marginal is "reparative therapy," or the attempt to turn gays straight, an approach rejected both by Debra Hirsch and by the GCN. In 2009, the governing council of the American Psychological Association voted 125 to 4 to reject treatments attempting to cure homosexuality.[11] In 2013, Exodus International, founded in 1976 and for decades the largest organization providing Christian treatment attempting to help gay people become heterosexuals, issued an apology and ended its operations.[12] In 2011, presidential candidate Michelle Bachmann's campaign was derailed in part by the revelation that her husband provided such therapy,[13] and by 2015, President Obama was responding to a petition by urging that reparative therapy for minors be banned.[14]

There are reactionaries who dissent. In *Saving Sex* (2015), scholar Amy DeRogatis highlights a 1999 book, *Holy Sex*, that identifies a biological basis for reparative therapy by claiming that any sexual misbehavior, including homosexuality, can result in demonic possession of genetic material, so that demons pass into new generations of people and remain, causing further sin, until they are exorcised. DeRogatis notes, however, that the claims of *Holy Sex* are "extreme and would be rejected by most readers of mainstream evangelical sex manuals."[15]

Even the macho realm of hip-hop by African-American men is being invaded by gay activism. One example is an out gay hip-hop artist, Fly Young Red, who was born Franklin Freeman Randall in 1991 and raised in Southern California as an active Baptist. Now based in Houston, Texas, Fly Young Red appears in gay clubs and released a single, "Throw That Boy Pussy," in 2014 that drew more than a million views on YouTube.[16] "Throw That Boy Pussy" features male dancers making their buttocks bounce in tight shorts and leggings while Fly Young Red raps about what he will do to these body parts; the song belongs to a genre sometimes called the "twerk anthem." On the other hand, the same young rapper has a video called "U Don't Want It" that affirms the dignity of gay and trans identities. He has also done a remix video of Taylor Swift's 2014 affirmation of life despite failure and rejection, "Shake It Off." Although some of the comments by Swift fans reject the effort, it seems clear that Fly Young Red is trying to continue an evangelistic mission that continues to distinguish American popular music.

Ever since rock and roll broke into the scene in the 1950s, American popular music has presented itself as a social and cultural movement. The very existence of the Rock and Roll Hall of Fame testifies to this. Unlike the writers of the Great American Songbook in the 1930s and 1940s, rock musicians often saw themselves and were generally seen by others as the voices of a generation.

Often rock music as a movement has seemed exclusive, in terms of musical style and in terms of sex, gender, and race. Female rockers were not welcome at first, misogyny was often prominent in rock lyrics, and no women were among the first ten inductees to the Hall of Fame. This has decisively changed in the last decades. Gay rockers continue to be marginalized, although there has been progress, as the career trajectories of Elton John, George Michael, K. D. Lang, and Melissa Etheridge attest. Black musicians, despite the role of gospel music in the birth of rock and the continuing prominence of African-American artists, have often been relegated to a separate category, such as "soul" or "rhythm and blues," primarily on the basis of race. When MTV began, it did not play black artists. That exclusion was defended on the grounds that MTV was dedicated to rock. One of the achievements of Michael Jackson's life was to break down this barrier, and that happened as recently as the 1980s.

Today, a merger of rock and hip-hop or rap music is taking place, and collaborations of white and black artists accompany this. The black rapper Snoop Dogg and the white rocker Katy Perry (who began as the Christian rocker Katy Hudson) collaborated in 2011 on the video "California Gurls," a new take on the Beach Boys classic. Madonna invited Trinidadian-American rapper Nicky Minaj, along with the Tamil rapper M.I.A., to take part in her 2012 Super Bowl show. Jay Z, the rapper who also calls himself J-Hova or Jehovah and who is married to Beyoncé, worked with Justin Timberlake on "Holy Grail" in 2013.

A rise of black artists and of rap music has also appeared on the business side of music. In a *New York Times* interview, Snoop Dogg said that when he started in 1992, ten percent of the popular music business was run by blacks, but "in 2015, it's 95 percent black-driven."[17] A fictional account of this development, a television series called *Empire*, loosely based on the life of Jay-Z, was the most popular broadcast television drama of spring 2015.[18]

Because American popular music sees itself as a movement with a mission but is always also a business, it runs the constant danger of losing its soul. In recent years, the world of rap and rock music has sometimes seemed crass, deliberately celebrating greed and physical pleasure. The Billboard Award winner for Best Rap Song of 2014, "My Anaconda" by Nicky Minaj, featured many women shaking their buttocks to the hook "My anaconda don't want none unless you got buns, hun," with a chorus of "Oh my gosh, look at her butt." Its message was that by having a good butt and being good at having sex, the singer found men (wealthy drug dealers) who dressed her in "Alexander McQueen" and in "Balmain," with outfits by both designers featured as their names were mentioned. In April of 2015, Nicky Minaj performed seven songs at a bar mitzvah in the Hotel Pierre in New York, where she also gave a talk urging the girls to never let a man take care of them, but to be their own women.[19] Affirming that women also can be crass about butts (as Fly Young Red did for gay men) seems to have become part of the hip-hop mantra to "keep it real."

Rap, pop, rock, and country music have all come together in the career of Taylor Swift, who at age twenty-five (in 2015) had already been under contract to record companies for ten years, since her 2005 debut at the Bluebird Café in Nashville. Swift's 2015 video, "Bad Blood," featured one male black rapper, Kendrick Lamar, and a troupe of sixteen female singers, models, and actresses. In late May of 2015, she was named by *Forbes* magazine as number sixty-four among the world's most powerful women.

Taylor Swift attained her first popularity as a teenager singing about her innocence, especially in "You Belong with Me," a narrative song about a female nerd who has always been friends with her male neighbor, a football star who dates the head cheerleader. Tall and thin, with a striking face and sharply shaped eyes, Swift can play awkward but beautiful and sincere very well, as in the 2014 video "Shake It Off." Her physical and emotional persona in many videos resembles that of Bella Swan, the character described by Stephanie Meyer in the *Twilight* books, and Anastasia Steel, the heroine modeled on Bella for *Fifty Shades of Grey*.

But Swift can also do harder images, such as the crazed woman destroying a boyfriend's car with a golf club in "Blank Space" (2014). She is known for revenge songs about males who have disappointed her, particularly "Dear John" (2010), publicly aimed at singer John Mayer. Unlike the fictional Bella Swan and Anastasia Steel, the real Taylor Swift has more than one persona, and does not live to redeem a man.

With the image projected by Swift, and the images of other young female stars like Nicky Minaj, Iggy Azalea, and M.I.A., and of males like Fly Young Red and Bruno Mars, innocent ecstasy has reached one logical conclusion. Where Madonna constantly worked, and continues to work, to overcome her sense of original sin, these millennials sing and dance as though they have never heard of any connection between original sin and sex. And in fact, most of their generation has not. They have heard the story of Adam and Eve, but they were not taught that the sin of Eden had a special effect on the sexual root of humanity, so that all children are conceived in a disordered lust that passes down corruption to all generations. Madonna's most direct successor in this generation, Lady Gaga, is an exception because of the deeply Catholic background with which she struggles and which she visibly uses in many videos, but for most millennials the battle of innocent ecstasy is over.

But Americans still feel that a message of liberation needs to be sent to the world. An American sense of mission appears in the conviction of many that sex must be improved, made more free and more perfect. Today, tens of thousands of evangelicals and medical missionaries from the United States are at work in many nations of Africa,[20] campaigning both for and against tolerance of homosexuality, working with AIDS victims and orphans, working against female genital mutilation, and trying to gain converts for religions like Mormonism and Pentecostal Christianity.

The enduring American missionary attitude with regard to sex appears in the work of Annie Sprinkle (born Ellen Steinberg in 1954), and in the reactions of students to her work over the last decades. In the 1980s, Annie Sprinkle was stripping as performance art. At the show's climax, she would insert a speculum into her vagina and invite each person in the audience to come to the edge of the stage and see her cervix. It was a strip without the "tease," a taking of power from those who gazed. Sprinkle also worked directly with women for decades in "Sluts and Goddesses Workshops," and produced an hour-long video version, *Sluts and Goddesses*, in 1992. The workshops were feminist analogs to the "Total Woman" courses that Marabel Morgan did in church basements in the 1970s. In the video, Sprinkle filmed herself having (with the aid of three of her female "transformation facilitators") a five-minute orgasm. The video and the workshops ended with all participants lying in a circle and bringing themselves to orgasms.

When I first used Annie Sprinkle's *Sluts and Goddesses* video in my classes on Sexuality and Religion in the 1990s, it made some students angry ("She isn't even pretty! I hate Annie Sprinkle!") and others very uncomfortable. But in recent years, my millennial students have responded with less shock and more good-humored appreciation. They asked what Annie Sprinkle was doing now, and we discovered that she is still working, now promoting something called EcoSex that encourages a sexual approach to environmental activism. For her, sexual liberation is still a mission.

The difference between American and other attitudes toward sex appears in the contrasting moods of recent English and American documentaries on the sex industry, *The Truth about Webcam Girls* (BBC, 2014) and *Kink* (Franco, 2014). In the English documentary, three young women who answer webcam calls and perform on camera express matter-of-fact attitudes about their work, their hopes, and their problems. None of them sees sex work as therapy or transformation. On the other hand, in *Kink*, which focuses on people working in a San Francisco company that makes pornographic films and fulfills individual fantasies, those who speak believe strongly in what they are doing. They are not simply making a living; they are exploring their spiritual capacities and helping others to do likewise. Perhaps the more extreme actions performed in *Kink*, using harnesses and sex machines, as opposed to the mundane masturbation and display in *Webcam Girls*, make part of the difference, but the contrast of attitudes also seems to grow out of the different sexual ethics of the United Kingdom and the United States.

Another video on the sex industry, *Hot Girls Wanted*, made by Jill Bauer and Ronna Gradus, premiered at the Sundance Film Festival in 2015. In interviews, Bauer and Gradus presented themselves as crusading investigative journalists.[21] They have discovered the new root of the pornographic film industry, in Craigslist ads by entrepreneurial young men promising free flights to Miami to eighteen- and nineteen-year-old girls who have never been on an airplane, who want to leave their towns, and who see nothing wrong with getting paid to have sex that they would be having anyway for nothing.

With an endless supply of girls turning eighteen and an endless appetite for fresh films on the Internet, Bauer and Gradus see this as a chronic social problem. They make the point that girls of eighteen have always done foolish things, but that making pornographic films may be harder to recover from than most. After a year or two the girls are cast aside by the filmmakers, who need new "amateur" talent to market. In a world where human trafficking and sexual slavery are rampant, the Internet porn industry may not seem seriously criminal, but it raises serious ethical issues.

The history that produced and supports the ethic of innocent ecstasy also made the morality of sex work and of pornography problematic. Margaret Sanger (1879–1966), the founder of Planned Parenthood, advocated for women's sexual pleasure and birth control as aspects of a *cure* for prostitution.[22] Until the purity crusades of the early twentieth century, prostitution was legal all over the United States. The same feminists and Christian organizations that succeeded in passing constitutional amendments allowing women to vote and prohibiting alcohol also passed laws raising the age of consent for sexual intercourse from ten (where it stood in English common law and in the United States in the 1880s) and banning prostitution.

Pornography was also tightly controlled. The Comstock Law of 1873 kept sexually explicit materials, including instructions on sex and contraception, out of the US mail into the third quarter of the twentieth century. When *Playboy* magazine first appeared, nudes had no genitals. Even today, travelers notice a greater prevalence of nudity on European television and on European beaches than in the United States. A limitation of innocent ecstasy remains: Americans love orgasm, but fear the body.

Much contemporary pornography, following a widely held ideal of beauty, has come to reject body hair on the genitals, and often on all parts of the body, for both sexes. The absence of hair can be seen as a further expression of innocence, but also as a symptom of oppression and perversity. Waxing establishments and advertisements for hair removal devices abound, and members of both sexes are taking part in the quest for a youthful, androgynous look. But the appearance of youth and innocence

may be associated with abuses. Pornography increasingly centers on violence and emphasizes depictions of forced sex, bondage, and degradation
rather than consensual scenes. Preferring hairless genitals and preferring
scenes of violent subjugation rather than sensual consent may both be
ways of pursuing ecstasy while rejecting the body.

Perhaps the answers to Internet pornography and webcam prostitution may be found in technology. Americans have long been attracted
by dreams of a future where sexual fantasy will liberate them from all
constraints. The early skyscrapers of Manhattan inspired German film-
maker Fritz Lang to make *Metropolis* (1927), which featured a sexually
attractive robot created to replace the female lead. Angel movies of the
1930s through the 1990s, an American specialty, expressed a longing for
sexual partners who transcend human limitations. In 2007, *Lars and the
Real Girl* presented a sympathetic portrayal of a shy man's relationship
with Real Girl sex doll, which he treated as real and brought to church.
Both the evangelical magazine *Christianity Today* and the Catholic News
Service found the film charming and humane.[23] In 2013, the movie *Her*
presented people falling in love with sentient operating systems in their
phones and being improved in their relations with each other by the experience. In 2015, the film *Ex Machina* located artificial intelligence in a
beautiful female robot, who rebelled against her creator and then escaped
the secret laboratory where she was made. The robot entered our world
undetected by humanity, with unknowable consequences.

Meanwhile, Matt McMullen, the leading creator of sex dolls for
RealDolls at Abyss Creations, near San Diego, was interviewed for the
May 2015 *Vanity Fair* and reported an exploding business. McMullen's
premium dolls started at $6,749, complete with real human hair and re-
alistic skin.[24] These dolls were being ordered by both women and men,
though men ordering female dolls still dominated the market. When ex-
perimental dolls have been made into robots, by programs and machinery
that vary their facial expressions or move their pelvises or make sounds
in response to touch, people have not liked them, through 2015. Robotic
dolls have fallen into what is called the "uncanny valley," a region where
the resemblance to humans is too close for comfort, so that people prefer
the inert doll. Nevertheless, the people working at RealDolls were still
trying for more. The prospect of sex with robots seemed increasingly real.

In the world of virtual reality, the San Francisco company that runs the
virtual world Second Life, where about a million active users all over the
world have been living parts of their lives on their computers as avatars

since 2003, has been developing new uses for the Oculus Rift, a headset that provides a fully immersive experience.[25] Headsets should soon connect the expressions of avatar faces with faces of real people. Surely, direct stimulation of real bodies by avatar bodies cannot be far behind. Second Life has from the outset been filled with people pursuing basic activities, especially music, visual art, religious rituals, gambling (until that was forbidden by the owners of Second Life, who feared government reprisals), and sex.

Spending time in Second Life stimulates dreams of escaping all bodily limitations, including those of sex, gender, species, and even mortality. Religion scholars already meet in "transhumanist" groups at conferences, and techies have long been writing about living forever by uploading into virtual reality.[26] Some of those committed to the merger of human and machine intelligence identify as "Singularitarians," and Singularitarian weddings are already happening.

Without doubt, technology will introduce new sources of sexual pleasure and new variants of moral conflict, but the goal of ecstatic experience without guilt will endure. If current trends continue, the distinction between sexuality as the means of communion with other people and spirituality as the means of communion with God will disappear. Sexual and spiritual ecstasy will become one, for good and ill.

Sexual + Spiritual

ecstacy

Notes

INTRODUCTION

1. This and the following quotations from McDowell's address are from the notes I took that night.
2. From Article IX of the Thirty-Nine Articles. My text from Protestant Episcopal Church in the United States, *The Book of Common Prayer* (New York: Church Pension Fund, 1945), p. 604.
3. Martin Luther, *Lectures on Romans*, trans. William Pauck (Philadelphia: Westminster Press, 1961), pp. 120–125.
4. Anthony Kosnik et al., *Human Sexuality: New Directions in American Catholic Thought* (New York: Paulist Press, 1977), pp. 120–125.
5. Adolphe Tanquerey, *The Spiritual Life* (Tournai: Desclée & Co., 1930), point 1453.
6. Marabel Morgan, *The Total Woman* (1973; Old Tappan, N.J.: Fleming H. Revell Company, 1975), p. 141.
7. Tom Wolfe, *Mauve Glories and Madmen, Clutter and Vine* (New York: Farrar, Straus & Giroux, 1976), p. 141.

CHAPTER 1

1. Francis P. Kenrick, *Theologiae Moralis* (Philadelphia: Eugene Cummiskey, 1843), vol. III, p. 310.
2. Ibid.
3. Thomas T. McAvoy, *A History of the Catholic Church in the United States* (Notre Dame, Ind.: University of Notre Dame Press, 1969), p. 142.
4. John T. Noonan Jr., *Contraception: A History of Its Treatment by Catholic Theologians and Canonists* (Cambridge: Harvard University Press, 1965), pp. 57ff.
5. Ibid., pp. 131–136.

6. Thomas Aquinas, *Summa theologiae*, 2–2.154.12.

7. Augustine, *On Marriage and Concupiscience*, 2.53–54, 59; also, *The City of God*, Book XIV, chaps. 16–24.

8. Noonan, *Contraception*, pp. 150–151.

9. Ibid., pp. 197, 252 n. 28.

10. Ibid., pp. 152–155, 162–170.

11. Aristotle, *Nicomachean Ethics*, 1175b 25–30, trans. by Martin Ostwald (Indianapolis: Bobbs-Merrill Company, 1962), p. 284.

12. Aquinas, *Summa theologiae*, 1–2.34.1 and 1.98.2.

13. Francis P. Kenrick, *Theologiae Moralis* (Philadelphia: Eugene Cummiskey, 1841), vol. I, p. 35.

14. Ibid., p. 17.

15. Noonan, *Contraception*, p. 313.

16. E.g., Alphonsus Liguori, *Theologia Moralis* (Graz, 1954), 6.912.

17. Noonan, *Contraception*, pp. 315–320.

18. Ibid., pp. 304–312.

19. Kenrick, *Theologiae Moralis*, vol. III, pp. 311–312; Liguori, *Theologia moralis*, 6.917.

20. H. Denzinger, *Enchiridion Symbolorum, Definitionem et Declarationem de Rebus Fidei et Morum)*, no. 1515 (in editions before 1963, no. 792).

21. Noonan, *Contraception*, p. 315.

22. Ibid., pp. 326–327.

23. Ibid., p. 320.

24. Ibid., p. 396.

25. Ibid.

26. Ibid.

27. Ibid., p. 397.

28. Kenrick, *Theologiae Moralis*, p. 308.

29. J. B. Hogan, *Clerical Studies* (Boston: Marlier, Callanan & Company, 1898), p. 242.

30. Liguori, *Theologiae Moralis*, 6.919.

31. Ibid.

32. Kenrick, *Theologiae Moralis*, p. 310.

33. Noonan, *Contraception*, pp. 296–297; see also John Humphrey Noyes, *Male Continence* (Oneida, N.Y.: Oneida Community, 1872).

34. Liguori, *Theologia Moralis*, 6.918.

35. Ibid.

36. Ibid.

37. Ibid.

38. Ibid.

39. Ibid.

40. Kenrick, *Theologiae Moralis*, p. 310.

41. Ibid.

42. Anthony Könings, *Theologiae Moralis* (Boston: Patrick Donahoe, 1874), 1651.4.

43. Jean-Pierre Gury, *Compendium Theologiae Moralis* (Rome, Turin: 1869; Ratisbon: Fr. Pustet, 1906), 939.2.

44. Thomas Slater, *A Manual of Moral Theology for English Speaking Countries* (New York: Benziger Brothers, 1908), p. 362.

45. Arthur Vermeersch, *Theologiae Moralis* (Rome: 1923), vol. IV, pp. 55–56; Heribert Jone, *Moral Theology*, rev. ed. by Urban Adelman (Westminster, Md.: Newman Press, 1946), p. 752; REFO:BKAntonio Ballerini, *Opus Theologicum Morale* (Prati, 1900), VI. 364.

46. Liguori, *Theologia Moralis*, 6.912.

47. Ibid, 6.940.

48. Ibid., 6.920.

49. Ibid., 6.928.

50. Ibid., 6.930.

51. Ibid., 6.927.

52. Ibid.

53. Kenrick, *Theologiae Moralis*, p. 313.

54. Noonan, *Contraception*, pp. 339–342.

55. Ballerini, *Opus*, VI. 358.

56. John C. Ford and Gerald Kelly, *Contemporary Moral Theology* (Westminster, Md.: Newman Press, 1964), vol. II, pp. 169–187.

57. Ibid.; also see Bernard Häring, *The Law of Christ*, trans. by Edwin G. Kaiser (Westminster, Md.: Newman Press, 1966), pp. 375, 362–363; and John A. McHugh and Charles J. Callan, *Moral Theology: A Complete Course* (New York: Joseph F. Wagner; London: B. Herder, 1929), I. 131 and II. 2618.

58. Pope Pius XI, *Casti Connubii* (1930), paragraphs 59, 97. Pope Paul VI, *Humanae Vitae* (1968), paragraphs 8–9, 11–12. Karol Wojtyla, *Fruitful and Responsible Love* (New York: Seabury Press, 1979), p. 31; also Noonan, *Contraception*, p. 499.

59. Liguori, *Theologia Moralis*, 6.913.

60. Ibid., 6.914.

61. Ibid., 6.935.

62. Alphonsus Liguori, *Praxis Confessarii* (Graz, 1954), paragraph 39.

63. Ibid., paragraph 41.

64. Kenrick, *Theologiae Moralis*, p. 314.

65. Liguori, *Theologia Moralis*, 6.934–935.

66. Ibid., 6.934.

67. Noonan, *Contraception*, pp. 491–492.

68. Kenrick, *Theologiae Moralis*, p. 313.

69. Ibid., pp. 305, 306.

70. Ibid., p. 306.

71. Joseph D. Brokhage, *Francis Patrick Kenrick's Opinion on Slavery* (Washington, DC: Catholic University of America Press, 1955).

72. Kenrick, *Theologiae Moralis*, p. 305.

73. Ibid.

CHAPTER 2

1. The estimate is conservative. See the bibliography of anti-Catholic books published in the United States from 1800 to 1860 in Ray Allen Billington, *The Protestant Crusade, 1800–1860* (New York: Macmillan, 1938), pp. 452–482.

2. [George Bourne], *The American Text-Book of Popery* (Philadelphia: Griffith & Simon, 1846), p. 344.

3. Ray Allen Billington, introduction to Maria Monk, *Awful Disclosures of the Hôtel Dieu Nunnery* (Hamden, Conn.: Archon Books, 1962), n.p.

4. Ibid., p. 29.

5. Ibid., pp. 41–42.

6. Ibid., in Introduction, n.p. See also Ray Allen Billington, "Maria Monk and Her Influence," in *Catholic Historical Review XXII* (October 1936), pp. 283–296.

7. Ibid.

8. James Hennesey, *American Catholics* (New York: Oxford University Press, 1981), pp. 96–98.

9. William Hogan, *Auricular Confession and Popish Nunneries* (1845; Hartford, Conn.: Silas Andrus and Son, 1847), vol. I, p. 33.

10. Ibid., p. 34.

11. *The Downfall of Babylon, or, the Triumph of Truth over Popery* (Philadelphia and New York), vol. II, no. 29 (October 15, 1836).

12. Alessandro Gavazzi, *The Lectures Complete of Father Gavazzi* (New York: M. W. Dodd, 1854), pp. 336–337, 385, 388.

13. Charles Chiniquy, *The Priest, the Woman, and the Confessional* (Chino, Calif.: Chick Publications, 1984).

14. Gilbert Barnes, *The Antislavery Impulse* (New York: D. Appleton-Century Co., 1933), p. 33.

15. George Bourne, *Lorette, the History of Louise, Daughter of a Canadian Nun, Exhibiting the Interior of Female Convents* (1833; New York: Charles Small, 1834), p. 53.

16. Ibid., p. 54.

17. Ibid., p. 57.

18. Ned Buntline, *The Beautiful Nun* (Philadelphia: T. B. Peterson & Brothers, 1866), pp. 57–75.

19. Ibid., p. 80.

20. Ibid., p. 82.

21. Ibid., p. 42.

22. Ibid., p. 47.

23. Ibid., p. 20.

24. Ibid., p. 52.

25. Nathaniel Hawthorne, *The Marble Fawn* (1860; New York: New American Library, 1961), p. 296.

26. Ibid., pp. 296–297.

27. Harriet Beecher Stowe, *Agnes of Sorrento* (1862; Boston: Houghton Mifflin, 1883), p. 384.

28. Ibid, pp. 142–143.

29. Ibid., pp. 47, 250.

30. Ibid., p. 51.

31. Ibid., pp. 58, 69.

32. Ibid., pp. 61–62, 73.

33. Billington, *The Protestant Crusade*, pp. 18–19.

34. Sydney E. Ahlstrom, *A Religious History of the American People* (New Haven, Conn.: Yale University Press, 1972), p. 749.

35. Billington, *The Protestant Crusade*, pp. 37, 240–241.

36. Lyman Beecher, *A Plea for the West* (Cincinnati: Truman and Smith, 1835), p. 68.

37. Samuel F. B. Morse, *Foreign Conspiracy against the Liberties of the United States* (New York: Leavitt, Lord & Co.; Boston: Crocker & Brewster, 1835). See also Billington, *The Protestant Crusade*, pp. 118–127.

38. Billington, *The Protestant Crusade*, pp. 313–314.

39. Buntline, *The Beautiful Nun*, p. 44.

40. W. C. Brownlee, *Popery an Enemy to Civil and Religious Liberty* (New York: Charles K. Moore, at the office of the *Protestant Vindicator*, 1839), p. 181.

41. Ibid.

42. Roland Bainton, *The Reformation of the Sixteenth Century* (Boston: Beacon Press, 1952), p. 256.

43. Henry Charles Lea, *The History of Sacerdotal Celibacy in the Christian Church* (1867; New York: Russell & Russell, 1957), pp. 1–3, 560.

44. Mary A. Cheney, *Life and Letters of Horace Bushnell* (New York: Harper & Brothers, 1880), p. 152.

45. W. C. Brownlee, Introduction to Joseph F. Berg, *Lectures on Romanism* (Philadelphia: D. Weidner, 1840), p. 6.

46. L. Larned, *The American Nun; or the Effects of Romance* (Boston: Otis, Broaders, & Co. 1836), p. 126.

47. J. W. Cunningham, "On the Practical Tendency of Popery," in *Lectures on the Points in Controversy between Romanists and Protestants* (Philadelphia: Presbyterian Board of Publication, 1840), pp. 236–237.

48. Francis P. Kenrick, *Theologiae Moralis* (Philadelphia: Eugene Cummiskey, 1843), vol. III, p. 319.

49. Ibid.

50. Adolphe Tanquerey, *Synopsis Theologiae Moralis et Pastoralis*, 7th ed. (Rome, 1920), vol. I, Supplementum, paragraphs 22, n. I; 32; 34; 24.

51. Ibid., vol. II, Supplementum, paragraph 28.

52. Ibid., paragraph 25. See also John A. McHugh and Charles Callan, *Moral Theology: A Complete Course* (New York: Joseph F. Wagner; London: B. Herder, 1929), vol. II, point 2501.

53. Arthur Vermeersch, *Theologiae Moralis* (Rome, 1923), vol. IV, point 56.

54. McHugh and Callan, *Moral Theology*, vol. II, point 2492.

CHAPTER 3

1. Sydney E. Ahlstrom, *A Religious History of the American People* (New Haven, Conn.: Yale University Press, 1972), p. 344.

2. Jeremy Taylor, *The Rule and Exercises of Holy Living* (1651), in *Works*, 3 vols., (London: Henry G. Bohn, 1844), vol. I, p. 428; William Ames, *Conscience*, Book V (London, 1639), p. 206; Robert Victor Schnucker, *Views of Selected Puritans, 1560–1630, on Marriage and Human Sexuality* (Ph.D. diss., University of Iowa, 1969), pp. 356–357, 360.

3. Jonathan Edwards, *Original Sin* (1758; New Haven, Conn.: Yale University Press, 1970), pp. 278, 140–146. See also Edwards, *The Nature of True Virtue.*

4. H. Shelton Smith, *Changing Concepts of Original Sin* (New York: Charles Scribner's Sons, 1955), pp. 3, 10–59.

5. Otho T. Beall, Jr., "*Aristotle's Master Piece* in America," *William and Mary Quarterly* XX (April 1963), pp. 207–222.

6. [Anonymous], *Aristotle's Master Piece.* Editions consulted were London: B. H., 1700; New York: Flying Stationers, 1788, 1817; and New England, 1831.

7. Ibid., 1817 ed., p. 7.

8. Ibid., 1831 ed., pp. 9–10.

9. Ibid., p. 16.

10. Ibid.

11. Ibid., p. 15.

12. George W. Corner, ed., *The Autobiography of Benjamin Rush* (Princeton, N.J.: Princeton University Press, 1948), pp. 165, 335.

13. Ibid., p. 337.

14. Benjamin Rush, *Three Lectures upon Animal Life* (Philadelphia: Budd and Bartram, 1799), p. 4.

15. Ibid., pp. 7, 81.

16. Ibid., pp. 67, 68.

17. Ibid., p. 21.

18. Ibid., p. 22.

19. Benjamin Rush, *Sermons to Gentlemen upon Temperance and Exercise* (Philadelphia: Dunlap, 1772); Benjamin Rush, *Thoughts upon Female Education* (Philadelphia: Pritchard & Hall, 1787).

20. Ellen Gould White, *Patriarchs and Prophets* (Mountain View, Calif.: Pacific Press Publishing Association, 1947), p. 68.

21. John Harvey Kellogg, *Plain Facts for Old and Young* (Burlington, Iowa: I. F. Segner & Co., 1888), p. 450.

22. Ann Douglas, *The Feminization of American Culture* (New York: Alfred A. Knopf, 1977), pp. 82–83.

23. Carleton Mabee, *The American Leonardo; a Life of Samuel F. B. Morse* (1943; New York: Octagon Books, 1969), pp. 157–158, 87–88.

24. Gerald Carson, *Cornflake Crusade* (New York: Rinehart & Company, 1957), pp. 44–45.

25. Sylvester Graham, *Lectures to Young Men on Chastity* (Boston: Light & Stearns, Crocker & Brewster; New York: Lord & Company, 1837), p. 33.

26. Ibid., p. 58.

27. Ibid.

28. Ibid., pp. 68–69, 161.

29. William A. Alcott, *The Physiology of Marriage* (Boston: John P. Jewett, 1857), p. 96.

30. Ibid., p. 64.

31. William A. Alcott, *The Young Husband* (Boston: George W. Light, 1839), p. 359.

32. Ibid., p. 364.

33. Dio Lewis, *Chastity; or, Our Secret Sins* (New York: Canfield Publishing, 1888), p. 157.

34. James C. Jackson, *The Sexual Organism* (Boston: B. Leverett Emerson, 1864), p. 8.

35. Mary S. Gove, *Lectures to Women on Anatomy and Physiology* (New York: Harper & Brothers, 1946), p. 173.

36. Ibid., p. 171.

37. Augustus K. Gardner, *Conjugal Sins against the Laws of Life and Health* (New York: J. S. Redfield, 1870), p. 80.

38. Elizabeth Blackwell, *The Laws of Life* (New York: G. P. Putnam, 1852), p. 43.

39. Horace Bushnell, *Nature and the Supernatural* (1858; New York: Charles Scribner's Sons, 1899), p. 178.

40. Ibid., pp. 177–178.

41. Ibid., pp. 182–183.

42. Horace Bushnell, *Christian Nurture* (New York: Charles Scribner's Sons, 1892), pp. 195–196.

43. Ibid., p. 213.

44. Ibid., p. 232.

45. Ibid., pp. 277–278.

46. Ibid., pp. 229–230.

47. Ibid.

48. Leonard Woods, *An Essay on Native Depravity* (Boston: William Pierce, 1835), pp. 225ff., esp. 228, 244. Charles Hodge, *Systematic Theology* (New York: Charles Scribner's Company, 1872), pp. 254–255.

49. Charles G. Finney, *Lectures on Systematic Theology* (Oberlin: James M. Fitch; Boston: Crocker & Brewster; New York: Saxton & Miles, 1846), vol. II, p. iii.

50. Charles G. Finney, *Lectures on Revivals of Religion* (1835; reprint Cambridge: Harvard University Press, 1960), p. 467.

51. Finney, *Systematic*, pp. 447–485.

52. Ibid., pp. 450–451.

53. Ibid., p. 484.

54. Ibid., vol. III, pp. 96–424.

55. Ibid., vol II, p. 414.

56. Donald Dayton, *Discovering an Evangelical Heritage* (New York: Harper & Row, 1976), p. 42.

57. Mary Baker Eddy, *Science and Health* (Boston: Mary Baker Eddy, 1875), chap. III, p. 64.

58. Mary Baker Eddy, *Miscellaneous Writings* (Boston, 1896), p. 286.

59. Alexander Campbell, *The Christian Baptist* (1823–1829; St. Louis: Christian Publishing Company, 1856), p. 470.

60. Ibid.

61. Ibid., pp. 470–471.

62. Ibid., p. 471.

63. Ibid., p. 470.

64. Ibid., p. 504.

65. Ibid., p. 654.

66. Theodore T. Munger, *The Freedom of Faith* (Boston, 1883), p. 62.

67. Lyman Abbott, *The Theology of an Evolutionist* (New York: Houghton Mifflin, 1897), p. 48.

68. Newman Smyth, *Through Science to Faith* (New York: Charles Scribner's Sons, 1902); George Harris, *Moral Evolution* (Boston: Houghton Mifflin, 1896), pp. 278–279.

69. [A Physician], *Satan in Society* (Cincinnati: C. F. Vent; Chicago: J. S. Goodman & Co., 1871), p. 203.

70. G. J. Barker-Benfield, *The Horrors of the Half-Known Life* (New York: Harper & Row, 1976), p. 166.

71. William T. Duryea, "Social Vice and National Decay," in *The National Purity Congress: Its Papers, Addresses and Portraits*, ed. Aaron Macy Powell (New York: Caulon, 1896).

72. Charles Knowlton, *The Fruits of Philosophy* (Philadelphia: F. P. Rogers, 1839), p. 107.

73. Reay Tannehill, *Sex in History* (New York: Stein & Day, 1980), p. 75.

74. Graham, *Lectures to Young Men on Chastity*, pp. 42–43.

75. Ibid., p. 51.

76. Ibid., pp. 60–61.

77. Ibid.

78. Ibid., pp. 71–73.

79. Ibid., pp. 58, 69, 161.

80. Knowlton, *The Fruits of Philosophy*, p. 105.

81. M. Larmont and E. Banister, *Medical Adviser and Marriage Guide* (New York, 1861), p. 93.

82. John Cowan, *The Science of a New Life* (New York: Cowan & Company, 1874), p. 116.

83. Ibid., pp. 153, 169.

84. Elizabeth Edson Evans, *The Abuse of Maternity* (Philadelphia: J. B. Lippincott, 1875).

85. Cowan, *The Science of a New Life*, after index, n.p.

86. Ibid.

87. Jackson, *The Sexual Organism*, p. 256; Kellogg, *Plain Facts*, p. 462; Mary Wood-Allen, *What a Young Woman Ought to Know* (Philadelphia: Vir, 1905), p. 154; Emma F. A. Drake, *What a Young Wife Ought to Know* (Philadelphia: Vir, 1908), pp. 86–87.

88. Evans, *The Abuse of Maternity*, pp. 128–129.

89. John S. Haller and Robin S. Haller, *The Physician and Sexuality in Victorian America* (Urbana: University of Illinois Press, 1974), pp. 131–132, 134.

90. E.g., [A Physician], *Satan in Society*, pp. 161–162.

91. Quoted in Haller and Haller, *The Physician and Sexuality in Victorian America*, p. 134.

92. Cowan, *The Science of a New Life*, p. 117.

93. James Reed, *From Private Vice to Public Virtue: The Birth Control Movement and American Society* (New York: Basic Book Publishers, 1978), p. 4; Daniel Scott Smith, "Family Limitation, Sexual Control, and Domestic Feminism in Victorian America," *Feminist Studies* 1 (Winter–Spring 1973), pp. 40–57.

94. Carl Degler, "What Ought to Be and What Was," *American Historical Review* 79 (1974), pp. 1467–1490.

95. Ibid., p. 1479.

96. Barker-Benfield, *The Horrors of the Half-Known Life*, pp. 130–132.

97. Barbara Ehrenreich and Deirdre English, *For Her Own Good: 150 Years of the Experts' Advice to Women* (Garden City, N.Y.: Doubleday, 1978), p. 123.

98. Haller and Haller, *The Physician in Victorian America*, pp. 97–98.

99. Mentioned in Tom Driver and Herbert Richardson, "The Meaning of Orgasm: A Dialogue," in *God, Sex, and the Social Project*, ed. James H. Grace (New York: Edward Mellen Press, 1978), p. 186.

100. Haller and Haller, *The Physician in Victorian America*, pp. 111–113.

101. David S. Pivar, *The Purity Crusade: Sexual Morality and Social Control, 1868–1900* (Westport, Conn.: Greenwood Press, 1973).

102. Ehrenreich and English, *For Her Own Good*, pp. 1–5.

103. Barker-Benfield, *The Horrors of the Half-Known Life*, pp. 91–119. J. Marion Sims, *The Story of My Life*, ed. J. Marion Sims (New York: D. Appleton Co., 1884).

104. Barker-Benfield, *Horrors*, pp. 91-119, quoting Sims.

105. Ibid., p. 89.

106. Ann Douglas, *The Feminization of American Culture*.

107. Ibid.

108. Evans, *The Abuse of Maternity*, p. 48.

109. Elizabeth Blackwell, *Counsel to Parents on the Moral Education of Their Children* (1879; New York: Brentano Brothers, 1883), p. 98.

110. Nancy F. Cott, "Passionlessness: An Interpretation of Victorian Sexual Ideology, 1790–1850," in *A Heritage of Her Own*, ed. Nancy F. Cott and Elizabeth H. Pleck (New York: Simon & Schuster, 1979), pp. 168–169.

111. William L. O'Neill, *Everyone Was Brave: A History of Feminism in America* (1969; Chicago: Quadrangle Books, 1971), pp. 31–34.

112. Carson, *Cornflake Crusade*; Wood-Allen, *What a Young Girl Ought to Know*, title page; Drake, *What a Young Wife Ought to Know*, title page.

113. Sylvanus Stall, *What a Young Husband Ought to Know* (1899; Philadelphia: Vir, 1907), p. 92.

114. Ibid., p. 97.

115. Ibid.

116. Ibid., p. 78.

117. Henry J. Spalding, "Sex-Hygiene and Eugenics," in *Moral Principles and Medical Practice*, ed. Charles Coppens (New York: Benziger Brothers, 1921), p. 297.

118. Ibid., p. 105.

119. Ibid., p. 106.

120. David F. Kelly, *The Emergence of Roman Catholic Medical Ethics in North America* (New York: Edward Mellen Press, 1979), pp. 110–117.

121. Fulton J. Sheen, *Peace of Soul* (New York: McGraw-Hill, 1949), pp. 101–102, 176ff.

122. Walter Elliott, *The Spiritual Life* (1914; New York: Paulist Press, 1918), pp. 18–29.

123. David Pivar, *Purity Crusade: Sexual Morality and Social Control, 1868–1900* (Westport, Conn.: Greenwood Press, 1973).

CHAPTER 4

1. Andrew J. Ingersoll, *In Health*, 4th ed. (1877; Boston: Lee and Shepard, 1898), p. 200.

2. Ibid.

3. Ibid.

4. Ibid., p. 201.

5. Ibid., pp. 100–101.

6. Ibid., p. 102.

7. Ibid., "Memoir," appendix to *In Health,* no author or pagination.

8. Ibid.

9. Ibid.

10. Ibid.

11. Ibid.

12. Ibid.

13. Ibid.

14. Ibid., pp. 164–165.

15. Ibid.

16. Ibid., pp. 23–24.

17. Ibid., pp. 105.

18. Ibid., p. 113.

19. Ibid., p. 106.

20. Ibid.

21. Ibid., p. 23.

22. Ibid., pp. 23–24.

23. Ibid., p. 24.

24. Ibid., pp. 24–34.

25. Ibid., p. 54.

26. Ibid., p. 22.

27. Ibid., p. 241.

28. Ibid., pp. 164–165.

29. Ibid., p. 38.

30. Ibid., p. 184.

31. Edward Bliss Foote, *Plain Home Talk* (1870; New York: Murray Hill Publishing Company, 1881), p. 489.

32. Ibid., p. 879.

33. Ibid., p. 607.

34. Ibid., p. 780.

35. Ibid., pp. 173, 805–829.

36. Ibid., pp. 452, 491.

37. Ibid., p. 872.

38. Ibid., p. 606.

39. Ibid., p. 607.

40. Frederick Hollick, *The Marriage Guide or Natural History of Generation* (New York: T. W. Strong, 1850), title page.

41. Ibid., p. 360.

42. Ibid., p. 362.

43. Ibid., p. 367.
44. Ibid.
45. Ibid., p. 357.
46. Ibid., p. 414.
47. Ibid., p. 415.
48. William A. Hammond, *Sexual Impotence in the Male and Female* (Detroit: George S. Davis, 1887), p. 302.
49. Denslow Lewis, *The Gynecologic Consideration of the Sexual Act* (Chicago: Henry O. Shepard Company, 1900), pp. 19–20.
50. Robert Latou Dickinson and Lura Beam, *A Thousand Marriages: A Medical Study of Sex Adjustment* (Baltimore: Williams & Wilkins, 1931), p. 144.
51. Ibid., pp. 10, 221.
52. James Reed, *From Private Vice to Public Virtue: The Birth Control Movement and American Society since 1830* (New York: Basic Book Publishers, 1978), p. 154.
53. Ibid.
54. Robert Latou Dickinson, *Control of Conception, Present and Future* (New York: New York Academy of Medicine, 1929), p. 9.
55. Reed, *From Private Vice to Public Virtue*, p. 151.
56. Dickinson, *Control of Conception*, p. 3.
57. Others included Horatio R. Bigelow, who published *Social Physiology* in 1891, and Joseph W. Howe, a professor at the City University of New York in the 1880s and 1890s.

CHAPTER 5

1. Carolyn Wahlstrom, *Sara's Story* (New York: Simon & Schuster, 1984), p. 179.
2. Aimée Semple McPherson, *This Is That: Personal Experiences, Sermons, and Writings* (Los Angeles: Bridal Call Publishing House, 1919), pp. 48–49.
3. Lonnie Garfield Barbach, *For Yourself: The Fulfillment of Female Sexuality* (New York: New American Library, 1975), pp. 171–173.
4. Mary Jane Sherfey, *The Nature and Evolution of Female Sexuality* (New York: Random House, 1972), pp. 68–71.
5. E.g., Tim and Beverly LaHaye, *The Act of Marriage* (Grand Rapids, Mich.: Zondervan Publishing House, 1976), pp. 67, 76.
6. Sherfey, *Female Sexuality*, pp. 104–108.
7. Shere Hite, *The Hite Report* (1976; New York: Dell Publishing Company, 1977), p. 129.
8. McPherson, *This Is That*, p. 29.
9. Ibid., pp. 27–30.
10. Peter W. Williams, *Popular Religion in America* (Englewood Cliffs, N.J.: Prentice-Hall, 1980), p. 162.

11. Phoebe C. Brent, describing a Pentecostal meeting of 1917 in Philadelphia, in McPherson, *This Is That*, p. 271.

12. Aimée Semple McPherson (with Georgia Stiffler), *The Foursquare Gospel* (Los Angeles: Echo Park Evangelistic Association, 1946).

13. McPherson, *This Is That*, p. 95.

14. Ibid., p. 97.

15. Ibid., p. 112.

16. Ibid., p. 12.

17. John L. Peters, *Christian Perfection and American Methodism* (New York: Abingdon Press, 1956), p. 155.

18. John Wesley, *Thoughts on Christian Perfection* (1760), question I, in *John Wesley*, ed. Albert C. Outler (New York: Oxford University Press, 1964), p. 284.

19. Ibid., p. 289.

20. Charles Edwin Jones, *Perfectionist Persuasion: The Holiness Movement and American Methodism, 1867–1936* (Metuchen, N.J.: Scarecrow Press, 1974), p. 2.

21. Journal entry for August 12, 1827, quoted in Richard Wheatley, *The Life and Letters of Mrs. Phoebe Palmer* (New York: W. C. Palmer, Jr., 1876), pp. 22–23.

22. Ibid., p. 18.

23. [Phoebe Palmer], *The Way of Holiness with Notes by the Way*, 34th ed. (New York, 1854), p. 76.

24. Peters, *Christian Perfection*, p. 98.

25. Jones, *Perfectionist Persuasion*, p. 2.

26. Palmer, *The Way of Holiness*, p. 109.

27. Ibid., p. 20.

28. Ibid., p. 21.

29. Ibid., p. 25.

30. Ibid., p. 28.

31. Ibid., p. 36.

32. Ibid., pp. 38, 40–41.

33. Ibid., p. 41–42.

34. Ibid., p. 42.

35. Timothy L. Smith, *Revivalism and Social Reform* (New York: Abingdon Press, 1957) pp. 122–124.

36. Jones, *Perfectionist Persuasion*, p. 4.

37. Wesley, *Thoughts on Christian Perfection*, p. 289.

38. Jones, *Perfectionist Persuasion*, p. 5. Also see Randolph Sinks Foster, *Christian Purity* (New York: Harper & Brothers, 1851), pp. 45–46, 48; and John A. Wood, *Purity and Maturity* (Philadelphia: National Publishing Association for the Promotion of Holiness; New York: W. C. Palmer, Jr.; London: F. E. Longley, 1876), p. 150.

39. Wesley, *Thoughts on Christian Perfection*, question 23, p. 292.

40. Phoebe Palmer, *Promise of the Father; or, A Neglected Specialty of the Last Days* (1859; New York: W. C. Palmer, 1868), pp. v–vi.

41. John Wesley, *Minutes* of Fourth Annual Conference, June 17, 1747, in *John Wesley*, ed. Outler, question 13, pp. 170–171.

42. Wesley, *Thoughts on Christian Perfection*, question 23, p. 292.

43. Ibid., p. 286.

44. Ibid., question 10, pp. 288–289.

45. Ibid., pp. 284–285.

46. Smith, *Revivalism*, p. 144.

47. Palmer, *The Way of Holiness*, pp. 50, 102, 158.

48. Ibid., p. 132.

49. Ibid., p. 93.

50. Lately Thomas, *Storming Heaven: The Lives and Turmoils of Minnie Kennedy and Aimée Semple McPherson* (New York: William Morrow & Co., 1970), p. 14.

51. T. H. Stockton, "The Gradations of Love," *The Guide to Christian Perfection* V:4 (June 1843), p. 86.

52. [Phoebe L. Upham], "Personal Experience," *The Guide to Christian Perfection* V:5 (November 1943), p. 117.

53. Ibid., V:10 (April 1844), pp. 217–218.

54. *The Guide to Christian Perfection* V:9, pp. 201, 204.

55. Smith, *Revivalism*, p. 145.

56. Jones, *Perfectionist Persuasion*, pp. 25–26, 33.

57. Peters, *Christian Perfection*, pp. 147–150.

CHAPTER 6

1. Franz Werfel, *The Song of Bernadette*, trans. Lewis Lewisohn (1942; New York: Avon Books, 1975), pp. 490–491.

2. Frances Parkinson Keyes, "Bernadette and the Beautiful Lady," in *A Woman Clothed with the Sun*, ed. John J. Delaney (Garden City, N.Y.: Doubleday, 1961), p. 136.

3. Don Sharkey, *The Woman Shall Conquer* (Kenosha, Wisc.: Franciscan Marytown Press, 1973), pp. 50–51.

4. Ethel Cook Eliot, "Our Lady of Guadalupe in Mexico," in Delaney, *A Woman Clothed with the Sun*, p. 39.

5. Werfel, *The Song of Bernadette*, p. 49

6. Henry Adams, *Mont-Saint-Michel and Chartres* (1905; Garden City, N.Y.: Doubleday, 1959), pp. 96–107

7. Quoted in Sharkey, *The Woman Shall Conquer*, p. 122

8. Ibid., p. 137.

9. Pope Pius IX, *Ineffabilis Deus* (1854), in H. Denzinger, *Enchiridion Symbolorum, Definitionem et Declarationem de Rebus Fidei et Morum*, rev. ed. by Adolf Schönmetzer (Rome: Herder, 1965), no. 2803 (in editions before 1963, no. 1641).

10. René Laurentin, *Court Traité de Théologie Mariale* (Paris, 1959), pp. 40ff.; Hilda Graef, *Mary: A History of Doctrine and Devotion*, 2 vols. (New York: Sheed and Ward, 1963–1965), vol. I, pp. 82, 97–98; Geoffrey Ashe, *The Virgin* (London: Routledge & Kegan Paul, 1976), pp. 172–174.

11. Laurentin, *Court Traité*, pp. 38–39.

12. Ashe, *The Virgin*, pp. 191, 193.

13. Carlo Balić, "The Mediaeval Controversy over the Immaculate Conception up to the Death of Scotus," in *The Dogma of the Immaculate Conception*, ed. Edward D. O'Connor (Notre Dame, Ind.: University of Notre Dame Press, 1958), p. 174. Also see Laurentin, in the same volume, p. 274.

14. Laurentin, *Court Traité*, p. 68, n. 199. Graef, *Mary*, vol. I, p. 303. Balić, "The Mediaeval Controversy."

15. Graef, *Mary*, vol. II, p. 72.

16. Joseph I. Dirvin, "The Lady of the Miraculous Medal," in Delaney, *A Woman Clothed with the Sun*, p. 69ff.

17. Sharkey, *The Woman Shall Conquer*, pp. 24–27.

18. William Bernard Ullathorne, *The Holy Mountain of La Salette* (1854; Hartford, Conn.: Fathers of La Salette, 1901), p. 55.

19. Sharkey, *The Woman Shall Conquer*, pp. 86–87.

20. Ibid., pp. 85–86.

21. Ibid., pp. 87–89.

22. Ibid., pp. 77–85, 91–92, 99–113 (describing apparitions at Knock, Castelpetroso, and Fatima).

23. J. Michael Phayer, *Sexual Liberation and Religion in Nineteenth Century Europe* (London: Croom Helm Ltd., 1977), pp. 95–98, 152–153.

24. Ibid., pp. 24–26. Also John T. Noonan, Jr., *Contraception* (Cambridge: Harvard University Press, 1966), pp. 387–388.

25. Sharkey, *The Woman Shall Conquer*, pp. 57–71.

26. H. Daniel-Rops, *The Church in an Age of Revolution, 1789–1870*, trans. John Warrington (1960; New York: E. P. Dutton 1965), pp. 252–255. On the connections of France, Pius IX, and Mary, see J. B. Bury, *History of the Papacy in the 19th Century* (London: Macmillan and Co., 1930), pp. 47–53.

27. Sharkey, *The Woman Shall Conquer*, pp. 233–234.

28. Henry Adams, *The Education of Henry Adams* (1904; Boston: Houghton Mifflin, 1918), pp. 383–385.

29. Henry Steele Commager, *The American Mind* (New Haven, Conn.: Yale University Press, 1950), p. 139.

30. Nathaniel Hawthorne, *The Marble Faun* (New York: New American Library, 1961), p. 240.

31. Ibid., p. 249.

32. Ibid., p. 250.

33. Ibid., p. 87.

34. Ibid., pp. 329–330.

35. Annette S. Driscoll, *Literary Convert Women* (Manchester, N.H.: Magnificat Press, 1928), pp. 130–132.

36. Quoted by James Cardinal Gibbons, in "The Position of the Blessed Virgin in Catholic Theology," *American Catholic Quarterly Review* III (1878).

37. Henry Wadsworth Longfellow, *Complete Poetical Works* (Boston: Houghton Mifflin, 1893), pp. 453–454.

38. James Russell Lowell, *Poetical Works* (Boston: Fields, Osgood, & Co., 1871), p. 445.

39. Ibid., p. 446.

40. Ibid., p. 451.

41. Harriet Beecher Stowe, *Agnes of Sorrento* (Boston: Houghton Mifflin, 1883), p. 294.

42. Ibid., p. 108.

43. Ibid., p. 212.

44. Ibid., p. 166.

45. Ibid., pp. 112–113.

46. Harriet Beecher Stowe, *Women in Sacred History* (New York: J. B. Ford & Company, 1874), Introduction.

47. Ibid., "Mary the Mythical Madonna."

48. Stowe, *Agnes of Sorrento*, p. 112.

49. Stowe, *Women in Sacred History*.

50. Harriet Beecher Stowe, "Footsteps of the Master," in *Religious Studies, Sketches and Poems* (Boston, 1896), pp. 39–40.

51. Henry Ward Beecher, *The Life of Jesus the Christ* (1871; New York, 1891), vol. I, pp. 34, 15.

52. Henry Ward Beecher, *The Sermons of Henry Ward Beecher in Plymouth Church, Brooklyn*. From Verbatim Reports by T. J. Ellinwood, 10 vols. (New York: J. B. Ford & Company, 1870–1874, vol. I [Sept. 1868–March 1869]), p. 203.

53. Horace Bushnell, "Mary, the Mother of Jesus," in *Sermons on Living Subjects* (New York, 1876), p. 10.

54. Ibid., pp. 32–33.

55. Ibid., pp. 35–36.

56. Ibid., p. 34.

57. Ibid.

58. Mary Baker Eddy, *Science and Health* (1875; Boston: Allison V. Stewart, 1917), pp. 16, 691–692.

59. Ibid., p. 29.

60. J. D. Bryant, *The Immaculate Conception ... A Dogma of the Catholic Church* (Boston: Patrick Donahue, 1855), p. x.

61. Ibid., p. 313.

62. Ibid., p. 311.

63. Ibid., p. 313.

64. John D. Bryant, *Redemption, A Poem* (Philadelphia: John Penington & Son, 1859), p. 66.

65. Ibid., p. 99.

66. Marie Josephine, *The Mystical Rose* (New York: D. Appleton Co., 1865), p. 19.

67. Alphonsus Liguori, *The Glories of Mary* (New York: P. J. Kenedy, 1852), p. 53.

68. Ibid., p. 417.

69. Ibid., pp. 415–416.

70. Ibid., p. 66.

71. Ibid., p. 422.

72. Ibid., p. 400.

73. Ibid., p. 417.

74. Ibid., p. 67.

75. Ibid., p. 12.

76. Alphonsus Liguori, *Homo Apostolicus*, (Mechlinae: S. Congregatio de Propaganda Fide, 1868), vol. III, p. 157.

77. Adolphe Tanquerey, *The Spiritual Life* (Tournai: Desclée & Co., 1930), pp. 90–91.

78. Ibid., p. 466.

79. Ibid., p. 529.

80. John L. Spalding, "The Virgin Mother," in *Lectures and Discourses* (New York: Catholic Publication Society, 1882), p. 217.

81. Peter Richard Kenrick, *The New Month of Mary* (Philadelphia: Eugene Cummiskey, 1840).

82. Ibid., p. 119.

83. Ibid., p. 121.

84. Ibid., pp. 128–129.

85. Ibid., p. 133.

86. Orestes Brownson, "Moral and Social Influence of Devotion to Mary," *Ave Maria*, June 1866, reprinted in *Works* (Detroit: Thorndike Nourse, 1884), vol. VIII, p. 89.

87. Orestes Brownson, "The Worship of Mary," *Brownson's Quarterly Review*, January 1853, reprinted in *Works*, vol. VIII, p. 80.

88. Ibid.

89. Ibid., p. 82.

90. Brownson, "Moral and Social Influence," p. 102.

91. Brownson, "The Worship of Mary," p. 83.

92. Ibid.

93. Ibid.

94. Orestes Brownson, "Our Lady of Lourdes," *Brownson's Quarterly Review*, July 1875, reprinted in *Works*, vol. VIII, pp. 105–108.

95. Isabella Beecher Hooker, *A Mother's Letters to a Daughter on Woman Suffrage* (Hartford, 1870), p. 11.

96. Spalding, "The Virgin Mother," p. 229.

97. Henry Adams, *Mont-Saint-Michel and Chartres* (1905; Boston: Houghton Mifflin, 1933), p. 321.

98. Ibid., pp. 321–322.

99. Adams, *The Education of Henry Adams*, p. 384.

100. Ibid.

101. Ibid., p. 385.

102. Ibid.

103. Walter Elliott, *The Life of Father Hecker* (New York: Columbus Press, 1891), pp. 69–70.

104. Ibid., p. 10.

105. Ibid., pp. 10–11, 14.

106. Ibid., p. 74.

107. Ibid., p. 96.

108. Ibid., p. 65.

109. Ibid., p. 70.

110. Ibid., pp. 192–193.

111. Richard Wheatley, *The Life and Letters of Mrs. Phoebe Palmer* (New York: W. C. Palmer, Jr., 1876), p. 47.

112. Bernard of Clairvaux, "Homilia tertia, super verba Evangelii: Missus est angelus," Latin text from Mabillon 1690, in *Saint Bernard et Notre Dame*, ed. P. Bernard (Paris: Desclée, 1953), p. 120.

113. Especially Psalms 44:12 (Vulgate) and Ecclesiasticus 24:25.

114. Jean Leclerq, *Monks and Love in Twelfth-Century France* (Oxford: Clarendon Press, 1979).

115. Amedée de Lausanne, *Huit Homélies Mariales* (Paris: Editions du Cerf, 1960), p. 103.

116. Ibid., p. 108.

117. Aelred de Rievaulx, *La vie de recluse*, texte Latin, introduction, traduction et notes par Charles Dumont (Paris: Editions du Cerf, 1956), pp. 80–81.

118. Guerric of Igny, *Liturgical Sermons*, trans. Monks of St. Bernard Abbey (Spencer, Mass.: Cistercian Publications, 1971), pp. 45–46.

119. Isaac de Stella, "Sermo in Assumptione Beatae Mariae," in *Patrologia ... latina*, ed. J. P. Migne (Paris: Garnier fratres, 1844–1903), vol. 194, col. 1863D–1864B.

120. Godfrey of Admont, "In Festum Nativitas S. Mariae Virginis," in Migne, *Patrologia ... latina*, vol. 174, col. 1025C.

121. Richard of St. Laurent, "De Laudibus Sanctae Mariae," in *B. Alberti Magni, ... Opera Omnia* (Paris, 1898), vol. 36, p. 88 (2.2.18).

122. Jean Leclerq, *Bernard of Clairvaux and the Cistercian Spirit* (Kalamazoo, Mich.: Cistercian Publications, 1976), p. 92.

123. J. Galot, "L'Immaculée Conception," in *Maria*, ed. Hubert du Manoir (Paris: Beauchesne, 1964), Tome VII, pp. 94–95.

124. Karl Rahner, *Theological Investigations*, trans. Cornelius Ernst (London: Darton, Longman, & Todd, 1961), vol. I, pp. 366, 375.

125. Elliott, *The Life of Father Hecker*, pp. 87–88.

126. Mother Seraphine, ed., *Immortelles of Catholic Columbian Literature* (Chicago: D. H. McBride & Company, 1897), p. 370.

127. Ibid., p. 371.

128. John D. Bryant, *Pauline Seward* (Baltimore: John Murphy; Pittsburgh: George Quigley; Dublin: R. Grace & Sons, 1847), vol. I, p. 242.

129. Ibid., p. 311.

130. Ibid., vol. II, pp. 147, 103–111.

131. Ibid., vol. I, p. 305.

132. Anna Hanson Dorsey, *The Sister of Charity* (New York: E. Dunigan, 1846), vol. I, pp. 45–46.

133. Paul R. Messbarger, *Fiction with a Parochial Purpose: Social Uses of American Catholic Literature, 1824–1900* (Boston: Boston University Press, 1971), pp. 32, 70.

134. Orestes Brownson, "Religious Novels, and Woman Versus Woman," *Brownson's Quarterly Review*, January 1873, reprinted in *Works* vol. XIX, pp. 565–566.

135. Ibid., pp. 568–569.

136. Ibid., p. 575.

137. Sarah Mary (Brownson) Tenney, *Marian Ellwood: or, How Girls Live, by One of Themselves* (New York: E. Dunigan, 1859), pp. 289–290.

138. *The Ursuline Manual*, rev. by John Power (New York: P. J. Kenedy, 1851), p. 107.

139. Joseph B. Code, *Great American Foundresses* (New York: Macmillan, 1929), pp. 409–410.

140. [A Sister], *The Life of Cornelia Connelly, 1809–1879* (New York: Longmans, Green & Co., 1922), p. 238.

141. Code, *Great American Foundresses*, p. 416.

142. Ibid., p. 427.

143. Ibid., p. 423.

144. Ibid., p. 426.

145. *The Life of Cornelia Connelly*, p. 234.

146. Code, *Great American Foundresses*, p. 434.

147. Gaspar Lefebvre, *Saint Andrew Daily Missal* (St. Paul, Minn.: E. M. Lohmann Co., 1951), p. 1931.

148. Elliott, *The Life of Father Hecker*, pp. 12–13.

149. Ibid., pp. 104–105.

150. Ibid., p. 340.

151. Ibid., pp. 100, 316.

152. Thomas J. McAvoy, *The Great Crisis in American Catholic History* (Chicago: Henry Regnery Company, 1957), p. 275. See also Pope Leo XIII, *Testem Benevolentiae, passim*.

153. Elliott, *The Life of Father Hecker*, p. 4.

154. Ibid.

155. Ibid., p. 100.

156. Charles Beecher, *The Incarnation; or Pictures of the Virgin and Her Son* (New York: Harper Brothers, 1849), pp. 53–54.

157. Charles Beecher, *The Eden Tableau, or Bible Object-Teaching* (Boston: Lee and Shepard, 1880), pp. 72, 108.

158. Charles Beecher, *Patmos or the Unveiling* (Boston: Lee and Shepard, 1896), p. 112.

159. Ella Wheeler Wilcox, *Men, Women, and Emotions* (1893; Chicago: W. B. Conkey Company, 1896), p. 298.

160. Henry Adams, *Letters to a Niece and Prayer to the Virgin of Chartres* (Boston: Houghton Mifflin, 1920), p. 133.

CHAPTER 7

1. Madeleine Gray, *Margaret Sanger* (New York: Richard Marek Publishers, 1979), p. 175.

2. Ibid., p. 262.

3. Margaret Sanger, *An Autobiography* (1938; Elmsford, N.Y.: Maxwell Reprint Company, 1970).

4. Ibid.

5. Ibid., p. 21.

6. Randall N. Saunders, *Remembering Claverack College* (Hudson, N.Y.: Hudson Evening Register, 1944), p. 18.

7. Sanger, *Autobiography*, p. 38.

8. Claverack College Handbook for 1893, pp. 26–27. Consulted in the Hudson Public Library, Hudson, New York.

9. Obituary of Professor William McAfee, in *The Vidette* I: 4 (January 15, 1896), p. 45.

10. Francis Wayland, *The Elements of Moral Science* (Cambridge, Mass.: Harvard University Press, 1963; reprint of 1837 edition), p. 270.

11. Ibid., p. 121.

12. Saunders, *Remembering Claverack College*, p. 12.

13. Henry Home, Lord Kames, *Elements of Criticism* (New York: A. S. Barnes & Company, 1855), pp. 1–71.

14. Saunders, *Remembering Claverack College*, p. 12.

15. Sanger, *Autobiography*, pp. 89–92.

16. David M. Kennedy, *Birth Control in America: The Career of Margaret Sanger* (New Haven, Conn.: Yale University Press, 1970), pp. 17–18. Also see Gray, *Margaret Sanger*, p. 55.

17. Kennedy, *Birth Control in America*, pp. 29–30; Gray, *Margaret Sanger*, pp. 158–159.

18. Margaret Sanger, *Happiness in Marriage* (New York: Blue Ribbon Books, 1939), p. 19.

19. Ibid., p. 133.

20. Ibid., p. 130.

21. Ibid., p. 126.

22. Ibid., pp. 139–140.

23. Ibid., p. 140.

24. Ibid., p. 141.

25. Ibid.

26. Ibid., p. 139.

27. Michael Gordon, "From an Unfortunate Necessity to a Cult of Mutual Orgasm: Sex in American Marital Education Literature, 1830–1940," in *Studies in the Sociology of Sex*, ed. James M. Henslin (New York: Appleton-Century-Crofts, 1971), pp. 53–77.

28. Sanger, *Happiness in Marriage*, p. 141.

29. Ibid., p. 143.

30. Margaret Sanger, *Woman and the New Race* (Elmsford, N.Y.: Maxwell Reprint Company, 1969; reprint of 1920 edition), p. 180.

31. Ibid., p. 230.

32. Ibid., p. 232.

33. Ibid., p. 234.

34. Margaret Sanger, *The Pivot of Civilization* (London: Jonathan Cape, 1923), p. 239.

35. Sanger, *Woman and the New Race*, p. 169.

36. Sanger, *Pivot of Civilization*, p. 244.

37. Sanger, *Woman and the New Race*, p. 174.

38. Ibid., pp. 178–179.

39. Ibid., p. 170.

40. Ibid., p. 179.

41. Ibid.

42. Kennedy, *Birth Control in America*, pp. 96–97, 148–150.

43. Ibid., pp. 97–98.

44. Sanger, *Woman and the New Race*, p. 185.

45. Ibid., p. 184.

46. Sanger, *Pivot of Civilization*, p. 243.

47. Ibid., p. 240.

48. Ibid., pp. 240–241.

49. Kennedy, *Birth Control in America*, p. 161.

50. Ibid., p. 154.

51. Ibid., pp. 153–171.

52. Ibid., p. 132.

53. Margaret Sanger, *What Every Girl and Boy Should Know* (Elmsford, N.Y.: Maxwell Reprint Company, 1969; reprint of 1927 edition), p. 70.

54. Margaret Sanger, *My Fight for Birth Control* (Elmsford, N.Y.: Maxwell Reprint Company, 1969; reprint of 1931 edition), pp. 11–12.

55. Gray, *Margaret Sanger*, p. 262.

56. Sanger, *Autobiography*, p. 22.

57. Gray, *Margaret Sanger*, p. 307.

58. Ibid.

59. Nathan G. Hale, Jr., *Freud and the Americans* (New York: Oxford University Press, 1971), pp. 4, 331, 332–368.

60. Dorothy Ross, *G. Stanley Hall: The Psychologist as Prophet* (Chicago: University of Chicago Press, 1972), p. 4.

61. Ibid., p. 3.

62. Ibid., pp. 34–35.

63. John Chynoweth Burnham, *Psychoanalysis and American Medicine: 1894–1918* (New York: International Universities Press, 1967), p. 7.

64. G. Stanley Hall, *Adolescence* (New York: D. Appleton & Co., 1904), vol. II, p. 123.

65. Ibid.

66. Ibid., pp. 123–124.

67. Ibid., p. 124.

68. Ibid.

69. Ibid., p. 125.

70. G. Stanley Hall, "The Needs and Methods of Educating Young People in the Hygiene of Sex," *The Pedagogical Seminary* XV (March 1908), p. 165.

71. Ibid., p. 177.

72. Ibid., p. 178.

73. Ibid., p. 168.

74. G. Stanley Hall, "Christianity and Physical Culture," *The Pedagogical Seminary* IX (September 1902), pp. 155–156.

75. Ibid., p. 155.

76. Ibid., p. 156.

77. Hall, *Adolescence*, vol. II, p. 102.

78. Ibid., p. 126.

79. Ibid.

80. Ibid., pp. 126–127.

81. Ibid., p. 293.

82. Ibid., p. 126.

83. Ibid., p. 127.

84. Ibid., p. 294.

85. Sigmund Freud, *Moses and Monotheism*, trans. Katherine Jones (New York: Random House and Alfred A. Knopf, 1939), pp. 90–117. See also Sigmund Freud, *Totem and Taboo* (1913).

86. Hall, *Adolescence*, vol. II, pp. 126, 294.

87. Ibid., pp. 120–121.

88. Ibid., p. 124.

89. Ibid., p. 125.

90. Ibid., p. 141.

91. Ibid., pp. 139–140.

92. Ibid., p. 139.

93. Ibid., p. 116.

94. Ibid., p. 122.

95. Ibid., pp. 636, 638, 642.

96. G. Stanley Hall, "Sex Hygiene in Infantile and Pre-Pubertal Life," *Transactions*, International Congress on School Hygiene (Buffalo, 1914), vol. IV, p. 14.

97. Hall, *Adolescence*, p. 646.

98. Ibid., pp. 646–647.

99. Hall, "Sex Hygiene," p. 10.

100. Ibid., p. 12.

101. Ibid., pp. 13–14.

102. Sigmund Freud, *New Introductory Lectures on Psychoanalysis*, trans. and ed. James Strachey (New York: W. W. Norton, 1965), pp. 134–135. The whole of lecture XXXIII, "Femininity," expresses Freud's regrets and ambiguities about the destiny he saw for women.

103. Hall, "Sex Hygiene," p. 10.

104. Hall, *Adolescence*, pp. 288, 292, n. 1.

105. Ibid., p. 280.

106. Ibid., p. 282.

107. Ibid., pp. 281–282.

108. Ibid., pp. 136, 129–136.

109. Hall, "The Needs and Methods of Educating Young People," p. 177.

110. Ibid., p. 164.

CONCLUSION

1. Tim and Beverly LaHaye, *The Act of Marriage* (1976; New York: Bantam Books, 1978), p. 122.

2. Marabel Morgan, *The Total Woman* (Old Tappan, N.J.: Fleming H. Revell Company, 1973), p. 238.

3. Andrew Greeley, *The Bottom Line Catechism for Contemporary Catholics* (Chicago: Thomas More Press, 1982), p. 304.

4. Ben B. Lindsey and Wainwright Evans, *The Companionate Marriage* (New York: Boni & Liveright, 1927), pp. 227–228.

5. Federal Council of Churches of Christ in America, Committee on Marriage and Home, *Ideals of Love and Marriage* (New York: Federal Council of Churches, 1929), p. 8.

6. George Marsden, *Fundamentalism and American Culture* (New York: Oxford University Press, 1980), pp. 85ff.

7. Ed Wheat and Gaye Wheat, *Intended for Pleasure* (Old Tappan, N.J.: Fleming H. Revell Company, 1977), p. 23.

8. Anthony Kosnik, William Carroll, Agnes Cunningham, Ronald Modras, and James Schulte, *Human Sexuality* (New York: Paulist Press, 1977), p. 78.

9. Ibid., p. 82.

10. Ibid., p. 95.

11. Morgan, *The Total Woman*, p. 133.

12. Ibid., pp. 130–131.

13. Mary Daly, *Beyond God the Father* (Boston: Beacon Press, 1973), pp. 33, 124–131; Rosemary Ruether, "Mother Earth and the Megamachine," and Phyllis Trible, "Genesis 2–3 Reread," in *Womanspirit Rising*, ed. Carol P. Christ and Judith Plaskow (New York: Harper & Row, 1976), pp. 74–83.

14. Judith L. Weidman, ed., *Christian Feminism* (New York: Harper and Row, 1984).

15. Lindsey and Evans, *The Compassionate Marriage*, p. 66.

16. Ibid., pp. 66–67.

17. Alfred C. Kinsey et al., *Sexual Behavior in the Human Female* (1953; New York: Pocket Books, 1973), pp. 298–299, 380, 403.

18. Carol Tavris and Susan Sadd, *The Redbook Report on Female Sexuality* (1975; New York: Dell Publishing Company, 1978), pp. 109–110.

19. Ibid., p. 141.

20. LaHaye, *The Act of Marriage*, p. 202.

21. Ibid., p. 207.

22. Ibid., p. 206.

23. Earl Ubell, "Sex in America Today," *Parade* (October 28, 1984), pp. 11–13.

24. LaHaye, *The Act of Marriage*, p. 67.

25. Ibid., p. 282.

26. Wheat and Wheat, *Intended for Pleasure*, pp. 217–218.

27. Ubell, "Sex in America Today," p. 13.

28. Michael Gordon, "From an Unfortunate Necessity to a Cult of Mutual Orgasm: Sex in American Marital Education Literature, 1830–1940," in *Studies in the Sociology of Sex*, ed. James M. Henslin (New York: Appleton-Century-Crofts, 1971), p. 69.

29. Alice K. Ladas and Beverly Whipple, *G. Spot: And Other Recent Discoveries about Human Sexuality* (New York: Holt, Rinehart & Winston, 1982).

30. Germaine Greer, *The Female Eunuch* (1970; New York: McGraw-Hill, 1972), pp. 34–35.

31. Ibid., p. 39.

32. Ibid., p. 37.

33. Barbara Welter, "The Cult of True Womanhood: 1820–1860," *American Quarterly* XVIII (Summer 1976), pp. 151–174; Ann Douglas, *The Feminization*

of American Culture (New York: Alfred A. Knopf, 1977), p. 67; Caroll Smith-Rosenberg, *Religion and the Rise of the American City* (Ithaca, N.Y.: Cornell University Press, 1971); William G. McLoughlin, introduction to *The American Evangelicals, 1800–1900* (New York: Harper & Row 1968), p. 18.

34. Welter, "The Cult of True Womanhood," p. 151.

35. Max Weber, *The Protestant Ethic and the Spirit of Capitalism* (London: G. Allen and Unwin, 1930).

36. Douglas, *The Feminization of American Culture*, p. 10.

37. *Genesis* 3.

38. *Genesis* 3:16.

39. Krister Stendahl, "Enrichment or Threat? When the Eves Come Marching In," in *Sexist Religion and Women in the Church*, ed. Alice L. Hageman (New York: Association Press, 1974), p. 117.

40. Thomas Aquinas, *Summa Contra Gentiles*, III, 51–52, especially 52.4.

SINCE 1985: REDEEMING THE BODY

1. http://rockhall.com/inductees/ceremonies/1986/ (December 26, 2014)

2. Larry Geller, *Leaves of Elvis' Garden: The Song of His Soul* (Beverly Hills, Calif.: Bell Rock Publishing). Quote found at http://elvispresleybiography.net/elvis-presley-history2.htm (January 6, 2015).

3. J. D. Davis, *Unconquered: The Saga of Cousins Jerry Lee Lewis, Jimmy Swaggart, and Mickey Gilley* (Dallas, Texas: Brown Books Publishing Group, 2012), pp. 75–76.

4. http://www.pbs.org/thisfarbyfaith/people/thomas_dorsey.html (January 16, 2015).

5. Don Cusic, *The Sound of Light: A History of Gospel and Christian Music* (Bowling Green, Ohio: Bowling Green State University Popular Press, 1990), pp. 88–89.

6. https://www.youtube.com/watch?v=hqKQ5OxYofE (January 18, 2015).

7. Albert J. Raboteau, *Slave Religion: The "Invisible Institution" in the Antebellum South* (New York: Oxford University Press, 1978), pp. 73–75. Joseph M. Murphy, *Working the Spirit: Ceremonies of the African Diaspora* (Boston: Beacon Press, 1994), pp. 148–149.

8. Michael J. McClymond, *Embodying the Spirit: New Perspectives on North American Revivalism* (Baltimore: Johns Hopkins University Press, 2004), pp. 25–29.

9. Daniel Silliman, "If I Did Not Believe God Loved the Blackest Negro Girl": Responses to American Racism among Early White Pentecostals," http://danielsilliman.blogspot.com/2014/02/if-i-did-not-believe-god-loved-blackest.html (May 24, 2015).

10. Jon Pareles and Bernard Weinraub, "Ray Charles, Bluesy Essence of Soul, Is Dead at 73," *New York Times*, June 11, 2004, Arts Section, http://www.nytimes.com/2004/06/11/arts/ray-charles-bluesy-essence-of-soul-is-dead-at-73.html (January 8, 2015).

11. Bob Herbert, "Loving Ray Charles," *New York Times*, June 14, 2004, op-ed page, http://www.nytimes.com/2004/06/11/arts/ray-charles-bluesy-essence-of-soul-is-dead-at-73.html (January 8, 2015).

12. J. D. Davis, *Unconquered*, pp. 128–130. Four minutes of the actual argument between Jerry Lee Lewis and Sam Phillips were recorded, and they can be heard at https://www.youtube.com/watch?v=N-wsEcmwJKo (January 19, 2015).

13. Rich Juzwiak, "Prince and His Gay Panic Took Over Last Night's Arsenio," *Gawker*, March 3, 2014, http://gawker.com/prince-and-his-gay-panic-took-over-last-nights-arsenio-1537896202 (January 25, 2015). On the symbolic name change, see Ronin Ro, "A Prince by Any Other Name," *Vanity Fair*, October 19, 2011, http://www.vanityfair.com/hollywood/features/2011/10/prince-bio-201110 (January 25, 2015).

14. Quoted in Marc Di Paolo, "Introduction: Meeting Madonna and C.S. Lewis Again, For the First Time," in *Unruly Catholics: Faith, Heresy, and Politics in Cultural Studies*, ed. Marc Di Paolo (Plymouth, UK: Scarecrow Press, 2013), p. xlv. Also accessible at http://www.rollingstone.com/music/news/the-rolling-stone-interview-madonna-19890323?page=3 (January 18, 2015).

15. Carmen R. Lugo-Lugo, "The Madonna Experience: A U.S. Icon Awakens a Puerto Rican Adolescent's Feminist Consciousness," *Frontiers: A Journal of Women Studies* 22, 2 (2001), p. 127.

16. Mary Lambert, *Behind the Music*, VH1, August 16, 1998. Cited in Lugo-Lugo, "The Madonna Experience," p. 130.

17. Matthew Jacobs, "How Madonna's 'Like a Virgin' Has Changed over 30 Years," *Huffington Post*, November 16, 2014, http://www.huffingtonpost.com/2014/11/06/madonna-like-a-virgin-evolution_n_6110764.html (January 8, 2015). Kenneth Partridge, "Madonna's 'Like a Virgin' at 30: Classic Track-by-Track Album Review," *Billboard*, November 12, 2014, http://www.billboard.com/articles/review/album-review/6312350/madonnas-like-a-virgin-at-30-classic-track-by-track-album (January 8, 2015).

18. Madonna, *Truth or Dare*, video-recording (Boy Toy, Miramax, Propaganda Films, 1991). Quotations from minutes 82 (1:22) to 85 (1:25). https://www.youtube.com/watch?v=Mlbyln43IWQ (January 9, 2015).

19. Georges-Claude Guilbert, *Madonna as Postmodern Myth: How One Star's Self-Construction Rewrites Sex, Gender, Hollywood and the American Dream* (Jefferson, NC: McFarland & Co., 2002), p. 166.

20. "Pepsi Cancels Madonna Ad," *New York Times*, April 5, 1989, http://www.nytimes.com/1989/04/05/business/pepsi-cancels-madonna-ad.html (January 25, 2015).

21. Andrew Greeley, "Madonna's Challenge to Her Church," *America*, May 13, 1989, http://americamagazine.org/issue/100/madonnas-challenge-her-church (January 9, 2015).

22. Maria Gagliano, "Madonna vs. the Virgin Mary" in *Madonna and Me*, ed. Laura Barcella (Berkeley, Calif.: Soft Skull Press, 2012), pp. 41–42.

23. Jamia Wilson, "Are You There, God? It's Me, Madonna," in *Madonna and Me*, ed. Barcella, pp. 44–45.

24. Ibid., p. 46.

25. Lucy O'Brien, *Madonna: Like an Icon* (New York: HarperCollins, 2007), p. 171.

26. Associated Press, "NBC: Debating Madonna Crucifix Scene," September 21, 2006, http://usatoday30.usatoday.com/life/television/news/2006-09-21-NBC-madonna-debate_x.htm (January 10, 2015).

27. Charles Henderson, "Madonna's Crucifixion: Blasphemy or Inspiration?," http://www.godweb.org/madonnacruci.htm (January 11, 2015).

28. BBC, October 20, 2006, http://news.bbc.co.uk/2/hi/entertainment/6069260.stm (January 10, 2015).

29. Based on an interview Lady Gaga did with Oprah Winfrey in March of 2012, http://www.fuse.tv/2012/03/things-lady-gaga-told-oprah (February 1, 2015).

30. Sister Christina Scuccio, "Like a Virgin," video-recording, https://www.youtube.com/watch?v=roe8Uve7cJU (January 17, 2015).

31. Lawrence K. Altman, "Rare Cancer Seen in 41 Homosexuals," *New York Times*, July 3, 1981, https://aids.gov/hiv-aids-basics/hiv-aids-101/aids-timeline/ (January 13, 2015).

32. http://history.nih.gov/NIHInOwnWords/docs/page_30.html (January 18, 2015).

33. Randy Shilts, *And the Band Played On: Politics, People, and the AIDS Epidemic* (New York: St. Martin's Press, 1987), pp. 575–582.

34. Indianapolis Star, "Ryan White's Life: A Timeline," April 8, 2010, http://archive.indystar.com/article/20100408/NEWS/4080374/Ryan-White-s-life-timeline (January 18, 2015). Also see http://ryan-white.memory-of.com/Timeline.aspx (January 18, 2015).

35. Dylan Matthews, "What 'Dallas Buyers' Club' Got Wrong about the AIDS Crisis," *Washington Post*, December 10, 2013, http://www.washingtonpost.com/blogs/wonkblog/wp/2013/12/10/what-dallas-buyers-club-got-wrong-about-the-aids-crisis/ (January 18, 2015).

36. Larry Kramer, *The Normal Heart* (New York: New American Library, 1985), pp. 37–38.

37. Susan E. Henking, "The Legacies of AIDS: Religion and Mourning in AIDS-Related Memoirs," in *Spirituality and Community: Diversity in Lesbian & Gay Experience*, ed. J. Michael Clark and Michael L. Stemmeier (Las Colinas, Texas: Monument Press, 1994), p. 5. In 1986, Falwell denied that he had ever said these widely reported lines: see Mark D. Jordan, *Recruiting Young Love: How Christians Talk about Homosexuality* (Chicago: University of Chicago Press, 2011), p. 172.

38. William F. Buckley, "Crucial Steps in Combating the AIDS Epidemic; Identify All the Carriers," *New York Times*, March 18, 1986, https://www.nytimes.com/books/00/07/16/specials/buckley-aids.html (January 15, 2015).

39. Donna Ferentes, "AIDS Is God's Punishment," in *AIDS: Opposing Viewpoints*, ed. Michael D. Biskup and Karin L. Swisher (San Diego: Greenhaven Press,

1992), pp. 66, 64. Reprinted from Donna Ferentes, "Death Control," *Fidelity*, March 1992.

40. Tony Kushner, *Angels in America, Part Two: Perestroika*, Act Two, Scene Two (New York: Theatre Communications Group, 1995), pp. 173–175.

41. Tony Kushner, *Angels in America, Part Two: Perestroika*, Act Four, Scene Ten (New York: Theatre Communications Group, 1995), p. 275.

42. Ibid., Epilogue, p. 279.

43. Ibid., Epilogue, p. 280.

44. Russell Berman, "The Awkward Clinton-Era Debate over 'Don't Ask Don't Tell,'" *The Atlantic*, October 10, 2014, http://www.theatlantic.com/politics/archive/2014/10/the-awkward-clinton-era-debate-over-dont-ask-dont-tell/381374/ (February 12, 2015).

45. Kay S. Hymowitz, "The Futile Crusade: The Rise and Fall of Joe Fernandez," *City Journal*, Spring 1993, http://www.city-journal.org/story.php?id=1495 (February 12, 2015).

46. Anna Livia and Kira Hall, eds., *Queerly Phrased: Language, Gender, and Sexuality* (New York: Oxford University Press, 1997), p. 338. On Heather and the Congressional Record, see Elon Green, "Lesléa Newman: So What Was That Like?" *New Yorker*, April 14, 2014, http://www.newyorker.com/culture/culture-desk/lesla-newman-so-what-was-that-like (February 12, 2015).

47. Claude J. Summers and Craig Kajorowski, "Bowers v. Hardwick / Lawrence v. Texas," *GLBTQ: An Encyclopedia of Gay, Lesbian, Bisexual, Transgender, and Queer Culture* (Chicago: GLBTQ, 2004), http://www.glbtq.com/social-sciences/bowers_v_hardwick.html (May 23, 2015).

48. James Dao, "Same-Sex Marriage Issue Key to Some G.O.P. Races," *New York Times*, November 4, 2004, http://www.nytimes.com/2004/11/04/politics/campaign/04gay.html?_r=0 (May 24, 2015).

49. Jesse McKinley and Kirk Johnson, "Mormons Tipped Scale in Ban on Gay Marriage," *New York Times*, November 14, 2008, http://www.nytimes.com/2008/11/15/us/politics/15marriage.html?pagewanted=all (May 25, 2015).

50. Daniel Allott, "The Millennial Divide: What Explains Young Americans' Divergent Views on Homosexuality and Abortion?" *American Spectator*, January 22, 2013, http://spectator.org/articles/34057/millennial-divide (May 25, 2015).

51. Richard Wolf, "Supreme Court Agrees to Rule on Gay Marriage," *USA Today*, January 16, 2015, http://www.usatoday.com/story/news/nation/2015/01/16/supreme-court-gay-marriage/21867355/ (May 23, 2015).

52. Margaret Ramirez, "Quincy Diocese among Latest to Depart Episcopal Church Episcopal Church at Crossroads after Defections," *Chicago Tribune*, November 17, 2008, http://articles.chicagotribune.com/2008-11-17/news/0811160208_1_rev-kendall-harmon-episcopal-diocese-rector-of-christ-church (May 25, 2013).

53. http://www.hrc.org/resources/entry/stances-of-faiths-on-lgbt-issues-united-church-of-christ (January 19, 2015).

54. http://www.cbsnews.com/news/mormon-leaders-vow-support-for-gay-rights-with-conditions/ (February 16, 2015).
55. http://www.adherents.com/people/pd/Ellen_DeGeneres.html (May 25, 2015).
56. Dan Savage, *American Savage: Insights, Slights, and Fights on Faith, Sex, Love, and Politics* (New York: Dutton, 2013), pp. 6–11.
57. Ibid., p. 228.
58. Ibid., p. 276.
59. Emily Steel, "Bruce Jenner's Transgender Announcement Draws 16.8 Million on ABC News," *New York Times*, April 25, 2015, http://www.nytimes.com/2015/04/26/business/media/bruce-jenners-transgender-announcement-draws-16-8-million-on-abc-news.html (May 25, 2015). For the buildup, see Sarah Lyall and Jacob Bernstein, "The Transition of Bruce Jenner: A Shock to Some, Visible to All," *New York Times*, February 6, 2015, http://www.nytimes.com/2015/02/07/sports/olympics/the-transition-of-bruce-jenner-a-shock-to-some-visible-to-all.html?_r=0 (February 12, 2015).
60. Mark Oppenheimer, "The Church of Oprah Winfrey and a Theology of Suffering," *New York Times*, May 27, 2011, http://www.nytimes.com/2011/05/28/us/28beliefs.html (January 19, 2015).
61. LaTonya Taylor, "The Church of O," *Christianity Today*, April 1, 2002, http://www.christianitytoday.com/ct/2002/april1/1.38.html (January 19, 2015).
62. Alice Walker, *The Color Purple* (1982; New York: Washington Square Press, 1983), p. 178.
63. Ibid., p. 179.
64. Kristopher Tapley, "Oprah Winfrey Reflects on 'The Color Purple,' America's Disinterest in News and 'Twelve Years a Slave," *HitFix*, February 6, 2014, http://www.hitfix.com/in-contention/oprah-winfrey-reflects-on-the-color-purple-americas-disinterest-in-news-and-12-years-a-slave (January 19, 2015).
65. Alice Walker, *The Color Purple*, pp. 44–47.
66. Tapley, "Oprah Winfrey Reflects on 'The Color Purple,' America's Disinterest in News and 'Twelve Years a Slave."
67. A Grammy-nominated video, "Oh Father," detailed this aspect of Madonna's childhood.
68. Bootie Cosgrove-Mather, "Ellen DeGeneres Molested as Teen," CBS/AP, May 18, 2005, http://www.cbsnews.com/news/ellen-degeneres-molested-as-teen/ (January 19, 2015).
69. John Calvin, *Commentary on Genesis*, chapter 6, and Jonathan Edwards, *A History of the Work of Redemption, Part I: From the Fall to the Flood*, both cited in Peter Gardella, *American Angels: Useful Spirits in the Material World* (Lawrence: University Press of Kansas, 2007), pp. 134, 257 n. 8.
70. Thomas Aquinas, *Summa Contra Gentiles*, Part IV.
71. Emanuel Swedenborg, *Heaven and Its Wonders and Hell, from Things Heard and Seen* (Latin edition, London 1758; 52nd printing, English edition, New York: Swedenborg Foundation, 1964).

72. The statue stands in the Corcoran Gallery in the District of Columbia. Further detail in Gardella, *American Angels*, pp. 135–136.

73. For more detailed accounts of these movies and songs, see Gardella, *American Angels*, pp. 137–161.

74. On Greeley's novel, see Gardella, *American Angels*, pp. 150–152. On Rice and Memnoch, see pp. 161–163.

75. Heinrich Kramer and Jacob Sprenger, *The Malleus Maleficarum*, translated and with an introduction by Montague Summers (London: Pushkin Press, 1948).

76. Elena Evans, "There's Power in the Blood," *Christianity Today*, February 2010, pp. 37–38.

77. Christine Seifert, "Bite Me! (or Don't)," December 2008, http://bitchmagazine. org/article/bite-me-or-dont (February 11, 2015). The article has been widely discussed.

78. Emily Eakin, "Grey Area: How 'Fifty Shades' Dominated the Market" *New York Review of Books Blog*, July 27, 2012, http://www.nybooks.com/blogs/nyrblog/2012/jul/27/seduction-and-betrayal-twilight-fifty-shades/ (February 15, 2015).

79. Linda S. Schearing and Valerie N. Ziegler, *Enticed by Eden: How Western Culture Uses, Confuses, (and Sometimes Abuses) Adam and Eve* (Waco, Texas: Baylor University Press, 2013), p. 67.

80. Ibid., p. 65.

81. Mark and Grace Driscoll, *Real Marriage: The Truth about Sex, Friendship, & Life Together* (Nashville, Tenn.: Thomas Nelson, 2012), pp. 177–203.

82. Cora Daniels and John L. Jackson, Jr., *Impolite Conversations: On Race, Politics, Sex, Money, and Religion* (New York: Atria Books, 2014).

83. Kathryn Lofton, "Everything Queer?" in *Queer Christianities: Lived Religions in Transgressive Forms*, ed. Kathleen T. Talvacchia, Michael F. Pettinger, and Mark Larrimore (New York: New York University Press, 2015), pp. 199, 203.

AFTERWORD: PROJECTING THE FUTURE

1. Aziz Ansari, with Erik Klinenberg, *Modern Romance* (New York: Penguin Press, 2015).

2. Donna Freitas, *Sex and the Soul: Juggling Sexuality, Spirituality, Romance, and Religion on America's College Campuses* (New York: Oxford University Press, 2008), p. 213.

3. Ibid., p. 236.

4. Christian Smith, *Lost in Transition: The Dark Side of Emerging Adulthood* (New York: Oxford University Press, 2011), pp. 16–17, 149.

5. Ibid., p. 193.

6. Hanna Rosin, "Boys on the Side," *The Atlantic*, September 2012, http://www. theatlantic.com/magazine/archive/2012/09/boys-on-the-side/309062/ (May 26,

2015). Also see Kathleen Bogle, *Hooking Up: Sex, Dating, and Relationships on Campus* (New York: NYU Press, 2008).

7. Rachel Donadio, "On Gay Priests, Pope Francis Asks, Who Am I to Judge?" *New York Times*, July 29, 2013, http://www.nytimes.com/2013/07/30/world/europe/pope-francis-gay-priests.html?_r=0 (May 26, 2015).

8. Sylvia Poggoli, "Catholic Synod Highlights Divisions, Sets Stage for Future Battles," npr.org, October 20, 2014. http://www.npr.org/sections/parallels/2014/10/20/357508863/catholic-synod-highlights-divisions-sets-stage-for-future-battles (May 26, 2015).

9. Jeff Gottlieb, "L.A. Diocese Is Steps Ahead of Catholic Debate over Homosexuality," Los Angeles Times, November 9, 2014, http://www.latimes.com/local/california/la-me-catholic-20141110-story.html (May 26, 2015).

10. Debra Hirsch, *Redeeming Sex: Naked Conversations About Sexuality and Spirituality*, Kindle Edition (Forge Partnership Books) (Kindle Locations 1836-1841), April 6, 2015. InterVarsity Press.

11. Associated Press, "Psychologists Reject Gay 'Therapy,'" August 5, 2009, printed in *New York Times*, August 6, 2009, p. A16, http://www.nytimes.com/2009/08/06/health/06gay.html (May 26, 2015).

12. Ed Payne, "Group Apologizes to Gay Community, Shuts Down 'Cure' Ministry," *CNN*, July 8, 2013, http://www.cnn.com/2013/06/20/us/exodus-international-shutdown/ (May 26, 2015).

13. Edward Schumacher-Matos, "The Furor over Gay Conversion Therapy," npr. org, August 4, 2011, http://www.npr.org/sections/ombudsman/2011/08/05/138963061/the-furor-over-gay-conversion-therapy (May 26, 2015).

14. https://petitions.whitehouse.gov/petition/enact-leelahs-law-ban-all-lgbtq-conversion-therapy (May 26, 2015).

15. Amy DeRogatis, *Saving Sex: Sexuality and Salvation in American Evangelicalism* (New York: Oxford University Press, 2015), p. 72.

16. http://www.thelgbtupdate.com/fly-young-red-breakdown-his-recent-success-with-clay-cane-bet/ (May 26, 2015).

17. Jon Caramanica, "Snoop Dogg Has More Than Money on His Mind," *New York Times Magazine*, May 7, 2015, http://www.nytimes.com/2015/05/10/magazine/snoop-dogg-has-more-than-money-on-his-mind.html?_r=0 (May 23, 2015).

18. Michael O'Connor, "TV Ratings: 'Empire' Finishes Unstoppable Season with More Growth," *Hollywood Reporter*, March 19, 2015, http://www.hollywoodreporter.com/live-feed/tv-ratings-empire-finishes-unstoppable-783023 (May 26, 2015).

19. "My Anaconda Don't Want None Unless You Got Yarmulkes, Son," *TMZ*, April 27, 2015, http://www.tmz.com/2015/04/27/nicki-minaj-bar-mitzvah-photo-video-nyc-matt-murstein/ (May 26, 2015).

20. Michel Martin, "Missionaries in Africa Doing More Harm Than Good?" *Tell Me More*, National Public Radio, July 20, 2012, http://www.npr.org/2012/07/20/157105485/missionaries-in-africa-doing-more-harm-than-good (May 26, 2015).

21. Ondi Timoner, *BYOD*, February 25, 2015, https://www.youtube.com/watch?v=2hnoy_hK6eM (May 28, 2015).

22. Margaret Sanger, *Woman and the New Race* (New York: Blue Ribbon Books,1920). Chapter V, p. 15: "What have large families to do with prostitution? Ask anyone who has studied the problem. The size of the family has a direct bearing on the lives of thousands of girls who are living in prostitution. Poverty, lack of care and training during adolescence, overcrowded housing conditions which accompany large families are universally recognized causes of 'waywardness' in girls," http://www.bartleby.com/1013/5.html (May 27, 2015).

23. Peter T. Chattaway, "Lars and the Real Girl," *Christianity Today*, October 12, 2007, http://www.christianitytoday.com/ct/2007/octoberweb-only/larsandtherealgirl.html (May 28, 2015). Harry Forbes, "Lars and the Real Girl," *Catholic News Service*, 2007, http://www.catholicnews.com/data/movies/07mv204.htm (May 28, 2015).

24. George Gurley, "Dawn of the Sexbots," *Vanity Fair*, May 2015, p. 160.

25. Stuart Dredge, "Virtual World Second Life to Be Reincarnated, with Oculus Rift," *The Guardian*, June 24, 2014, http://www.theguardian.com/technology/2014/jun/24/second-life-oculus-rift-virtual-world (May 28, 2015).

26. For transhumanist activities, see the website of the American Academy of Religion. Positive hope for immortality through technology can be found in Ray Kurzweil, *The Singularity Is Near* (New York: Viking Books, 2005), and in Frank Tipler, *The Physics of Immortality* (New York: Doubleday, 1994). The mathematician Vernor Vinge has written negative fictions about this quest for immortality in many books.

Bibliography

PRIMARY SOURCES

Abbott, Lyman. *The Theology of an Evolutionist.* New York: Houghton Mifflin, 1897.

Acton, William. *The Functions and Disorders of the Reproductive Organs.* 1857; London: J. A. Churchill, 1875.

Adams, Henry. *The Education of Henry Adams.* 1907; Boston: Houghton Mifflin, 1918.

Adams, Henry. *Letters to a Niece and Prayer to the Virgin of Chartres.* Boston: Houghton Mifflin, 1920.

Adams, Henry. *Mont-Saint-Michel and Chartres.* 1905; Boston: Houghton Mifflin, 1933.

Adams, Henry. "Primitive Rights of Women," in *Historical Essays.* New York: Charles Scribner's Sons, 1891.

Addams, Jane. *The Spirit of Youth and the City Streets.* New York: Macmillan, 1909.

Alcott, William A. *The Moral Philosophy of Courtship and Marriage.* 1856; Boston: John P. Jewett; Cleveland: H. P. B. Jewett; New York: Sheldon, Blakeman and Company, 1857.

Alcott, William A. *The Physiology of Marriage.* Boston: John P. Jewitt, 1857.

Alcott, William A. *The Young Husband.* Boston: George W. Light, 1839.

Ames, William. *Conscience.* London: 1639.

Aristotle's Master-Piece, editions consulted: London: B. H., 1700; New York: Flying Stationers, 1788; New England, 1831.

Ballerini, Antonio. *Opus Theologicum Morale,* 6 vols. Prati: 1890–1900.

Beecher, Charles. *The Eden Tableau, or Bible Object-Teaching.* Boston: Lee and Shepard, 1880.

Beecher, Charles. *The Incarnation; or Pictures of the Virgin and Her Son.* New York: Harper & Brothers, 1849.

Beecher, Charles. *Patmos or the Unveiling.* Boston: Lee and Shepard, 1896.

Beecher, Henry Ward. *The Life of Jesus the Christ*. 1871; New York, 1891.

Beecher, Henry Ward. *The Sermons of Henry Ward Beecher, in Plymouth Church, Brooklyn*. From Verbatim Reports by T. J. Ellinwood. New York: J. B. Ford, 1876.

Bigelow, Horatio R. *Social Physiology; or, Familiar Talks on the Mysteries of Life*. New York: Union Publishing House, 1891.

Blackwell, Elizabeth. *Counsel to Parents on the Moral Education of Their Children*. 1879; New York: Brentano Brothers, 1883.

Blackwell, Elizabeth. *Essays in Medical Sociology*. London: Ernest Bell, 1902.

Blackwell, Elizabeth. *The Human Element in Sex*. London: J. A. Churchill, 1894.

Blackwell, Elizabeth. *The Laws of Life*. New York: P. Putnam, 1852.

Brownson, Orestes. *Charles Elwood; or, The Infidel Converted*. Boston: Little, Brown, 1840.

Brownson, Orestes. *Works*, 20 vols. Detroit: Thorndike Nourse, 1882–1907.

Bryant, John D. *The Immaculate Conception of the Most Blessed Virgin ... A Dogma of the Catholic Church*. Boston: Patrick Donahoe, 1855.

Bryant, John D. *Pauline Seward*. Baltimore: John Murphy; Pittsburgh: George Quigley; Dublin: R. Grace & Sons, 1847.

Bushnell, Horace. *Christian Nurture*. 1847; New York: Charles Scribner's Sons, 1892.

Bushnell, Horace. *Sermons on Living Subjects*. New York, 1876.

Bushnell, Horace. *Woman's Suffrage: The Reform against Nature*. New York: Charles Scribner and Company, 1869.

Capellmann, Carl. *Pastoral Medicine*. New York: Pustet, 1879.

Code, Joseph B. *Great American Foundresses*. New York: Macmillan, 1929.

Coppens, Charles. *Moral Principles and Medical Practice*, ed. and enlarged by Henry J. Spalding. 1897; New York: Benziger Brothers, 1921.

Corner, George W., ed. *The Autobiography of Benjamin Rush*. Princeton, N.J.: Princeton University Press, 1948.

Cowan, John. *The Science of a New Life*. New York: Cowan & Co., 1874.

Daniels, Cora, and Jackson, John L.Jr. *Impolite Conversations: On Race, Politics, Sex, Money, and Religion*. New York: Atria Books, 2014.

Delaney, John J., ed. *A Woman Clothed with the Sun*. Garden City, N.Y.: Doubleday, 1961.

Dickinson, Robert L., and Beam, Lura. *A Thousand Marriages: A Medical Study of Sex Adjustment*. Baltimore: Williams & Wilkins, 1931.

Dix, Morgan. *Lectures on the Calling of a Christian Woman*. New York: D. Appleton & Co., 1883.

Dorsey, Anna Hanson (McKenney). *The Sister of Charity*. New York: E. Dunigan, 1846.

Drake, Emma F. A. *What a Young Wife Ought to Know*. 1901; Philadelphia: Vir, 1908.

Driscoll, Mark and Grace. *Real Marriage: The Truth about Sex, Friendship, & Life Together*. Nashville, Tenn.: Thomas Nelson, 2012.

Duffey, Eliza B. *The Relations of the Sexes*. New York: Wood & Holbrook, 1876.

Dunlap, Knight. *Social Psychology*. Baltimore: Williams & Wilkins, 1925.

Eddy, Mary Baker. *Miscellaneous Writings 1883–1896*. Boston, 1896.

Eddy, Mary Baker. *Retrospection and Introspection*. Boston, 1891.

Eddy, Mary Baker. *Science and Health*. Boston, 1875.

Edwards, Jonathan. *Original Sin*. 1758; New Haven, Conn.: Yale University Press, 1970.

Elliott, Walter. *The Life of Father Hecker*. New York: Columbus Press, 1891.

Ellis, John. *Marriage and Its Violations*. 1859; New York: Samuel R. Wells, 1873.

Evans, Elizabeth Edson. *The Abuse of Maternity*. Philadelphia: J. B. Lippincott, 1875.

Federal Council of the Churches of Christ in America, Committee on Marriage and Home. *Ideals of Love and Marriage*. New York: Federal Council, 1929.

Finney, Charles G. *Lectures on Revivals of Religion*. 1835; reprint Cambridge: Harvard University Press, 1960.

Foerster, Friedrich Wilhelm. *Marriage and the Sex-Problem*. New York: Frederick A. Stokes, 1936.

Foote, Edward Bliss. *Plain Home Talk*. 1870; New York: Murray Hill Publishing Co., 1881.

Ford, John C, and Kelly, Gerald. *Contemporary Moral Theology*, 2 vols. Westminster, Md.: Newman Press, 1964.

Foster, Randolph Sinks. *Christian Purity*. New York: Harper & Brothers, 1851.

[Franciscus], "De Actibus Conjugum Qui Dicuntur Imperfecti," *American Ecclesiastical Review* III (Aug. 1925), pp. 178–190.

Freud, Sigmund. *Moses and Monotheism*, trans. Katherine Jones. New York: Random House and Alfred A. Knopf, 1939.

Freud, Sigmund. *New Introductory Lectures on Psychoanalysis*, trans. and ed. James Strachey. New York: W. W. Norton, 1965.

Gardner, Augustus K. *Conjugal Sins against the Laws of Life and Health*. New York: J. S. Redfield, 1870.

Geller, Larry. *Leaves of Elvis' Garden: The Song of His Soul*. Beverly Hills, CA: Bell Rock Publishing, 2007.

Gibbons, James. *Our Christian Heritage*. Baltimore: John Murphy, 1889.

Gibbons, James. "The Position of the Blessed Virgin in Catholic Theology," *American Catholic Quarterly Review* III (1878), pp. 594–614.

Gove, Mary S. *Lectures to Women on Anatomy and Physiology*. New York: Harper & Brothers, 1846.

Gray, George Zabriskie. *Husband and Wife, or the Theory of Marriage and Its Consequences*. 1885; Boston: Houghton Mifflin, 1886.

Greer, Germaine. *The Female Eunuch*. New York: McGraw-Hill, 1970.

Gury, Jean Pierre. *Compendium Theologiae Moralis*. Rome: 1869.

Gury, Jean Pierre. *Compendium Theologiae Moralis*, rev. and ed. by Aloysius Sabetti and Timothy Barrett. New York: Pustet, 1906.

Hall, G. Stanley. *Adolescence*. New York: D. Appleton & Co., 1904.

Hall, G. Stanley. "Christianity and Physical Culture," *The Pedagogical Seminary* IX (Sept. 1902).

Hall, G. Stanley. "The Needs and Methods of Educating Young People in the Hygiene of Sex," *The Pedagogical Seminary* XV (March 1908).

Hall, G. Stanley. "Sex Hygiene in Infantile and Prepubertal Life," *Transactions of the International Congress on School Hygiene* IV (1914).

Hammond, William A. *Sexual Impotence, in the Male and Female.* Detroit: George S. Davis, 1887.

Häring, Bernard. *The Law of Christ,* trans. Edwin G. Kaiser. Westminster, Md.: Newman Press, 1966.

Harris, George. *Moral Evolution.* Boston: Houghton Mifflin, 1896.

Hawthorne, Nathaniel. *The Marble Faun.* 1860; New York: New American Library, 1961.

Higginson, Thomas Wentworth. *Common Sense about Women.* Boston: Lee and Shepard; New York: Charles T. Dillingham, 1892.

Hildebrand, Dietrich von. *In Defense of Purity.* New York: Sheed & Ward, 1935.

Hodge, Charles. *Systematic Theology.* New York: Charles Scribner & Co., 1872.

Hogan, J. B. *Clerical Studies.* Boston: Marlier, Callanan & Co., 1898.

Holcombe, William H. *The End of the World.* Philadelphia: J. B. Lippincott, 1881.

Hollick, Frederick. *The Marriage Guide or Natural History of Generation.* New York: T. W. Strong, 1850.

Hollick, Frederick. *The Marriage Guide.* New York: T. W. Strong, 1850.

Holmes, Oliver Wendell. *Elsie Venner.* New York: Grossett & Dunlap, 1883.

Home, Henry, Lord Kames. *Elements of Criticism.* New York: A. S. Barnes & Co., 1855.

Hooker, Isabella Beecher. *A Mother's Letters to a Daughter on Woman Suffrage.* Hartford, 1870.

Hooker, Isabella Beecher. *Womanhood: Its Sanctities and Fidelities.* Boston, 1874.

Howe, Joseph, W. *Excessive Venery, Masturbation, and Continence.* 1887; New York: E. B. Trent, 1896.

Ingersoll, Andrew J. *In Health.* 1877; Boston: Lee & Shepard, 1899.

Ireland, John. *The Church and Modern Society.* Chicago: D. H. McBride & Co., 1896.

Jackson, James Caleb. *The Sexual Organism.* 1861; Boston: B. Leverett Emerson, 1864.

Jone, Heribert. *Moral Theology,* rev. by Urban Adelman. 1929; Westminster, Md.: Newman Press, 1946.

Kellogg, John Harvey. *Plain Facts for Old and Young.* 1877; Burlington, Iowa: J. F. Segner & Co., 1888.

Kenrick, Francis Patrick. *Theologiae Moralis.* Philadelphia: Eugene Cummiskey, 1841–1843.

Kenrick, Peter Richard. *The New Month of Mary.* Philadelphia: Eugene Cummiskey, 1840.

Knowlton, Charles. *The Fruits of Philosophy.* Philadelphia: F. P. Rogers, 1839.

Könings, Anthony. *Theologia Moralis*. Boston: Patrick Donahoe, 1874.

Kramer, Heinrich, and Sprenger, Jacob. *The Malleus Maleficarum*, trans. and with an introduction by Montague Summers. London: Pushkin Press, 1948.

Kramer, Larry. *The Normal Heart*. New York: New American Library, 1985.

Kushner, Tony. *Angels in America, Part Two: Perestroika*. New York: Theatre Communications Group, 1995.

Larmont, M., and Banister, E. *Medical Adviser and Marriage Guide*. New York, 1861.

Lewis, Denslow. *The Gynecologic Consideration of the Sexual Act*. Chicago: Henry O. Shepard Company, 1900.

Lewis, Dio. *Chastity, or, Our Secret Sins*. 1874; New York: Canfield Publishing, 1888.

The Life of Cornelia Connelly, . . . Foundress of the Society of the Holy Child Jesus, by A Member of the Society. New York: Longmans, Green and Co., 1922.

Liguori, Alphonsus. *The Glories of Mary*. New York: P. J. Kenedy, 1852.

Liguori, Alphonsus. *Homo Apostolicus*. Mechlinae: S. Congregatio de Propaganda Fide, 1868.

Liguori, Alphonsus. *Praxis Confessarii*. Graz, 1954.

Liguori, Alphonsus. *Theologia Moralis*. 1748; Graz, 1954.

Lindsey, Ben. B., and Evans, Wainwright. *The Companionate Marriage*. New York: Boni & Liveright, 1927.

Lofton, Kathryn. "Everything Queer?," in *Queer Christianities: Lived Religions in Transgressive Forms*, ed. Kathleen T. Talvacchia, Michael F. Pettinger, and Mark Larrimore. New York: New York University Press, 2015.

Longfellow, Henry Wadsworth. *Complete Poetical Works*. Boston: Houghton Mifflin, 1893.

Lowell, James Russell. *Poetical Works*. 1857; Boston: Fields, Osgood, & Co., 1871.

Madonna. *Truth or Dare*, video-recording. Boy Toy, Miramax, Propaganda Films, 1991.

Mahan, Asa. *The Scripture Doctrine of Christian Perfection*. 1839; Boston: Waite, Pierce, 1849.

Marie Josephine. *The Mystical Rose*. New York: D. Appleton & Co., 1865.

McHugh, John A., and Callan, Charles. *Moral Theology: A Complete Course*. New York: Joseph F. Wagner, 1929–1930.

McKeever, Paul E. "Seventy Five Years of Moral Theology in America," *American Ecclesiastical Review* CLII: 1 (Jan. 1965), pp. 17–32.

McPherson, Aimée Semple. *This Is That: Personal Experiences, Sermons and Writings*. Los Angeles: Bridal Call Publishing House, 1919.

McPherson Aimée Semple, and Stiffler, Georgia. *The Foursqure Gospel*. Los Angeles: Echo Park Evangelistic Association, 1946.

Merritt, Timothy, and King, D. S., eds. *The Guide to Christian Perfection*, Vols. 5–12 (Nov. 1843–June 1844).

Messbarger, Paul R. *Fiction with a Parochial Purpose: Social Uses of American Catholic Literature, 1884–1900*. Boston: Boston University Press, 1971.

Morgan, Marabel. *The Total Woman*. Old Tappan, N.J.: Fleming H. Revell Company, 1973.

Mother Seraphine, ed. *Immortelles of Catholic Columbian Literature*. Chicago: D. H. McBride & Company, 1897.

Napheys, George, H. *The Physical Life of Woman*. 1873; Philadelphia: David McKay, 1888.

Napheys, George H. *The Transmission of Life*. 1871; Philadelphia: David McKay, 1889.

Nichols, Thomas L. *Human Physiology, the Basis of Sanitary and Social Science*. London: Trübner & Co., 1872.

Nichols, Thomas L. *Women in All Ages and Nations*. 1849; New York: Fowlers and Wells, 1855.

Nichols, Thomas L., and Gove, Mary S. *Marriage: Its History, Character, and Results*. New York: T. L. Nichols, 1854.

Norton, Carol. *Woman's Cause*. Boston: Dana Estes & Company, 1895.

Noyes, John Humphrey. *Male Continence*. New York: Gordon Press, 1975.

O'Malley, Austin, and Walsh, James J. *Pastoral Medicine*. New York: Longmans, Green, 1906.

Outler, Albert C., ed. *John Wesley*. New York: Oxford University Press, 1964.

Palmer, Phoebe. *Promise of the Father, or, a Neglected Specialty of the Last Days*. 1859; New York: W. C. Palmer, 1868.

Palmer, Phoebe. *The Way of Holiness, with Notes by the Way*, 36th ed. New York, 1856.

Pomeroy, H. S. *The Ethics of Marriage*. New York: Funk & Wagnalls, 1888.

Presbyterian Church in the U.S.A. *Twenty-Four Views of Marriage*. New York: Macmillan, 1930.

Putnam, James Jackson. *Human Motives*. Boston: Little, Brown, 1915.

Rush, Benjamin. *Sermons to Gentlemen upon Temperance and Exercise*. Philadelphia, 1772.

Rush, Benjamin. *Thoughts upon Female Education*. Philadelphia: Pritchard & Hall, 1787.

Rush, Benjamin. *Three Lectures upon Animal Life*. Philadelphia: Budd and Bartram, 1799.

Sanger, Margaret. *An Autobiography*. 1938; Elmsford, N.Y.: Maxwell Reprint Co., 1970.

Sanger, Margaret. *The Pivot of Civilization*. London: Jonathan Cape, 1923.

Sanger, Margaret. *What Every Girl and Boy Should Know*. 1931; Elmsford, N.Y.: Maxwell Reprint Co., 1969.

Sanger, Margaret. *Woman and New Race*. 1920; Elmsford, N.Y.: Maxwell Reprint Co., 1969.

Sanger, William, W. *The History of Prostitution*. New York: Harper & Brothers, 1859.

[A Physician]. *Satan in Society*. Cincinnati: C. F. Vent; Chicago: J. S. Goodman & Co., 1871.

Saunders, Randall, N. *Remembering Claverack College.* Hudson, N.Y.: Hudson Evening Register, 1944.

Savage, Dan. *American Savage: Insights, Slights, and Fights on Faith, Sex, Love, and Politics.* New York: Dutton, 2013.

Sharkey, Don. *The Woman Shall Conquer.* Kenosha, Wisc.: Franciscan Marytown Press, 1973.

Sims, J. Marion. *The Story of My Life*, ed. H. Marion-Sims. New York: D. Appleton & Co., 1884.

Slater, Thomas. *A Manual of Moral Theology for English-Speaking Countries.* New York: Benziger Brothers, 1908.

Smyth, Newman. *Through Science to Faith.* New York: Charles Scribner's Sons, 1902.

Stall, Sylvanus. *What a Young Husband Ought to Know.* 1899; Philadelphia: Vir., 1907.

Stockton, T. H. "The Gradations of Love," *The Guide to Christian Perfection* V: 4 (June 1843).

Storer, Horatio R. *The Causation, Course, and Treatment of Reflex Insanity in Women.* Boston: Lee and Shepard, 1871.

Storer, Horatio R. *Is It I? A Book for Every Man.* 1867; Boston: Lee and Shepard, 1868.

Stowe, Harriet Beecher. *Agnes of Sorrento.* 1862; Boston: Houghton Mifflin, 1883.

[Stowe, Harriet Beecher]. "Bodily Religion: A Sermon on Good Health," in *The Chimney-Corner.* 1868; Plainview, N.Y.: Books for Libraries Press, 1972.

Stowe, Harriet Beecher. *Religious Poems.* Boston: Ticknor and Fields, 1867.

Stowe, Harriet Beecher. *Religious Studies, Sketches, and Poems.* Boston, 1896.

Stowe, Harriet Beecher. *Woman in Sacred History.* New York: J. B. Ford, 1874.

Swedenborg, Emmanuel. *Heaven and Its Wonders and Hell, from Things Heard and Seen.* Latin edition, London 1758; 52nd printing, English edition, New York: Swedenborg Foundation, 1964.

Tanquerey, Adolphe. *The Spiritual Life.* Tournai: Desclée & Co., 1930.

Thomas Aquinas. *Summa Contra Gentiles*, Book Four: Salvation, trans. Charles J. O'Neill. Notre Dame, Ind.: University of Notre Dame Press, 1975.

Walker, Alice. *The Color Purple.* 1982; New York: Washington Square Press, 1983.

Secondary Sources

Ahlstrom, Sydney E. *A Religious History of the American People.* New Haven, Conn.: Yale University Press, 1972.

Ansari, Aziz, with Klinenberg, Erik. *Modern Romance.* New York: Penguin Press, 2015.

Ashe, Geoffrey. *The Virgin.* London: Routledge & Kegan Paul, 1976.

Barcella, Laura, ed. *Madonna and Me.* Berkeley, Calif.: Soft Skull Press, 2012.

Barker-Benfield, G. J. *The Horrors of the Half-Known Life.* New York: Harper & Row, 1976.

Beall, Otho T., Jr. "Aristotle's Master Piece in America," *William and Mary Quarterly* XX (April 1963).

Billington, Ray Allen. *The Protestant Crusade, 1800–1860.* 1938; Gloucester, Mass.: Peter Smith, 1963.

Biskup, Michael D., and Swisher Karin L., eds. *AIDS: Opposing Viewpoints.* San Diego: Greenhaven Press, 1992.

Bogle, Kathleen. *Hooking Up: Sex, Dating, and Relationships on Campus.* New York: NYU Press, 2008.

Burlage, Dorothy D. "Judaeo-Christian Influences on Female Sexuality," in *Sexist Religion and Women in the Church,* ed. Alice Hageman. New York: Association Press, 1974.

Burnham, John Chynoweth. *Psychoanalysis & American Medicine: 1894–1918.* New York: International Universities Press, 1967.

Carson, Gerald. *Cornflake Crusade.* New York: Rinehart & Co., 1957.

Caskey, Marie Carpenter. *Faith and Theology in the Beecher Family.* Ph.D. diss., Yale University, 1974.

Chinnici, Joseph P. "Organization of the Spiritual Life: American Catholic Devotional Works, 1791–1866," *Theological Studies* 40: 2 (June 1979), pp. 229–255.

Clark, J. Michael, and Stemmeier, Michael L., eds. *Spirituality and Community: Diversity in Lesbian & Gay Experience.* Las Colinas, Texas: Monument Press, 1994.

Cott, Nancy F. "Passionlessness: An Interpretation of Victorian Sexual Ideology, 1790–1850," in *A Heritage of Her Own,* ed. Cott and Elizabeth H. Pleck. New York: Simon & Schuster, 1979.

Cusic, Don. *The Sound of Light: A History of Gospel and Christian Music.* Bowling Green, Ohio: Bowling Green State University Popular Press, 1990.

Daly, Mary. *Beyond God the Father.* Boston: Beacon Press, 1973.

Davis, J. D. *Unconquered: The Saga of Cousins Jerry Lee Lewis, Jimmy Swaggart, and Mickey Gilley.* Dallas: Brown Books Publishing Group, 2012.

Degler, Carl. "What Ought to Be and What Was," *American Historical Review* 79 (1974), pp. 1467–1490.

DeRogatis, Amy. *Saving Sex: Sexuality and Salvation in American Evangelicalism.* New York: Oxford University Press, 2015.

Di Paolo, Marc, ed. *Unruly Catholics: Faith, Heresy, and Politics in Cultural Studies.* Plymouth, UK: Scarecrow Press, 2013.

Dillenschneider, R. P. Clément. *La Mariologie de S. Alphonse de Liguori.* Fribourg, 1931.

Ditzion, Sidney. *Marriage, Morals, and Sex in America: A History of Ideas.* New York: Bookman Associates, 1953.

Douglas, Ann. *The Feminization of American Culture.* New York: Alfred A. Knopf, 1977.

Ehrenreich, Barbara, and English, Deirdre. *For Her Own Good: 150 Years of The Experts' Advice to Women.* Garden City, N.Y.: Doubleday, 1978.

Foster, Charles H. *The Rungless Ladder: Harriet Beecher Stowe and New England Puritanism*. Durham, N.C.: Duke University Press, 1954.

Freitas, Donna. *Sex and the Soul: Juggling Sexuality, Spirituality, Romance, and Religion on America's College Campuses*. New York: Oxford University Press, 2008.

Gardella, Peter. *American Angels: Useful Spirits in the Material World*. Lawrence: University Press of Kansas, 2007.

Geiger, Louis-B. *Le Probleme de l'Amour chez Saint Thomas d'Aquin*. Montreal: Institute d'Études médiévales, 1952.

Gilson, Etienne. *The Mystical Theology of St. Bernard*, trans. A. H. C. Downes. London: Sheed and Ward, 1940.

Ginder, Richard. *Binding with Briars: Sex and Sin in the Catholic Church*. Englewood Cliffs, N.J.: Prentice-Hall, 1975.

Gordon, Michael. "From an Unfortunate Necessity to a Cult of Mutual Orgasm: Sex in American Marital Education Literature, 1830–1940," in *Studies in the Sociology of Sex*, ed. James M. Henslin. New York: Appleton-Century-Crofts, 1971.

Graef, Hilda. *Mary: A History of Doctrine and Devotion*, 2 vols. New York: Sheed and Ward, 1963–1965.

Gray, Madeleine. *Margaret Sanger*. New York: Richard Marek Publishers, 1979.

Guilbert, Georges-Claude. *Madonna as Postmodern Myth: How One Star's Self-Construction Rewrites Sex, Gender, Hollywood and the American Dream*. Jefferson, N.C.: McFarland & Co., 2002.

Hale, Nathan G. *Freud and the Americans*. New York: Oxford University Press, 1971.

Haller, John S., and Haller, Robin S. *The Physician and Sexuality in Victorian America*. Urbana: University of Illinois Press, 1974.

Hirsch, Debra. *Redeeming Sex: Naked Conversations about Sexuality and Spirituality*. Downers Grove, Ill.: InterVarsity Press, 2015

Howe, Daniel Walker. *The Unitarian Conscience: Harvard Moral Philosophy, 1805–1861*. Cambridge: Harvard University Press, 1970.

Jones, Charles Edwin. *Perfectionist Persuasion: The Holiness Movement and American Methodism, 1867–1936*. Metuchen, N.J.: Scarecrow Press, 1974.

Jordan, Mark D. *Recruiting Young Love: How Christians Talk about Homosexuality*. Chicago: University of Chicago Press, 2011.

Kennedy, David M. *Birth Control in America: The Career of Margaret Sanger*. New Haven, Conn.: Yale University Press, 1970.

Kinsey, Alfred C., et al. *Sexual Behavior in the Human Female*. 1953; New York: Pocket Books, 1973.

Kosnik, Anthony, et al. *Human Sexuality*. New York: Paulist Press, 1977.

Laurentin, René. *Court Traité de Théologie Mariale*. Paris, 1959.

Livia, Anna, and Hall, Kira, eds. *Queerly Phrased: Language, Gender, and Sexuality*. New York: Oxford University Press, 1997.

Manoir, Hubert du, ed. *Maria: Études sur la Sainte vierge*, 6 vols. Paris: Beauchesne, 1964.

Masters, William H., and Johnson, Virginia E. "The Role of Religion in Sexual Dysfunction," in *Sexuality and Human Values*, ed. Mary S. Calderone. New York: Association Press, 1974.

McClymond, Michael J. *Embodying the Spirit: New Perspectives on North American Revivalism*. Baltimore: Johns Hopkins University Press, 2004.

Murphy, Joseph M. *Working the Spirit: Ceremonies of the African Diaspora*. Boston: Beacon Press, 1994.

Noonan, John T., Jr. *Contraception*. Cambridge: Harvard University Press, 1966.

O'Brien, Lucy. *Madonna: Like an Icon*. New York: HarperCollins, 2007.

O'Connor, Edward, ed. *The Dogma of the Immaculate Conception*. Notre Dame, Ind.: University of Notre Dame Press, 1958.

O'Neill, William L. *Everyone Was Brave: A History of Feminism in America*. 1969; Chicago: Quadrangle Books, 1971.

Peters, John L. *Christian Perfection and American Methodism*. New York: Abingdon Press, 1956.

Phayer, J. Michael. *Sexual Liberation and Religion in Nineteenth Century Europe*. London: Croom Helm Ltd., 1977.

Raboteau, Albert J. *Slave Religion: The "Invisible Institution" in the Antebellum South*. New York: Oxford University Press, 1978.

Rahner, Karl. *Theological Investigations*, vol. I, trans. Cornelius Ernst. London, 1974.

Reed, James. *From Private Vice to Public Virtue: The Birth Control Movement and American Society since 1830*. New York: Basic Books, 1978.

Ross, Dorothy. *G. Stanley Hall: The Psychologist as Prophet*. Chicago: University of Chicago Press, 1972.

Rugoff, Milton. *Prudery and Passion*. New York: G. P. Putnam's Sons, 1971.

Schearing, Linda S., and Ziegler, Valerie N. *Enticed by Eden: How Western Culture Uses, Confuses, (and Sometimes Abuses) Adam and Eve*. Waco, Texas: Baylor University Press, 2013

Schnucker, Robert Victor. *Views of Selected Puritans, 1560–1630, on Marriage and Human Sexuality*. Ph.D. diss., University of Iowa, 1969.

Sherfey, Mary Jane. *The Nature and Evolution of Female Sexuality*. New York: Random House, 1972.

Shilts, Randy. *And the Band Played On: Politics, People, and the AIDS Epidemic*. New York: St. Martin's Press, 1987.

Smith, Christian. *Lost in Transition: The Dark Side of Emerging Adulthood*. New York: Oxford University Press, 2011.

Smith, Daniel Scott. "Family Limitation, Sexual Control, and Domestic Feminism in Victorian America," *Feminist Studies* 1 (Winter–Spring 1973).

Smith, H. Shelton. *Changing Concepts of Original Sin*. New York: Charles Scribner's Sons, 1955.

Smith, Timothy L. *Revivalism and Social Reform*. New York: Abingdon Press, 1957.

Stendahl, Krister. "Enrichment or Threat? When the Eves Come Marching In," in *Sexist Religion and Women in the Church*, ed. Alice L. Hageman. New York: Association Press, 1974.

Tannehill, Reay. *Sex in History*. New York: Stein & Day, 1980.

Tavris, Carol, and Sudd, Susan. *The Redbook Report on Female Sexuality*, 1975; New York: Dell Publishing Co., 1978.

Thomas, Lately. *Storming Heaven: The Lives and Turmoils of Minnie Kennedy and Aimée Semple McPherson*. New York: William Morrow & Co., 1970.

Warner, Marina. *Alone of All Her Sex*. New York: Alfred A. Knopf, 1976.

Welter, Barbara. "The Cult of True Womanhood, 1820–1860," *American Quarterly* XVIII (Summer 1976), pp. 151–174.

Williams, Peter W., *Popular Religion in America*. Englewood Cliffs, N.J.: Prentice-Hall, 1980.

Acknowledgments

FOR INSPIRING THIS work, I thank my mother, who taught me to pray to the Virgin Mary, and my father, who showed me that faith could be tolerant. Professor Sydney Ahlstrom opened the field of American religious history to me. He helped me get the temporary teaching appointments that supported me while I researched and wrote, and insisted that I should produce a popular book of about two hundred pages. My students at Miami University of Ohio, Indiana University, Colgate University, and Manhattanville College encouraged me with their interest. Just after I took the Foreign Service Test in an attempt to escape from my notes and drafts, my first love, Lorrie Greenhouse, came back into my life, married me, listened to the best prose I could write, and told me when it was good enough. When I was in need of friends to turn the text into a manuscript, Min Houts and Charles Mulholland volunteered to be those friends. Finally, Cynthia Read became a collaborator as well as an editor in turning the manuscript into a book.

Over the years of gathering material, many librarians helped me, especially those at Harvard, Yale, the Graduate Theological Union, the Pacific School of Religion, the University of California at Berkeley, the Marian Library of the University of Dayton, the Kinsey Institute for Sex Research, and Syracuse University. I promise that I will now mail back all my overdue books.

West Haven, Connecticut
P.G.
January 1985

For the updated edition, I again thank Cynthia Read of Oxford University Press, who gave the project her immediate and continuing support. I also thank my wife, Lorrie Greenhouse Gardella, and my son, William

Gardella, for reading drafts of the new material and giving wise editorial advice. William's friend, Amanda Gregg, and my niece Molly Greenhouse also read the Afterword and shared their perspectives.

Hamden, Connecticut
P.G.
May 2016

Index

Abbott, Lyman, 54

abortion, 2, 35, 128, 131, 171

The Abuse of Maternity (Evans), 57, 61

Adam (Book of Genesis). *See also* Eve: descendants of, 176; God's warning to, 179; Millennial generation and, 189; offspring of, 52–53; original sin and, 3, 38, 40, 42, 93; prelapsarian nature of, 63, 143; shame and, 155; as slave to passion, 52

Adams, Henry, 97–98, 112–113, 124–125

Adolescence (Hall), 137, 140–142, 144

adultery: mental, 19, 55; purity through avoiding, 39; as sin, 8, 13, 16; suspicion of, 20–21

Adventists, 42, 46, 50, 62

Aelred of Rievaulx (abbot), 116

Agnes of Sorrento (Stowe), 28–29, 102–103, 106

Ahlstrom, Sydney E., 6

AIDS (Acquired Immunodeficiency Syndrome): Christians' condemnation of homosexuality and, 169; early history of, 167–168; gay community and, 168–169; global campaign to combat, 189; heterosexuals with, 169; Madonna's concert drawing attention to, 166–167; treatments for, 168

Albert the Great, 12

Albigensian heresy, 13–14

Alcott, Bronson, 114

Alcott, William A., 45–46

Alphonsus Liguori (Catholic saint). *See* Liguori, Alphonsus

Amadeus of Lausanne (Catholic saint), 116

American Bible Society, 44

American Episcopal Prayer Book, 39

American Gynecological Society, 60

American Home Missionary Society, 44

The American Nun; or, The Effects of Romance, 33

American Romanticism: harmony with nature as ideal for, 114; human desire and, 118–119; Marian devotion and, 97, 99–104, 106, 111, 114–115; marriage and, 100; Victorian sexual restraints and, 110; women as ideal in, 91, 96, 103, 129, 141–142, 154; women's passion and, 124

American Savage (Savage), 173

American Sunday School Union, 44, 49

American Tract Society, 44

Ames, William, 37

amplexus reservatus (restricted form of
    intercourse), 13–15
Andriveau, Apolline, 96
Angels in America (Kushner),
    169–170, 176
angels in American popular culture,
    176–177
Anglican Articles of Religion, 50–51, 82
Anglican Communion, 171
Annie Sprinkle (performance artist),
    189–190
annunciation. *See under* Virgin Mary
"Annunciation Night" (Sister Marie
    Josephine), 107
"Another Saturday Night" (Cooke), 161
Ansari, Aziz, 183
Aquinas, Thomas, 8–12, 156, 176
Aristotle, 9
Aristotle's Master-piece, 38–39, 43
Assemblies of God denomination, 89
Augustine (Catholic saint): Catholic
    sexual doctrine and, 8–9; on
    "daughters of men" in Genesis,
    176; Liguri and, 12; on marriage
    and procreation, 17; original sin
    and, 3, 54; passion distrusted
    by, 10, 18, 156; on sin as concu-
    piscence, 116–117; on the Virgin
    Mary, 94
*Awful Disclosures of the Hotel Dieu
    Nunnery* (Monk), 23–24
Azalea, Iggy, 189

Bachmann, Michele, 186
"Bad Blood" (Swift), 188
Ballerini, Antonio, 17
Baptists, 77, 160. *See also* Evangelicals
Bauer, Jill, 190–191
The Beatles, 163
The Beautiful Nun (Buntline), 26–27
Beecher, Charles, 123–124
Beecher, Henry Ward, 104, 137

Beecher, Lyman, 31
Bellarmine, Robert, 11
Bernadette Soubirous (Catholic
    saint), 91–94, 118. *See also Song of
    Bernadette*
Bernard of Clairvaux (Catholic saint),
    93, 112, 115–118
Berry, Chuck, 159
bestiality, 8
Biden, Joe, 171
birth control. *See also* abortion; contra-
    ceptives: advocacy of, 1, 75, 79, 113,
    126–136, 148, 155, 191; *amplexus re-
    servatus and*, 13–15; Comstock Laws
    and, 75; in France, 96; movement,
    1, 4, 191 (*See also* Sanger, Margaret);
    natural law and, 129; opposition to,
    61, 133; Protestants' acceptance of,
    63, 148; Roman Catholic Church
    and, 35, 96, 133, 148
Bisqueyburu, Justine, 95
The Black Domino (Auber), 122
Blackwell, Elizabeth, 47, 61
"Blank Space" (Swift), 189
Blond Ambition World Tour
    (Madonna), 164
Book of Common Prayer, 3, 147
The Book of Mormon (musical), 173
"Born This Way" (Lady Gaga), 167
Boston (Massachusetts), 30
*Bottom Line Catechism for Contemporary
    Catholics* (Greeley), 146–147
Bourne, George, 25
"Bring It on Home to Me" (Cooke), 161
Brisse, Adele, 96
Brook Farm commune, 53, 113–114
Brown, Brian, 173
Brown, James, 159
Brown, Norman O., 140
Brownlee, W.C., 31–32
Brownson, Orestes: Brook Farm
    and, 114; on Catholic novelists,

120–121; redemption and, 125; on
the Virgin Mary, 111–112; wom-
en's rights movement criticized
by, 111

Brownson, Sarah, 120–121

Brownson's Quarterly Review, 120

Bruno Mars (musician), 189

Bryant, John D., 106–107, 119

Buckley, William F., 169

Budapest, Zsuzsanna, 178

Buffy the Vampire Slayer (television
show), 178

Buntline, Ned, 26–28, 31

Bush, George W., 171

Bushnell, Horace: consecration in the
womb concept of, 72, 133; on diet,
48–49; Ingersoll and, 71; Italian
travels of, 32–33; on original sin,
47–48, 51; perfectionist emphasis
of, 64; on physical forms of redemption, 48; Virgin Mary and,
97, 104–105, 119; women's suffrage
and, 112

Businessman's Revival (New York,
1858), 85

Cabrini, St. Frances Xavier, 122

"California Gurls" (Perry), 188

Calvin, John, 176

Campbell, Alexander, 52–53, 64

Campbellite movement, 52–53

Campus Crusade for Christ, 1–2, 4

"The Cathedral" (Lowell), 101

Catholics. *See also* Roman
Catholicism: ecstatics, 91–97, 110;
homosexuality and, 152, 171; novels
intended for, 120; sexual repression and, 63–64; U.S. immigration and, 6, 21, 30–31, 90, 97–98;
violence against, 31

Catholic Theological Society of
America, 4, 149

celibacy. *See also* chastity: communes
and, 53; missionaries and the
Catholic doctrine of, 132; priests
and, 20, 31–32; Protestant suspicion of, 31–32

Charles, Ray, 159, 161–162

Charlestown (Massachusetts), 31

Charmed (television show), 178

Chartres Cathedral (France), 98, 101

chastity. *See also* celibacy: concupiscence and, 116; Hall on, 141; Luther
on, 32; marriage and proper levels
of, 55–56; nuns' vow of, 31; Virgin
Mary and, 111; virtue of, 34, 114–115

Chastity; or, Our Secret Sins (Lewis), 46

Chicago (Illinois), 30

childbirth, dangers of, 60–61

"Children of the Rainbow" curriculum
(New York City public schools), 170

Chiniquy, Charles, 25

Christian Domestic Discipline movement, 180–181

Christian Feminism (1984 volume), 150

Christianity. *See also specific
sects*: American version of, 6; definition of, 5; medicine and, 37–65

Christian motherhood, 103–105, 140

Christian Nurture (Bushnell),
48–49, 72

Christian perfection, 51, 82–89,
136, 144

Christian Science, 52, 105–106, 175

Christus (Longfellow), 101

"The Church and the Republic"
(Hecker), 123

Churches of Christ denomination, 52

Church of England, 3, 39. *See also*
Episcopalianism

Church of God in Christ
denomination, 89

Church of the Nazarene
denomination, 89

Cincinnati (Ohio), 30

The Claiming of Sleeping Beauty
    (Rice), 180

Clairvaux, Bernard of, 93, 112, 115–118

Claverack College, 127, 136

Clinton, Bill, 170

clitoris: clitoridectomy and, 58, 60;
    function of, 39, 72–74, 152–153

Code, Joseph B., 122

coitus interruptus, 57, 66

The Color Purple (Walker), 174–175

Common Prayer, Book of, 3, 147

communes in nineteenth-century
    America, 53–54

The Companionate Marriage (Lindsey),
    147–148

Comstock Laws, 75, 191

conception. *See also* immaculate con-
    ception; procreation: Catholic
    doctrine regarding, 8, 10, 12–14;
    female orgasm and, 12–15; preven-
    tion of, 15, 66, 129; as purpose of
    sex, 8, 10, 12–14, 71, 138

concupiscence: Council of Trent on, 11;
    definition of, 10, 116; of God, 116–118;
    marital sex as remedy for, 17; sin
    and, 3, 11, 63, 147; virtue of, 10

Condomblé, 160

condoms, 57

confession: guidance for priests hear-
    ing, 7, 9, 15, 19; Hogan's criticism
    of, 24–25; penance and, 11; privacy
    of, 9; Protestant suspicion of, 23–
    25, 28, 31–32; sex discussed in, 11

Confessions on a Dance Floor
    (Madonna), 166–167

Congregationalism, 77

*Conjugal Sins against the Laws of Life
    and Health* (Gardner), 47

Connelly, Cornelia, 121–122

Connelly, Pierce, 121

contraceptives. *See also* birth con-
    trol: Catholic doctrine on, 17;
    coitus interruptus and, 57, 66;
    condoms and, 57; douches and, 56;
    prevalence of, 58

convents, 26–27, 29, 31

Cooke, Sam, 159, 161

Coppens, Charles, 63

copulation, 8, 19. *See also* fornication;
    intercourse; sex

Council of Trent (1546), 11

Covenant of the Goddess, 178

Covenant of Unitarian Universalist
    Pagans, 178

Cowan, John, 56–57

Cox, Laverne, 173

Cromwell, Oliver, 30

Culbertson, Rosamond, 25

Daddy's Romance, 170

Daly, Mary, 150

Daniels, Cora, 181

Darwin, Charles, 53

Daughters of Charity at Paris, 95–96

"Dear John" (Swift), 189

Deering, Annie J., 57

Defense of Marriage Act (1996),
    170–171

DeGeneres, Ellen, 172, 174–176

Degler, Carl, 58

Delta of Venus (Nin), 180

Democratic Party (United States), 31

Dempster, John, 85

depravity: evil and, 43; Finney's ar-
    gument against the notion of,
    50–51; hereditary forms of, 48, 71,
    186; sexual pleasure and, 16, 47;
    shame and, 72; "voluntary" forms
    of, 44–45

DeRogatis, Amy, 186

Dickinson, Robert Latou, 58, 74–75

diet, Christianity and, 42–43, 45, 48–
49, 51, 57, 59, 114. *See also* Graham,
Sylvester; Kellogg, John Harvey
Disciples of Christ denomination, 52
Discipline (Methodist doctrinal
book), 83
Dominican order, 94, 177
Donohoe, Bill, 166
"Don't Ask, Don't Tell" (U.S. military
policy on gay service members),
170–171
Dorsey, Anna Hanson, 120
Dorsey, Thomas A., 160
Douglas, Ann, 154–155
The Downfall of Babylon (newspaper), 25
Dracula (Stoker), 178
Drake, Emma F.A., 57, 62
Driscoll, Mark and Grace, 180–181
Duryea, William T., 54

ecstasy. *See also* innocent ecstasy: Catholic women and, 91–97;
definition of, 3; Evangelicals and,
3, 76–89, 110; of incarnation,
107–108; Ingersoll's therapy practices and, 69, 71; methamphet-
amine named for, 167; momentary
nature of, 3; musical forms of,
159–162, 167; orgasm and, 3, 5, 64,
134; religious forms of, 33, 76–
89, 91–97, 112, 122, 130, 159–160;
sexual forms of, 73, 129–131, 157,
165; speaking in tongues and, 3,
77–79, 89, 159; spiritual love and,
113; suspension of the senses in, 5
ecstatics. *See also* evangelicals: Catholic,
91–97, 110; Protestant, 108–110;
sanctification and, 145; spiritual
love and, 113
Eddy, Mary Baker, 52, 61, 64,
105–106, 155

Eden: as allegory for decadence of
love, 139; expulsion from, 52–53,
139, 148–149, 155; innocence
of, 149–150; marriage and, 39;
passion in, 41
The Education of Henry Adams
(Adams), 97–98, 112–113, 124–125
Edwards, Jonathan: on "daughters of
men" in Genesis, 176; emotions in
religious worship and, 33; on life's
dependence on an external force,
40; original sin and, 38, 40, 54; on
physical depravity, 50; on selfishness, 38; on supernatural capacity
of the "elect," 138; on "true virtue,"
144–145
Elders, Jocelyn, 181
Elements of Criticism (Home), 128
Elements of Moral Science (Wayland),
127–128
Elliott, Walter, 114, 123
Ellis, Havelock, 129, 135
Elton John (musician), 187
Empire (television show), 188
The Enlightenment, 37, 97
Ephraim of Syria (Catholic saint), 94
Episcopalianism: Articles of Religion
and, 3, 70, 147; evangelism and,
77; gay clergy and, 171
equiprobabilism, 12, 14
Etheridge, Melissa, 187
Ethics (Aristotle), 9
Evangelicals. *See also* ecstatics;
Methodism: in the American
middle class, 6; Christian perfec-
tion and, 138; early twentieth cen-
tury retrenchment by, 90; ecstasy
and, 3, 76–89, 110; faith healing
and, 80; gospel of desire and, 123;
"Great Reversal" (twentieth century) and, 148; Holiness movement

Evangelicals (*Cont.*)
and, 110; homosexuality and, 153, 171, 186, 189; innocent ecstasy and, 180–181; marriage and, 148–149; masturbation and, 153; medical Christianity and, 50–51; music of, 160; pornography and, 153; rebirth emphasis of, 76–77, 132; redemptive power of women emphasized by, 4–5; restraint and, 80; Rock and Roll Hall of Fame inductees and, 159; sadomasochism and, 180; sex and, 9, 73, 90, 148–149, 151–152, 156, 180–181; sexual advice among, 152–153, 180–181; worship style among, 49

Evangeline (Longfellow), 101, 106

Evans, Elizabeth Edson, 57, 61

Eve (Book of Genesis). *See also* Adam: Alcott's analysis of, 45; fall of, 141–142; Millennial generation and, 189; offspring of, 52–53; original sin and, 38, 42, 45, 93; prelapsarian nature of, 63, 143; shame and, 155; in *Twilight* novels, 179; Virgin Mary contrasted with, 94

Everly Brothers, 159

evil, origin of, 3, 42–43, 45

evolution, 53–54, 90

Ex Machina (film), 192

Exodus International, 186

faith healing, 66, 80

fall of humanity, 5, 18, 41, 71. *See also* original sin

Falwell, Jerry, 169

fan fiction, 179

Fantasia (film), 98

Fats Domino (musician), 159

Federal Council of Churches of Christ, 134, 147–148

feminism: birth control and, 136; free love and, 61; theology and, 150; twentieth century political activism and, 191; Victorian Era and, 156; Virgin Mary and, 98; witchcraft and, 178

Fernandez, Jose, 170

Fifty Shades series (James), 179–180, 189

Fillmore, Millard, 31

Finney, Charles Grandison, 45, 49–51, 64, 85

First Corinthians, 16

Flack, Arthur H., 127–128

Fly Young Red (musician), 189

Foote, Edward Bliss, 71–72, 75, 139

Ford, John C., 17

fornication, 8

Fourth Lateran Council (1215), 9

Francis (Catholic pope), 172, 185–186

Franciscan order, 94

Francis of Assisi (Catholic saint), 112

Franklin, Aretha, 162

Freitas, Donna, 184

French, Daniel Chester, 177

Freud, Sigmund: American audience of, 136; on hysteria, 65–66; infantile sexuality and, 136, 138–139, 143; Oedipal complex and, 136, 140; on orgasms, 136; pansexualism and, 137; psychoanalysis and, 143–144; on religion and sex, 140; on sex and the release of tension, 141; sexual development stages and, 143

Fromm, Erich, 140

Frothingham, Octavius B., 57

Fruitlands commune, 53, 114

Fruits of Philosophy (Knowlton), 56

Gabriel (angel in Incarnation story), 115

Gardner, Augustus K., 47

Garrison, William Lloyd, 57

Gavazzi, Alessandro, 25
Gay Christian Network (GCN), 186
Gaye, Marvin, 162
gay marriage, 170–173, 186
gay rights movement, 169–172, 185–186
Geller, Larry, 159
General Council of the Congregational and Christian Churches, 134
General Synod of the United Church of Christ, 171–172
Genesis, Book of, 155–156, 176. *See also* Eden
Gilley, Mickey, 160
Gilman, Charlotte Perkins, 136
Giraud, Maximin, 95
The Glories of Mary (Ligouri), 108–109
Godfrey of Admont (abbot), 117
Goldman, Emma, 128–129
Gove, Mary S., 46–47
Gradus, Ronna, 190–191
Graham, Sylvester: dietary advice of, 44, 49, 51, 57, 114; on marriage and frequency of intercourse, 55–56; on masturbation, 44; medical Christianity and, 44–45; on orgasm, 55; on "voluntary depravity," 44–45
Grand Street tenement (New York City), 128
Great American Foundresses (Code), 122
Great Awakening, 33, 144
The Great Christian Doctrine of Original Sin Defended (Edwards), 38
"Great Reversal" (Evangelicals in twentieth century), 148
Greeley, Andrew, 24, 146–147, 165, 177
Greer, Germaine, 153–154
Gregory I ("Gregory the Great"; pope), 9, 11
Gregory XVI (pope), 12, 121
Grindr (hookup app), 185
Guadalupe (Mexico), apparition of Mary at, 92, 94

Guerric of Igny (monk), 116–117
The Guide to Holiness (magazine), 85, 88
guilt: Catholicism and, 165; equiprobabilism and, 12; freedom from, 1–2, 174, 193; hereditary forms of, 151; Oedipal complex and, 140; original sin and the inheritance of, 38; overcoming feelings of, 70–71, 83; priests and, 32; sin and, 10; Virgin Mary and, 94
Gury, Jean-Paul, 15, 17, 20
gynecology, 60

Hall, G. Stanley: biographical background of, 137; on Eden and the fall, 141–142; on Edwards and "true virtue," 144–145; Freud's stages of sexual development and, 143; on the holy nature of sex, 137–138, 140–141, 145; on infantile sexuality, 138–139; on New Testament's sexual meaning, 139–140; original sin and, 138; on psychoanalysis and rebirth, 144; on religion and health, 139; on sex and rebirth, 138–139; on sex roles, 142–144; on sex's hereditary effects, 141; on sex's rightful place in religion, 139
Hammond, William, 74
Happiness in Marriage (Sanger), 129
Harris, George, 54
Harrison, Beverly Wildung, 150
Hawthorne, Nathaniel. *See also specific works*: Catholicism in the novels of, 24, 27–28, 99–100, 106; harmony with nature as ideal for, 114; Virgin Mary and, 97, 99–101, 106
Heather Has Two Mommies, 170
Hecker, Isaac: Brook Farm and, 114; "free grace" doctrine and, 123; on gratification of the true wants of

Hecker, Isaac: Brook Farm and (*Cont.*) humanity, 123; as Paulist priest, 114, 123; Protestant pessimism criticized by, 123; redemption and, 125; self-mortification of, 114–115; on "the birth of feminine" in man, 118; vision experienced by, 113–115

Hemenway, Abby Maria, 107

Hepburn, Audrey, 122

Her (film), 192

Herbert, Bob, 161

Higgins, Margaret. *See* Sanger, Margaret

Higgins, Michael, 126–127

Hirsch, Debra, 186

History of Sacerdotal Celibacy (Lea), 32

Hodge, Charles, 49

Hogan, William, 24–25

Holiness movement, 110, 127, 137

Hollick, Frederick, 73, 75

Holly, Buddy, 159

Holy Spirit, reception of, 77–80, 134

Home, Henry (Lord Kames), 128

homosexuality: AIDS crisis and, 168–169; gay rights movement and, 169–172, 185–186; hip hop and, 187; "hookup culture" and, 185; religious denomination and, 152–153; "reparative therapy" and, 186; as sin, 8, 153, 169, 173

Hooker, Isabella Beecher, 112

"hookup culture," 183–185

Hot Girls Wanted (Bauer and Gradus), 190–191

Hudson, Rock, 168

Human Sexuality (Kosnik), 123, 149

"Human Sexuality and Mutuality" (Harrison), 150

Huntington, Frederick Dan, 89

Huntington, Lucy Irwin, 118–119

I Am Charlotte Simmons (Wolfe), 184

"If I Can Dream" (Presley), 160

"I Got a Woman" (Charles), 161

immaculate conception: Bryant on, 106; contemporary levels of belief in, 151; the fall and, 143; as official Catholic dogma, 97; original sin conquered by, 91; Romantic Era revival in doctrine of, 94–95; Virgin Mary's freedom from sin and, 93, 109, 112, 117

"imperfect acts" (Ligouri), 20

incarnation: concupiscence of God and, 118; ecstasy of, 107–108; Gabriel the Angel and, 115; immaculate conception doctrine and, 94; seduction and, 108; sin and, 157; Virgin Mary and, 104–105

Industrial Revolution, sexual attitudes affected by, 60–61, 154

Ingersoll, Andrew J.: biographical background of, 66–67; clergy as patients of, 70; on contraception, 66; ecstasy in the therapy practice of, 69, 71; "hanging the head" practice of, 69, 72, 75; on marriage, 68–69; natural law and, 66; on original sin, 70; perfectionist emphasis of, 70–71; salvation views of, 68; sex therapy practice of, 65–67, 69–70, 139; societal impact of, 71

Ingersoll, Robert, 127

In Health (Ingersoll), 68–69, 71

innocence. *See also* innocent ecstasy: childhood and, 139, 151–152; definition of, 2; durable forms of, 4; equiprobabilism and, 12; forgiveness compared to, 3; prepubescence and, 191–192; proper mental condition and, 20; sexual pleasure and, 39; virginity and, 2; Virgin

Mary and, 113; women viewed as embodiment of, 5, 96, 135–136

innocent ecstasy: advantages of, 3–4; AIDS and, 168–169; American public opinion and, 1–2; American *versus* European culture and, 190–191; disadvantages of, 4; Evangelicals and, 180–181; "hookup culture" and, 183–185; LGBT community and, 168–169, 172–173; Madonna as proponent of, 163–167; Millennial generation and, 183–185, 189; pornographic novels and, 180; redemption and, 174; sensuality neglected in, 5; sex between angels and humans and, 177; women as embodiment of, 150

Innocent XI (pope), 11, 17

Intended for Pleasure (Wheat and What), 148–149

intercourse. *See also* sex: *amplexus reservatus* (restricted form of intercourse), 13–15; anal, 19, 35, 173, 181, 185; angels and, 176; breastfeeding and, 11, 57; Catholic doctrine regarding, 8, 12–18, 35; dangers of, 55–60; duration of, 58–59; fantasy before, 19; frequency of, 45, 55–57; love and, 20; marital, 2–5, 7–10, 12–20, 34, 42–43, 55–57, 61, 68–72, 74, 126, 129–130, 132, 149, 151, 181; masturbation compared to, 72; menstruation and, 11, 35, 57; pleasure and, 10; positions in, 11, 35, 37; premarital, 4, 150; reproduction and, 35, 57; sanctification and, 145; self-abandonment in, 78; sin and, 3, 9; spiritual significance of, 2, 137–138, 141; young people and, 141

International Church of the Foursquare Gospel (Los Angeles), 81

Isaac of Stella, 117

Jackson, James Caleb, 46, 57

Jackson, Janet, 162

Jackson, Michael, 162, 187

Jackson 5 (music group), 162

James, E.L., 179

Jansenism, 10–11

Jay Z (musician), 188

Jenner, Bruce (Caitlyn), 174

Jerome (Catholic saint), 116

Jesuits, 10–11, 15, 30

"Jesus Walks" (West), 162

Johnson, Earvin "Magic," 169

Johnson, Herrick, 63

Johnson, James Weldon, 174

Johnson, Virginia E. *See* Masters and Johnson

Jones, Jennifer, 91

"Judas" (Lady Gaga), 167

"Justify My Love" (Madonna), 166

Kellogg, John Harvey, 42–43, 49–50, 57, 62

Kelly, Gerald, 17

Kelly, Howard A., 74

Kelly, Leah, 180

Kenrick, Francis Patrick: on Alphonsus Liguori's influence, 12; on "the facts of marriage," 34; on fostering love through intercourse, 20–21; on married women's right to orgasm, 7, 12–13, 15; on migration and marriage, 21; on natural goodness of sex, 17, 35; on passion and moral goodness, 10; on the psychological state accompanying passion, 18–19

Kenrick, Peter, 110–111

Kink (documentary), 190

Kinsey report, 59, 150–151

Klinenberg, Eric, 183

Knowlton, Charles, 56

"Know-Nothings" (anti-Catholic political party), 31

Könings, Anthony, 15
Kosnik, Anthony, 123, 149
Kostka, Saint Stainslaus, 111
Kramer, Heinrich, 177
Kramer, Karry, 168
Kushner, Tony, 169–170, 176

Labouré, Catherine, 95
Lady Gaga (musician), 167, 189
LaHaye, Beverly, 151–152
LaHaye, Tim, 146, 151–152
Lamar, Kendrick, 188
Landers, Ann, 172
Lang, Fritz, 192
Lang, K.D., 187
Lange, Jessica, 146–147
Lankford, Sarah Worrall, 83
Lars and the Real Girl (film), 192
La Salette, apparition of Mary at, 95–97, 112
Lateran Council (1215), 9
Lathrop, Rose Hawthorne, 100
Lawrence v. Texas (2003), 170–171
Laws of Life (Blackwell), 47
laxists, 10–12, 18
Lea, Henry Charles, 32
Lectures on Revivals of Religion (Finney), 49–50
Lectures to Women on Anatomy and Physiology (Gove), 46
Lectures to Young Men on Chastity (Graham), 44
Leonard, Erika, 179
Leo XIII (pope), 123
"Let's Pray for Sexually Active Daughters" (Daniels), 181
Lewis, Denslow, 74
Lewis, Dio, 46
Lewis, Jerry Lee, 159–160, 162
Liguori, Alphonsus: on *amplexus reservatus*, 14; canonization of, 12;

equiprobabilism of, 12, 14; on fantasy before intercourse, 19; on "imperfect sexual acts," 20; on married women's right to orgasm, 12–14; moral and sexual theology of, 11–13, 15–22, 25, 35, 108–110; on the psychological state accompanying passion, 18–19; Redemptorist order founded by, 11; on refusal of sex in marriage as a sin, 16; on the Virgin Mary, 108–109, 119
"Like a Prayer" (Madonna), 164–165, 167
"Like a Virgin" (Madonna), 163–165
Lindsey, Ben B., 147–148, 150
Litany of Loretto, 110
Little Birds (Nin), 180
Little Richard (musician), 159
"Live to Tell" (Madonna), 166
"Living for Love" (Madonna), 181
Lofton, Kathryn, 181
Longfellow, Henry Wadsworth, 97, 101, 106
Lorette (Bourne), 25
Lost in Transition (Smith), 184
Lourdes (France), apparition of Virgin Mary at, 91–93, 96–97, 112. *See also* Bernadette Soubirous
love: Catholic doctrine regarding, 19–22; free, 62, 129, 134, 169; marriage and, 20–21; medieval gospel of, 124–125; perfect, 6, 86, 88, 115; religion as, 112–113, 140–141, 145; sex and, 18–21; spiritual, 18
Lowell, James Russell, 97, 101
Luther, Martin, 3, 32, 103

Maddow, Rachel, 171
Madonna (pop singer). *See also specific songs*: AIDS-themed crucifixion concert scene of, 166–167; angels in the music of, 177; Blond

Ambition World Tour (1990) of, 164; Catholic identity of, 163; Confessions World Tour (2006) of, 166–167; Grammy Awards (2015) and, 181; Greeley on, 165; innocent ecstasy and, 163–167; masturbation and, 164; MDNA World Tour (2012) and, 167; sexual assault of, 175–176; on sin, 164, 189; Super Bowl show (2012) and, 167, 188; *Truth or Dare* documentary and, 164

Madonna and Me (2012 book), 165

Madonna di San Sisto (Raphael), 104

Malleus Maleficarum (Kramer and Sprenger), 177

Manichean heresy, 70

The Marble Faun (Hawthorne), 27–28, 99–100, 106

Marcuse, Herbert, 140

Marian Ellwood: or How Girls Live (Sarah Brownson), 120–121

Marie Josephine (nun and author of *The Mystical Rose*), 107

marriage: advice books on, 180–181; American Romanticism and, 100; birth control and, 129; Catholic doctrine of, 8, 132, 155–156; companionate forms of, 147–148; divorce and, 4, 148; Eden and, 39; fantasies about others within, 19; gay marriage and, 170–173, 186; infidelity as threat to, 20; love and, 20–21; orgasm and, 7–8, 35, 146; passion and, 74; of "perfect Christians," 86; polygamy and, 53; Protestant doctrine and, 37, 41–42; redemption and, 145; refusal of sex in, 16–17; sexual intercourse and, 2–5, 7–10, 12–20, 34, 42–43, 55–57, 61, 68–72, 74, 126, 129–130, 132, 149, 151, 181; in the United States,

21–22; of the Virgin Mary and God, 117–118

The Marriage Guide (Hollick), 73

Mars Hill megachurch (Seattle, WA), 180

Martin de Porres (Catholic saint), 164

Marx, Karl, 132

Mary (mother of Jesus). *See* Virgin Mary

Mary (queen of Great Britain), 30

Master of the Universe (Leonard), 179

Masters and Johnson (William H. Masters and Virginia E. Johnson), 2, 78, 153

masturbation: Aquinas on, 8; Catholic doctrine regarding, 35; "cure" for, 58, 67; Evangelicals' attitudes toward, 153; fantasies and, 19; insanity and, 54; intercourse compared to, 72; Madonna's on-stage performance of, 164; phobias regarding, 44, 54–55; release of pressure through, 141; as sin, 8, 13, 16, 19, 153; Surgeon General controversy regarding, 181; survey data regarding, 152–153; women and, 12–13, 15

Mathieu, Melanie, 95

"Maximum Sex" (McDowell), 1–2

May, Rollo, 140

Mayer, John, 189

McDowell, Josh, 1–2

McHugh, John, 35

McLuhan, Marshall, 93

McMullen, Matt, 192

McPherson, Aimée Semple: Christian perfection doctrine and, 87, 90, 109; depression suffered by, 80; ecstasy and Holy Spirit reception story of, 77–80, 130; evangelical performances of, 79–81; faith healing by, 80; "marriage to God" of, 115;

McPherson, Aimée Semple: Christian
       perfection doctrine and (*Cont.*)
       Pentecostal movement and, 77, 80;
       radio broadcasts of, 81; restraint
       preached by, 79–80; sexual scandal
       involving, 81
Medical Adviser (Larmont), 56
Medical Responsibility (Blackwell), 47
Memnoch the Devil (Rice), 177
menstruation, 11, 35, 57
Merritt, Timothy, 83
Methodism: American culture influ-
       enced by, 89; Christian perfection
       doctrine and, 82–84, 90, 108;
       evangelism and, 77; Methodist
       Conference of 1812 and, 83;
       middle-class adherents to, 6; pop-
       ularity of, 81; pursuit of perfect
       love and, 6; religion of health and,
       87; on sin and grace, 82
Metropolis (film), 192
Meyer, Stephanie, 178, 189
M.I.A. (musician), 188–189
Michael, George, 187
Millennial generation, 171, 183–185, 189
Milwaukee (Wisconsin), 30
Minaj, Nicky, 188–189
Modern Romance (Ansari and
       Klinenberg), 183
Monk, Maria, 23–25
Mont-Saint-Michel and Chartres
       (Adams), 98
Moody, Dwight L., 62
Moral Majority, 146, 169
*The Moral Philosophy of Courtship and
       Marriage* (Alcott), 45
Moral Principles and Medical Practice
       (Coppens), 63
Morgan, Marabel, 5, 146, 149, 190
Mormon Church, 53, 171–172
Morse, Samuel F.B., 31, 44
Mosher, Celia Duel, 58

Munger, Theodore Thornton, 53–54
"My Anaconda" (Minaj), 188
My Fight for Birth Control (Sanger),
       134–135
The Mystical Rose (Sister Marie
       Josephine), 107

National Baptist Convention (1930), 160
National Camp Meeting
       Association, 89
natural law: birth control and, 129;
       Catholic doctrine and, 8–9, 11,
       13–18, 35; Ingersoll and, 66; mas-
       turbation and, 13; orgasm and, 18,
       20, 73; sex and, 8, 11, 13–18, 20, 35,
       143, 155–156; sin and, 34; skepti-
       cism regarding knowability of, 156
Nature and the Supernatural (Bushnell),
       47–48, 71
New Harmony commune, 53
The New Month of Mary (Peter
       Kenrick), 110
The New Psyche (Huntington), 118–119
Nicene Creed, 5
Nietzsche, Friedrich, 181
Nin, Anais, 180
Noonan, John, 17, 20
The Normal Heart (Kramer), 168
nuns: American cultural celebration
       of, 122; fiction depicting priests's
       sexual relationships with, 25–26;
       Protestant suspicions of, 23; publi-
       cations featuring "escaped," 23–25
The Nun's Story (film), 122

Obama, Barack, 171, 186
Obergefell v. Rogers (2015), 171
Oculus Rift (virtual reality headset), 193
Oedipal complex, 136, 140
"Of Christian Perfection" (Wesley), 83
Olin, Stephen C., 85
O'Malley, Austin, 63

Oneida Community, 14, 53

online dating, 183

oral sex, 20, 35, 151–153, 181, 184–185

Orange Is the New Black (television show), 173

orgasm. *See also* sexual pleasure: *amplexus reservatus* and, 14–15; *Angels in America* and, 169–170; as "a spark of the Divine," 6; avoidance of, 14–15; as disease, 55; ecstasy and, 3, 5, 64, 134; female, 7, 12–16, 35, 37, 39, 72–74, 130–131, 136, 146, 151, 153–155, 190; Freud on, 136; "hookup culture" and, 184; liberation through, 5; in marriage, 7–8, 35, 146; medical warnings regarding, 54–55; mutual, 13–15, 35, 130–131, 153; natural law and, 18, 20, 73; non-genital organs and, 8; obligation to, 1, 13, 146, 152; prostration and, 55; religiosity and, 151; religious experience as, 78–79; *Sluts and Goddesses'* depiction of, 190; stimulation of wives to, 12–13, 15–16, 35, 153; women's right to, 12–13

original sin: baptism and, 33, 39; Christian perfection doctrine and, 87; concupiscence and, 116; conquest of, 63–64, 91, 93; health and, 50–54; immaculate conception's conquering of, 91; as "infection from nature," 70, 93–94, 147, 156; as invention of man, 175; liberation of sex from, 2–4, 18, 62, 131–132, 136, 149, 159, 176, 178, 189; Madonna on, 163; materialism and, 52; medical Christianity and, 42–43, 45–49, 138; Methodist doctrine on, 86; Millennial generation and, 189; Protestant doctrine on, 3, 38–40; reduction to sex of, 3, 42–47, 51, 54, 68, 138; sex and, 1,

9, 36, 53, 71, 132, 146–150, 152, 155; struggle against, 53; traditional view of, 3, 49–50, 54, 151; transmission of, 43; Virgin Mary's exemption from, 95, 117

Origin of Species (Darwin), 53

Palmer, Phoebe: biographical background of, 82–83; Businessman's Revival (1858) and, 85; Christian perfection doctrine and, 83–87, 90, 108, 123, 134; "marriage to God" of, 115; on original sin, 155; on redemption, 84, 89; religious ecstasy and, 108–110, 130; on "second blessing," 87; tours by, 85; Tuesday Meeting for the Promotion of Holiness and, 85; Wesley interpreted by, 85–87

Palmer, Walter C., 85–86

pansexualism, 68, 137, 153

Parade Magazine sex survey (1984), 152–153

Paradise Lost (Milton), 107

passion. *See also* ecstasy; love; sexual pleasure: control of, 14, 41, 51–52, 68, 128, 130–132, 141, 150, 152; corrupt forms of, 20; danger of, 8, 58; delivery from, 53; depravity and, 43; as disease, 42, 53–59; divine, 116–120; in Eden, 41; fear of, 54–64, 70, 75; health and, 45; marriage and, 74; original sin and, 48, 51; psychological state of, 18–19; reason *versus,* 9–10, 53, 64; sanctification of, 127; sin and, 8–10, 13, 36, 42, 46, 90, 147; suspicion of, 9, 16, 18; virtue of, 10, 124–125; women in American Romanticism and, 124; women's levels of, 61, 156; young people and, 141

Pastoral Medicine (Walsh), 63

Paul (Catholic apostle and saint), 16–17, 48

Pauline Seward (Bryant), 119

Paulist Fathers, 114, 123

Pentecostal First Assembly of God (Tupelo, MS), 161

Pentecostal movement, 77, 80, 109, 159–162. *See also* McPherson, Aimée Semple

perfectionism: duty of happiness and, 122; Finney and, 50–51, 64; innocent ecstasy and, 66, 71–73, 88–89; religion of health and, 64; sexual redemption and, 70; sexual restraint and, 71; spiritual love and, 18; Victorian feminism and, 156

Perkins, William, 37

Perry, Katy, 187–188

Phayer, J. Michael, 96

Phillips, Sam, 162

The Physiology of Marriage (Alcott), 45

Pius IX (pope): on Alphonsus Liguori, 12; in Hawthorne's *The Marble Faun*, 99; on the Virgin Mary's immaculate conception, 93, 97, 136; Washington Monument and, 31

The Pivot of Civilization (Sanger), 132

Plain Home Talk (Foote), 71

pleasure. *See also* sexual pleasure: morality of, 9–10; self-denial and, 80; sin and, 10–21

Poe, Edgar Allen, 100

pornography: anti-Catholic forms of, 1, 23–30; industry producing, 190–191; innocent ecstasy and, 180; the Internet and, 183, 190–191; survey data regarding, 152–153; violence and, 192; young women exploited by, 190–191

The Practice of the Confessor, 19

Presbyterianism, 53, 77, 172

Presley, Elvis, 159–161

The Priest, the Woman, and the Confessional (Chiniquy), 25

priests: advice to, 7, 9, 12, 15, 19; celibacy and, 20, 31–32; confession and, 7, 9, 15, 19, 23–25; fiction depicting nun's sexual relations with, 25–26; former, anti-Catholic, 24–25; Protestant suspicions regarding, 23; sexual counseling of parishioners by, 7, 35

Prince (musician), 162

probabiliorism, 12

probabilism, 12

procreation: Catholic doctrine and, 132; liberation of sex from, 126; marriage and, 17; as reason for sex, 8–9, 17, 57, 132; Virgin Mary and, 113

The Promise of the Father (Palmer), 85

Proposition 8 (California ballot measure against gay marriage), 171–172

prostitution, efforts to eliminate, 59; feminist crusades against, 191

The Protestant Ethic (Weber), 154

Protestantism. *See also* Protestants: Catholic arguments against, 11; divorce and, 148; medical Christianity and, 42–50; sexual doctrine and, 34, 36–38, 66, 72, 138, 148

Protestants. *See also* Evangelicals; Protestantism; *specific denominations*: birth control and, 63, 148; Catholic sexual doctrines scrutinized by, 6, 23–24, 34; convents as source of suspicion for, 26–27, 29, 31; ecstatics and, 108–110; homosexuality and, 152; sexual repression and, 63–64; Virgin Mary and, 97–107, 123–124; worship styles among, 32–33, 49

psychoanalysis, 1, 113, 136, 143–144

Puritans, 130, 144
Pusey, Edward Bouverie, 103

Quakers, 5

Rahab (harlot in the Book of Joshua), 117
Rahner, Karl, 118
Randall, Franklin Freeman, 187
Raphael (Renaissance painter), 104
Ray of Light (Madonna), 166
RealDolls at Abyss Creations, 192
Real Marriage (Driscolls), 180
rebirth: deliverance from sin and, 138;
    Evangelicals' emphasis on, 76–77,
    132; McPherson's account of,
    77–79; need for, 148; psychoanaly-
    sis and, 144; rapture of, 76–81, 130;
    sex and, 163
recovery from sexual abuse, ix; in lives
    of Oprah Winfrey, Madonna, Ellen
    DeGeneres, 174–176
Redbook survey (1975), 151
Redeeming Sex (Hirsch), 186
redemption: complete, 88–89; ecstasy
    and, 163–167; hereditary deprav-
    ity and, 48; innocent ecstasy and,
    174; marriage and, 145; medical
    Christianity and, 42, 47; physical
    forms of, 34, 40–41, 48, 116; sex
    and, 5, 66, 68, 70, 75, 116–118, 124–
    146, 149–150, 154–155, 168–169, 176,
    181, 186; Virgin Mary and, 5, 124;
    whole being and, 84; will and, 51–
    52; women viewed as agents of, 4–5
Redemption (Bryant), 107
Redemptorists, 11, 17
The Reformation, 103, 156
The Religion of Health (Blackwell), 47
"Religious Novels, or Woman *versus*
    Woman" (Orestes Brownson), 120
"reparative therapy" for
    homosexuality, 186

reproduction without sex, 52
Revelation (New Testament book), 124
revivalism, 33, 51, 144, 161
Rice, Anne, 177–178, 180
Richard of St. Laurent, 117
rigorists, 10–12, 18
Robinson, Gene, 171
Rock and Roll Hall of Fame, 159–160,
    162, 187
The Rolling Stones, 163
Roman Catholicism: anti-Catholic por-
    nography and, 1, 23–30; contem-
    platives and, 138; in France, 96;
    gospel of desire and, 123; guilt and,
    165; heretical groups competing
    with, 8, 10–11, 13–14; marriage and,
    1; moral teachings of, 1, 6, 34–35;
    natural law and, 8–9, 11, 13–18,
    35; on passion, pleasure and sin,
    10–19; prejudice against, 29–34;
    sensuality of, 7–22, 33–35; sexual
    doctrine in, 1, 4, 7–24, 34, 63,
    132–133, 146, 149, 153; in the United
    States, 7, 21, 24, 30, 35, 97–98, 106;
    Virgin Mary and, 91–117, 135, 142–
    143; women's role in, 29, 120–122
Roman Penitentiary (Catholic confes-
    sional court), 11–12
Romanticism. *See* American
    Romanticism
Ruether, Rosemary, 150
Rush, Benjamin, 39–43, 53–54
Ruskin, John, 71

sadomasochism, 179–180
Saint Louis (Missouri), 30
Salvation Army, 79
sanctification: the body and, 46, 51;
    ecstasy and, 86–87; entertainment
    and, 89; inherited forms of, 134;
    intercourse and, 145; piety and, 110;
    from the womb, 48, 72

Sanger, Margaret: biographical background of, 126–127, 135; birth control promoted by, 126, 128–136; on Catholic Church's sexual doctrine, 132–133; Dickinson on, 75; Grand Street tenement and, 128; on male sexuality, 134–135; on Marx, 132; on original sin, 155; on prostitution, 191, 226n22; Protestant churches and, 134; on sex as the consummation of love, 129–130, 138, 145; on sex's hereditary effects, 141; on simultaneous orgasm, 130–131; Virgin Mary and, 126–127, 135

Sanger, William, 128

Santeria, 160

Santorum, Rick, 172

Savage, Dan, 173

Saving Sex (DeRogatis), 186

Schori, Katherine Jefferts, 171

Science and Health (Eddy), 52, 105–106

Science of a New Life (Cowan), 56

"the second blessing," 86–88

Second Life (virtual world), 192–193

seduction, 8, 32, 108. *See also* concupiscence

segregation in the United States, 161

seminatio (female orgasm), 13, 15

Semple, Robert, 80

sensuality: Catholic worship and, 32–34, 133; ecstatics' denial of, 113; Greer on women's detachment from, 154; innocent ecstasy's denial of, 5; political repression and, 112; sexual pleasure and, 16

Sermons to Gentlemen on Temperance and Exercise (Rush), 41

Seventh-Day Adventists, 42, 46, 50, 62

sex. *See also* intercourse; sexual pleasure: Christian Science's goal of overcoming, 52; in colonial America, 37–42; death and,

62–63; as disease, 40, 42–47; excess in, 46, 62–63; frequency of, 45, 55–58, 61; guilt and, 2–3; health and, 17, 35; Industrial Revolution and changing attitudes toward, 60–61; marriage and, 2–5, 7–10, 12–13, 16–19, 34, 55–57, 61, 68–72, 74, 126, 129–130, 132, 149, 151, 181; mechanical, 154; medical advice and, 38–40; medical Christianity and, 43; medical view of, 65–66, 68–75; mysticism and, 1, 115, 157; natural law and, 8, 11, 13–18, 20, 35, 143, 155–156; oralgenital, 20, 35, 151–153, 181, 184–185; passion and, 10; pregnancy and, 48; procreation and, 35, 57; psychology of, 136–145; reciprocity and, 72; redemptive powers of, 5, 66, 68, 70, 75, 116–118, 124–146, 149–150, 154–155, 168–169, 176, 181, 186; refusal of, 16; religion and, 130–136, 139–140; sacredness and, 4; sin and, 1–2, 7, 9–10, 13, 16–17, 19, 37–47, 62–63, 93–94, 138, 146, 149, 152, 155–156, 164–165, 167; Victorian attitudes toward, 154–155

Sex (Madonna), 166

Sex and the Soul (Freitas), 184

sex dolls, 192

sex roles, 58, 134, 142–144, 153–154, 156

sexual advice: Evangelicals and, 152–153, 180–181; medical and, 38; popular dispensers of, 172–173; popular literature and, 97; religious, 34, 146; Victorian, 1

sexual ethics: Christian influences on, 5; contemporary America and, 18, 75, 148, 156; procreation and, 141

Sexual Impotence in the Male and Female (Hammond), 74

sexuality: abuse of, 149; female, 143, 146, 156; Holy Spirit and, 78; homosexuality and, 8, 152–153, 169–170, 173, 186, 189; infantile, 136, 138–139, 143; male, 134–135, 143; spirituality distinguished from, 193

sexual pleasure. *See also* orgasm: American ethic of, 5–6, 159; Catholic doctrine and, 7–8, 11, 13–18, 22, 24, 35, 43, 63; *delectationem veneream* and, 15; ecstatic religious experience and, 157; encouragement of, 13, 17, 66, 74–75, 126–127, 135, 139, 141, 147–148, 150, 154, 156, 191; Evangelicals and, 2, 90, 151–152; medical advice and, 38–39; modern ethic of, 22, 24, 35, 43, 90; prophets of, 150–157; Protestant doctrine regarding, 37, 41–42; rock music and, 162; sin and, 9–10, 16, 155–156; technology and, 192–193

sexual repression: Catholicism and Protestantism's similarities in supporting, 63–64; evangelism and, 53; Freud on, 143; medical Christianity and, 48; prostration and, 65–66; Sanger's criticism of Catholic Church for, 132–133; Victorian Era's increasing levels of, 59, 61–65

"Shake It Off" (Swift), 187, 189

Shakers, 53

Shakur, Tupac, 162

shame: children's instinct of, 63; depravity and, 72; overcoming feelings of, 71, 132–133, 149; prelapsarian absence of, 9, 149, 155; sin and, 132

Shaw, George Bernard, 135

Sheen, Fulton J., 63

Sheldon, Charles M., 63

Sims, J. Marion, 60

sin. *See also* original sin: adultery as, 8, 13, 16; conscious intention and, 11, 19; as disease, 66; freedom from, 5, 51, 79, 109, 112, 123, 129, 155; free will and, 50; grace and, 82; hierarchy of, 8; as "infection of nature," 70, 82, 93–94, 147, 155; Madonna on, 163; masturbation as, 8, 13, 16, 19, 153; medical Christianity and, 45–46; mortal forms of, 7, 13, 15–16, 19; natural law and, 34; passion and, 8–10, 13, 36, 42, 46, 90, 147; Protestant doctrines and, 50–51; selfishness as, 38; sex and, 1–2, 7, 9–10, 13, 16–17, 19, 37–47, 62–63, 93–94, 138, 146, 149, 152, 155–156, 164–165, 167; venial forms of, 7, 9–10, 13, 17

Sister Christina (nun covering Madonna's "Like a Virgin"), 167

The Sister of Charity (Dorsey), 120

Slater, Thomas, 15

Sluts and Goddesses (Annie Sprinkle), 190

Smet, Pierre de, 96

Smith, Bob, 170

Smith, Christian, 184

Smith, Samuel B., 25

Smyth, Newman, 54

Snoop Dogg (musician), 187–188

Society of the Holy Child Jesus, 121–122

sodomy, 19, 35, 171

The Song of Bernadette, 91–92, 98

Song of Solomon, 152

Song of Songs, 91, 119

"The Sons of God Saw the Daughters of Men That They Were Fair" (French), 177

Soubirous, Bernadette, 91–94, 118. *See also Song of Bernadette*

Soul Stirrers (music group), 161

Spalding, Henry J., 63

Spalding, John L., 112

The Spiritual Life (Tanquerey), 109–110

Sprenger, Jacob, 177

Stainslaus Kosta (Catholic saint), 111

Stall, Sylvanus, 62–63

Stanton, Elizabeth Cady, 57

Starhawk, 178

Stendahl, Krister, 156

Stockton, Reverend Mr., 88

Stoker, Bram, 178

Storer, Horatio, 66

Stowe, Harriet Beecher. *See also specific works*: Catholicism in the novels of, 24, 28–29, 101–103; convents depicted by, 29; on original sin, 155; on sexual issues, 61; Virgin Mary and, 97, 102–104, 106, 110

Swaggart, Jimmy, 160

Swedenborg, Emanuel, 176

Swift, Taylor, 187–189

Systematic Theology (Finney), 50–51

Tamburinius, 19

Tanquerey, Adolphe, 34–35, 109–110

Taylor, Jeremy, 37

Taylor, Nathaniel William, 45

Teish, Luisah, 178

temperance movement, 53, 59

Theologiae Moralis (Kenrick), 7

Theologia Moralis (Ligouri), 11

Theology of an Evolutionist (Abbott), 54

This Is That (McPherson), 109

The Thorn Birds (McCullough), 24

Thoughts upon Female Education (Rush), 41

Three Essays on Sexuality (Freud), 139

Three Lectures upon Animal Life (Rush), 40

"Throw That Boy Pussy" (Fly Young Red), 187

Timberlake, Justin, 188

Tinder (hookup app), 185

Tissot, Simon André, 54–55

Todd, John, 62

tongues, speaking in, 3, 77–79, 89, 159

The Total Woman (Morgan), 5

Transcendentalists, 53, 111

transgender population, 173–174

Transparent (television show), 173

Trible, Phyllis, 150

Truslow, Sarah, 74–75

The Truth about Webcam Girls (documentary), 190

Truth or Dare (documentary film), 164

Tuesday Meeting for the Promotion of Holiness, 85

Twilight series (Meyer), 178–180, 189

"U Don't Want It" (Fly Young Red), 187

Uncle Tom's Cabin (Stowe), 23, 103

Unitarians, 5

Updike, John, 177

Upham, Thomas C., 85, 87

The Ursuline Manual, 121

vampires in American popular culture, 178

Van Buren, Abigail ("Dear Abby"), 172

venereal disease, 38, 40, 61

Vermeersch, Arthur, 35

Vincent, John H., 63

Virgin Mary. *See also* immaculate conception: Americans and devotion to, 1, 6, 90–91, 97–113; annunciation of, 102, 107–108; Christian motherhood and, 140; devotion to, 1, 4–5–6, 90–91, 94, 96–113, 126–127; Eve contrasted with, 94; feast celebrating birth of, 94; France and devotion to, 96–97; freedom from sin of, 93, 107, 109–110, 112, 136; God's desire for, 108,

113, 115–120; guilt and, 94; marriage to God of, 117–118; Middle Ages' views of, 97, 115–118, 143; miraculous appearances of, 91–97, 112; as mystic, 143; Protestants and, 97–107, 123–124; redemption through, 5, 124; as Romantic ideal, 91, 96, 99–105, 114–118, 142–143; Sanger on, 126–127; sexuality of, 112–113; Victorian sexual restraints and, 110; women's rights movement and, 111–112

"The Virgin Mother" (Spalding), 112

Voudou, 160

Walsh, James J., 63

Washington, George, 30

Wayland, Francis, 127–128

The Way of Holiness (Palmer), 84–85, 109

Weber, Max, 154

Welter, Barbara, 154

Werfel, Franz, 92–93

Wesley, John: Christian perfection doctrine and, 82–83, 85–87, 89; emotions in religious worship and, 33, 90; "free grace" doctrine and, 123; on grace and sin, 82; lay teaching encouraged by, 127; on marriage of "perfect Christians," 86; Methodism founded by, 81; Palmer's interpretation of, 85–87

West, Kanye, 162

Westheimer, Ruth ("Dr. Ruth"), 173

What a Young Husband Ought to Know (Stall), 62

What a Young Man Ought to Know (Stall), 62

"What'd I Say?" (Charles), 161

What Every Girl and Boy Should Know (Sanger), 134

Wheat, Ed, 148–149, 152

Wheat, Gaye, 148–149

When Harry Met Sally (film), 185

White, Ellen Gould, 42, 46

White, Ryan, 168

Whitefield, George, 33

Whittier, John Greenleaf, 71

Wilcox, Ella Wheeler, 124

Willard, Frances, 61

Will & Grace (television show), 171

Winfrey, Oprah, 174–176

witches in American popular culture, 177–178

The Witches of Eastwick (Updike), 177

Wolfe, Tom, 6, 184

Woman and the New Race (Sanger), 131–132

Woman's Suffrage: The Reform Against Nature (Bushnell), 112

women: in anti-Catholic fiction, 26–28; ecstatic Catholic, 91–97; fallen, 4, 156; fulfillment in marriage of, 136; gynecology and, 60, 75; Industrial Revolution and, 60–61; innocence and, 5, 96, 135–136; leadership by, 110, 122; masturbation and, 12–13, 15; needs and desires of, 4–5, 118, 120, 124, 141–142; orgasms and, 7, 12–16, 35, 37, 39, 72–74, 130–131, 136, 146, 151, 153–155, 190; preachers, 77–90; as redemptive agents, 4–5; Romantic ideal of, 91, 96, 103, 129, 141–142, 154; sex roles and, 2, 4, 58, 143–144, 146, 149–150, 154, 156; sexuality of, 143, 146, 156

Women in Sacred History (Stowe), 103

Women's Christian Temperance Union, 61–62

women's rights movement, 6, 111–112, 155

Wonder, Stevie, 162

Wood-Allen, Mary, 57, 62
Woodard, Alfre, 174
Woodhull, Victoria, 129
Woods, Leonard, 49–51
Wordsworth, William, 69, 71
Worrall, Henry, 82–83

Yeezus (West), 162
Yoruba people (West Africa), 160
"You Belong with Me" (Swift), 188–189
The Young Husband (Alcott), 45–46
The Young Wife (Alcott), 45
"You Send Me" (Cooke), 161